"Synthia and Colin Andrews are am
rary authors who really understand the
found changes affecting our world today
ical insight with the latest scientific research to produce this highly
intriguing, wide-ranging yet accessible book. If you aren't afraid to take
a good, hard look at where our society and planet are rapidly heading,
then I urge you to read this now."

—Dr. Simeon Hein, PhD, founder of Mount Baldy Institute

"To compare Colin Andrews to a modern Paul Revere or Charles
Fort would be an understatement. Colin is the one who first brought
the crop circle phenomenon to the world attention when no hoax was
involved. He is also the one who not only courageously exposed the
hoaxing happening in the later years but also had the insight to look
more thoroughly into this phenomenon and understood its deeper
meaning. This earned him to be ostracized and crucified by many
researchers who had become too engrained in their own belief system.
Now Colin is giving us another outstanding example of his dedication
to truth, deep insight, integrity, and talent in *On the Edge of Reality* he
wrote with his equally talented wife Synthia. When I started reading
this book, I could not put it down as I was so taken by the flowing quality of the writing and the exceptional way in which Colin is opening our
eyes to what is really happening in our world. He is truly connecting
the dots to build an amazing picture of what is already here and what
is to come, along with providing ample documentation to support his
points. It is a must-read for those who are ready to welcome a change
in paradigm and really want for humanity to evolve to a higher status."

—Dr. Jean-Noel Aubrun, PhD, senior aerospace consultant.

"This book is a provocative mind-opening experience and a synop-
sis of many of the exciting breakthroughs taking place in paraphysical
exploration."

—J.J. Hurtak, PhD,The Academy For Future Science

ON THE EDGE of REALITY

Hidden Technology, Powers of
the Mind, Quantum Physics,
Paranormal Phenomena, Orbs,
UFOs, Harmonic Transmissions,
and Crop Circles

By

COLIN ANDREWS
WITH SYNTHIA ANDREWS

New Page Books
A division of The Career Press, Inc.
Pompton Plains, NJ

ON THE EDGE OF REALITY
EDITED BY JODI BRANDON
TYPESET BY EILEEN MUNSON
Cover design by Howard Grossman/12E Design
Printed in the U.S.A.

To order this title, please call toll-free 1-800-CAREER-1 (NJ and Canada: 201-848-0310) to order using VISA or MasterCard, or for further information on books from Career Press.

The Career Press, Inc.
220 West Parkway, Unit 12
Pompton Plains, NJ 07444
www.careerpress.com
www.newpagebooks.com

Library of Congress Cataloging-in-Publication Data

CIP Data Available Upon Request.

Synthia and I are dedicating this book to Reg Presley, the front man of the famous 1960s pop band The Troggs. Reg's big hits include "With a Girl Like You," "Love Is All Around" (which was prominent in the movie *Four Weddings and a Funeral*), and the biggest of them all: "Wild Thing."

Reg was a good friend and the best man at Synthia's and my wedding; he was also a kind, generous person, who sadly departed ahead of time on February 4, 2013.

Reg Presley and Colin Andrews. Best man at Colin and Synthia's wedding, 1993.

I am honored to have spent some of my fondest memories with him and his lovely family in Andover, England, where we both lived. The subjects that primarily connected us were research into the paranormal, crop circles, UFOs, and human consciousness. Reg and I also felt strongly about the environment and both held strong views on modern politics.

Reg was a funny man who enjoyed putting real human events into his own words and joke form, which would usually transpose unpleasant events into reflections of ourselves from which we could laugh. He was curious, opinionated, and not afraid to express his views. He once telephoned to tell me of a profound new idea: Society could function without money. Little did he know the global economy would soon be bankrupt and we would be functioning without money—just the kind of thing Reg's jokes were made of.

Love is the only thing in the Universe that is real and not an emotion in progress. It is the glue of life that creates everlasting development. It is the creative force with which we can make a difference to our world and our surroundings. Reg left us with "Love Is All Around" and now we must ensure that is so.

Acknowledgments

T his book represents a collective 100 years of study and experience. The experiences that directly contributed to my lifetime of investigation started young and the same is true of my wife and co-author, Synthia. This book would not and could not have been written without our particular synthesis. Synthia and I came together with our joint mission already set. I love her dearly. I am indebted for the extraordinary amount of work she put into *On the Edge of Reality,* as she reliably does for any project she undertakes.

Synthia and I are deeply indebted to our close friend Johanna Sayer, professional editor, who has helped with our words, research, and morale. She has been an invaluable springboard for our thoughts. Also we greatly thank Wayne Mason, who created the exquisite art for the parts introductions.

Many people have contributed to this book, among them professional colleagues and friends. My deepest thanks to all of them, acknowledged here in no particular order and with apologies for any unintentional oversights:

Johanna Sayer, Wayne Mason, Busty Taylor, the late Reg Presley of the pop band The Troggs, Dr. Bruce Maccabee, the late Dr. James Harder, Steve Rapetti, Julian Richardson, Dr. Jean-Noel Aubrun, Dr. Jesse Marcel, Jr., Malcolm Treacher, Ron Russell, the late Stephen Balon, Matthew Williams, The late Prof. Gerald Hawkins, Peter Sorensen, my brother the late David Andrews, Valenya, the late Susan Ramsby, Steve and Robin, David Haith, Derek James, Bob Schindler and Kenneth John Parson of BEAMS (UK), Thomas E. Bearden, Masahiro Kahata, Lindy Tucker, the Australian Government Bureau of Meteorology, Larry Frascella, Dr. Steven Greer, Dr. Edward Belbruno, the late Pat Delgado, the Website The Crop Circle Connector run by Mark Fussell and Stuart Dike, Stephen Hannard at DiscloseTV.org, Dr. Ted Loder, Dr. Lynne Kitei, Dr. Melih Arici, Conchita, Travis Walton, the late Paul Vigay, Graham Prichard, Dr. J.J. Hurtack, Dr. Desiree Hurtak, Paul O'Brien, and not to forget the exceptional support at Career Press. Thanks also to my agent, John White, for making this possible.

A special thank you to my daughter and her husband, Mandy and Peter Butcher, who have put Synthia and me up in their wonderful friendly home in Hampshire, England, during our many years of research visits. Also, many thanks to my stepdaughters, Erin and Adriel Infantino, who tended the horses, dogs, cats, and rabbits on the home front when we traveled.

Contents

Great spirits
have always encountered
violent opposition
from mediocre minds.

—Albert Einstein

I believe that we are engaged in a process of integration with a higher mind. What this higher intelligence is and where it originates are unknown. The process of integration has been especially evident over the past 50 years with the exponential increase in high-strangeness events. The ultimate purpose is discerned through the interactions we are having as orchestrated events lead us toward a paradigm shift and a new view of reality.

This book is not written with irrefutable proof to convince the reader of the events described. It moves beyond the question of whether the events are real and asks instead: What does it mean to us that they are? When we talk about paradigm shifts, we tend to look at social, scientific, and technological trends that usher in new thinking. However, trends ultimately reflect changes in people who are altered through events. Whereas new information engages our mind, events engage our emotions and emotional shifts push us to expand.

The integration of higher mind is occurring through individual encounters with non-ordinary reality. These encounters are called high-strangeness events. While they boggle the mind, they also engage our emotions and stimulate our creative capacity. Our mind races to catch up with what our body and emotions already know. Some say the frequency of the planet is changing. It is. A new reality is on the horizon; a new time is being born.

The majority of my life has been spent investigating high-strangeness events. I am best known for helping bring crop circles into worldwide awareness. My belief is that the intelligence driving events has been influencing individuals for some time. We are at a turning point and now people's personal stories must come forward. Each of us holds a small piece of a larger picture, and it is time to put the pieces together to see the entirety. It's not about what we can theorize or prove; it is what we experience and how we feel about it. It's about the changes our experiences create within us and how that alters the way we see the world.

What are high-strangeness events? They are events that defy the laws that govern our physics and the expectation of our experience. They include UFOs, orbs of light, strange sounds and altered states of awareness and perception. The events represent an interface with the unknown, an interaction with parts of reality we do not yet understand. They are not paranormal or supernatural, although both words are used to describe them. Rather, they are normal and natural to a worldview that we are presently being introduced to and will one day inhabit.

The hallmark of high-strangeness events is that the encounters leave us permanently altered. For some, being altered means turning off and disappearing into a fog of denial. For most, being altered means being enlivened as inner parts that were asleep, wake up. In some cases, such as mine, an initial encounter early in our lives plants a seed in our subconscious for the awakening that is underway.

This book details what I see as the major factors in the shift. I view us as at a crossroads; we can awaken and move forward into a new paradigm, or collapse back to the mistakes of our past. I believe an interface with a higher intelligence is driving us toward the shift in paradigm. This might be for our own sake, or this might be because we are part of a larger reality and what we do on this planet effects more than we can understand at this time. The subjects and experiences covered in this book reflect this belief.

Most of the topics discussed within have existed for millennia, yet they are emerging today in new and unimagined ways. Some of what is coming forth relates to advances in science and technology that extend our senses further into the world. New technology allows us to record events and transmit them worldwide, helping us see the extent of the evolving phenomena. A great deal of what we are discovering, however, represents a change in humans.

Mental conditioning affects what we are able to see; our inability to perceive outside of our beliefs is called inattentional blindness. Rather than believing what we see, we see what we believe. Right now, what we believe is changing. We are opening to new vistas and challenging the boundaries of what is real. This represents a breakthrough in conditioning.

When I glanced left into a wheat field in 1983, I saw five unusual circles that changed my life. Hundreds of other drivers glanced left and saw only a wheat field. Thirty years later, the term *crop circle* is a worldwide household term and the average person in England, both resident and tourist, now looks to the fields anticipating a design. The emergence of crop circles, wherever you believe they come from, encourages people to look for patterns in nature and consequently see the world in new ways. Was the crop circle phenomenon a hoax, a government conspiracy to condition society, or an interaction with an unknown reality that expanded expectations? What we know for sure is that people now look and see differently than they did before crop circles were commonly seen.

Synthia and I chose to write this book from the perspective of my research and my personal experience; however, Synthia is part of every piece. Ideas, observations, concepts, and conclusions represent the unique synthesis of our experience. Our coming together is itself an orchestrated event that broadened our combined perspective. Many of the conclusions that I slowly came to realize are the basis of the work Synthia has been immersed in for the past 30 years. She is an integral part of all aspects of this book.

Isolation is the greatest impediment to reaching a better state. People who have been separated from making bonds with family, friends, animals, nature, and their own spirit suffer from isolation. They are not recognized for who they are and this is not only a loss to them; it is a loss to us all. The flow of energy that creates the matrix of life requires all of us to be engaged. In holographic reality, either all of us make it or none of us do. As we reach out with our minds and hearts to find new realities, we need to reach out to each other to forge bonds based on respect, trust, and a shared future. If we don't like what we see in another, we must change the reflection within ourselves. Make peace. In the shift underway, no one will be left behind.

The Crossroads

The Crossroads *by Wayne Mason.*

We are on the edge of a new paradigm where new truths are becoming self evident. The direction of this shift is not a given; we are creating it with every choice we make. The hand of higher intellegence is directing our attention to greater possibilities. Right now we are at the crossroads; the choices we make will set the direction for a new cycle of human endeavor. There is much to be grateful for in today's world and much to be improved. As you look at what we have created, ask yourself: Is this the best we can imagine?

We are on the brink of a paradigm shift. Everything we currently understand to be true is changing. A paradigm is a model or conceptual framework that organizes how we perceive reality. When a paradigm shifts, our perceptions change. This is not the same as the small, eureka moments each of us has nearly every day—moments that expand our view of a problem, plan, or idea. A paradigm shift reorganizes the foundations of life. It is precipitated by two things: increasing pressure of external limitations resulting from our current thinking, and the innate desire to grow.

My friend and colleague, the late Dr. Gerald Hawkins, called dramatic and irreversible paradigm shifts mindsteps. In his 1987 book, *Mindsteps to the Cosmos,* Hawkins states that a mindstep permanently changes how we fit ourselves into the larger context of the universe.[1] It represents a shift in how we identify ourselves. The paradigm shift we are stepping into is such a mindstep. Once engaged, our ideas of what humanity is and what the universe is will be forever altered.

Historically, our sense of self expanded in small steps: first extending beyond the boundaries of family, tribe, culture, and nation until eventually we began to search off-planet for our origins, capabilities, and destiny. Each paradigm shift created new technology that expanded our reach further and enabled us to engage reality in previously unimaginable ways, traveling farther and faster to explore greater vistas, and adding to our picture of the universe. Imagine the leaps involved as our ancestors moved from observing the night sky in awe and fear to creating telescopes, spaceships, and eventually the Hubble Telescope to assist in our exploration of galaxies. Many believe our current shift in paradigm involves finding unequivocal proof that we are not alone in the universe.

Mindsteps represent a shift in perception; how we think is altered. We connect the dots differently, linking information together into new arrangements. Another aspect is the development of new faculties of awareness. More than perceiving from a different perspective, we actually *perceive* differently and make new neural connections that expand our capabilities. Reality expands because the faculty we use to perceive, our consciousness, expands first. We see, touch, and understand a new layer—a deeper one that still only represents a small fraction of what is actually present.

A new paradigm gives birth to new understanding from which new technology is derived. A period of growth is initiated that escalates until the limits of our new understanding are reached and the resultant restriction drives a new leap forward. Hawkins observed that the time between mindsteps became exponentially shorter with each one. Consider the tens of thousands of years that passed with people living in small, mobile bands relying on clubs, spears, and other primitive tools. Then, seemingly out of nowhere, a leap in understanding results in the simultaneous eruption of civilization across the planet and the advent of the agricultural age. Five thousand years later, the industrial age emerged, to be followed within a hundred years by the current era of electronics, and within a few decades, quantum physics. The diminished amount of time between shifts represents an acceleration of change.

The mindstep we are presently experiencing surpasses any previous in its scope and magnitude. It involves all the foundations of life and culture: ecological, social, scientific, religious, and economic. The acceleration of change is racing forward at unprecedented speed. The stakes are tremendous. Never before have we struggled with the ability to destroy the planet with nuclear weapons; never before has the planet tried to support a population of more than seven billion people. Our international activities in forestry, mining, agriculture, and fossil fuel production and consumption disrupt the planet's life-sustaining capabilities. We have reached the global limits of our ability to expand exponentially as a species. Consequently, the need for a paradigm shift has never been more critical, and the immensity of what we stand to gain or lose, never greater.

Though many people might disagree with the specifics of global difficulty or the reality of expanding consciousness, everyone agrees that we are undergoing accelerated change, predicted by Hawkins as signaling the advent of a new mindstep. Exponential acceleration is seen in the quickening pace of each day and the ever-increasing complexity of what the average person is expected to manage. The amount of change a modern person is confronted with in a year or even a month is more than a person 100 years ago would have faced in a lifetime. When regarded this way, we don't have to ask whether other signs of a shift are real. Two questions immediately arise: Is it possible to adapt to incessant and accelerating change and complexity without a radical shift in consciousness, and how much acceleration can we absorb before this shift must occur?

Native Consciousness

The times we are in may be unprecedented, but they are not unexpected. The prophecies of many ancient cultures such as the Maya, Egyptian, Hindu, and several Native American tribes predict this paradigm shift. Examining ancient wisdom clarifies the stakes and the steps that will help us adjust to the transition underway.

Using different terms and cultural metaphors, all ancient texts basically warn of a "Day of Purification" where the imbalances of human consciousness are eradicated in a cleansing process. This is commonly interpreted as End Times and described as a period of massive disruption. More precisely, all that does not sustain life is collapsed in ruin, allowing movement through the bottleneck into a new and ostensibly better era.

According to most prophecy, catastrophe is caused by our loss of connection to spiritual reality and neglected awareness of the sacred. As humans we are out of balance with our own spirit and consequently with the forces of nature. Restoration is required to avert destruction. My wife and I have discussed this with many Native people who work with traditional prophecy. Each has said the same thing: The prophecies do not predict doom or punishment. Rather, they warn of the consequences of being out of balance and encourage us to return to a path of inner and outer harmony. At any point along the path we can change direction. We only need to make a choice. We can choose to live in recognition of the interconnection of all life, or we can choose to act from greed and fear. The prophecies are calling for a change in consciousness; however, the bottom line is that when the mindstep occurs, by choice or by consequence, we will change.

With some exceptions, the timing of prophecy is discerned through the arrival of predicted events that portend the transition. People often wonder whether various prophecies actually relate to the current time period. It is not our purpose in writing this book to prove or disprove prophecy; we offer the following as examples only.

Hopi Prophecy

The Hopi Prophecy is carried on by an oral tradition that is supported by a drawing on the "Prophecy Rock," thought to be at least 1,500 years old. The prophecy is extensive, revealing many aspects of the Hopi path and the imbalance that creates the need for Purification. The prophecy reveals signs and omens that provide a time line of events to alert the People (those who live in accordance with spiritual law) when the time is at hand. The following list is a very short sample of the type of detail found in the prophecy. It comes from a combination of published and unpublished sources. For those who want in-depth information, *Hotevilla: Hopi Shrine of the Covenant-Microcosm of the World* by Thomas E. Mails and Dan Evehems is the only published source that is sanctioned by traditional Hopi Elders. Information that is taken from Hotevilla is sourced.

- *A gourd of ashes will fall from the sky causing great destruction.* This is commonly thought to relate to the dropping of the atomic bomb.

- *The Bear and Eagle will build a ladder to the Moon.* This is thought to represent the Russian and American space programs.

- *The Eagle will bring back rocks from the Moon.* This happened with the Apollo 11 Moon landing.

- And Purification is close when *"Nature will speak to us with its mighty breath of wind. There will be earthquakes and floods causing great disasters, changes in the seasons and in the weather; disappearance of wildlife, and famine in different forms. There will be gradual corruption and confusion among the leaders and the people all over the world, and wars will come about like powerful winds.*"[2] As we explore the trend lines in Chapter 2, we see that the seasons have shifted, the weather is changing, natural disasters abound, and there are corruption and confusion among our leaders.

The Calendar of the Maya

Most people today have heard some rendition of the prophecy connected with the Maya of Central America and the end of their Long Count calendar in 2012. The Maya tracked the cycles of celestial events: the movement of planets and constellations through the night sky. Celestial cycles such as the phases of the moon, the Earth's revolution around the Sun, the movement of Venus as the morning and evening star, and, most importantly, the 26,000 year Precession of the Equinox, were all tracked with individual calendars. The Maya are said to have 17 different calendars tracking various celestial cycles. How they knew the length of longer cycles like the Precession of the Equinox is one of the mysteries of their advanced mathematical and astronomical culture.

For the Maya, the endings and beginnings of cycles contained meanings and were celebrated. The Long Count calendar marks one-fifth of the Precession of the Equinox and the completion of five Long Count calendars represents the completed Precession called a Grand Cycle, Age, or World. The end of the current Long Count in 2012 represents the end of such an age. According to Creation stories found in Mayan codices such as the *Popul Vuh,* the Earth has already gone through four previous ages. Each age ended with some type of calamity as life transitioned into the new age. The current thought that the end of the Long Count calendar represents the end of the World is purely a media induced interpretation; however, it is not a stretch to say it represents the end of a current paradigm and therefore the world as we know it.

There is speculation as to the exact date the Long Count calendar ends. The continuity of Day-keepers, those who kept the calendars, was disrupted and the meanings of original documents were altered with the arrival of Spanish missionaries in the 1500s. Also, archeological date correlations are controversial. However, exact dates and years are not as important in a 26,000-year cycle as periods of transition. The changes associated with the endings and beginnings of cycles do not occur on one date; they arrive along a continuum, one that we can clearly see is underway.

If the end of the current Long Count is the end of an age and is correctly interpreted as 2012, Mayan texts provide indications of how things might transpire in the years leading up to and immediately after as "the old crumbles to make way for the new," so to speak. This includes:

- Earth changes such as floods, volcanoes, earthquakes, and fires resulting in famine and plague.

- Corruption of governments and religions such that the populations no longer trust their leaders.

- Widespread social unrest and war.

- The beginning of a "Golden Age" where spiritual "Masters" that lived in the past return to share gifts and wisdom.

Original sources for this information can be found in modern interpretations of the *Popul Vuh, The Dresden Codex,* and *The Chillum Balaam, The Book of the Jaguar Priest.* For the last, we used Maud Worchester Makemson's translation (Henry Schuman, Inc., 1951).

Hawkins's Mindstep Prediction

Gerald Hawkins also predicted a time frame for the next mind-step: 2021. He determined the date using a mathematical formula based on the ratio of accelerated change from one era to the next. Hawkins relates mindsteps to advancing awareness of our place in the cosmos and writes, "If rationality is any guide, one might expect the fifth mind-step to be communication with extra-terrestrial intelligence."[3]

Astrological Indicators

How does modern astrology relate to that of the ancient Maya? We asked astrologer Alan Ouimet. Alan is a retired FBI Special Agent in counter-intelligence and terrorism, a member of the Secular Franciscan Order, and founder and president of the Franciscan Family

Apostolate, providing support to families in India. He began studying astrology in 1972. As one might expect he is highly intelligent, serious, and not one for nonsense.

At my request Alan did a detailed astrological chart on the date December 21, 2012, including the years before and after. The following is summary of his report, which can be read on my Website (*www. colinandrews.net*).

At the center of the chart is an unusual astrological configuration called a *Yod,* or *Double Quincunx,* commonly known as the *Finger of God.* It involves three key planets: Jupiter, Saturn, and Pluto. Alan quotes astrologer Bil Tierney as stating that the configuration is symbolic of society meeting an unrecognized necessity and arriving at a fork in the road, having to proceed in one direction without knowing where it leads.[4] Alan explains that this astrological configuration—the *Finger of God*—was joined by a square aspect suggesting "the need for the physical manifestation of a reality which promises to be deep and revolutionary."[5]

It is further suggested that society's conflict is between secularism and religion, capitalism and socialism, conservatism and progressivism. The reconciling of these forces will require dropping long held ideologies that are blocking our ability to move forward. The tensions demand a shift in paradigms. The chart warns against bad judgment, overconfidence, and overreaching in material, economic, and political concerns.

The activation of the *Finger of God* at this time and under these conditions suggests the need to let go of limiting psychological beliefs, interests, and habits in order to become involved in whatever is appearing on the horizon. Any part of self or society that is destructive will most likely surface and actively struggle in the environment.[6]

One problem with astrological prediction is that we interpret it in light of known facts. However, the manner in which an astrological impulse will actually express is unknown and results often fall short of their expected impact. For example, in his 2009 report, Alan suggests that in the fall of 2010 there might be an Israeli and Iranian conflict involving a stealth attack on Iran's nuclear facility. Of course we imagined a military attack. In fact, in November 2010, Iranian President

Mahmoud Ahmeadinejad reported a stealth attack of malicious software against Iran's uranium enrichment centrifuges. According to a January 15, 2011, report in the *New York Times* quoting Reuters news agency, the software was an Israeli test of a computer virus/worm hoped to slow Iran's ability to develop a nuclear device. The *Times* reported that the tests of the destructive Stuxnet worm had occurred over the previous two years at the heavily guarded Dimona complex in the Negev desert. Apparently it was a joint Israeli–U.S. effort to undermine Iran's nuclear ambitions. The *Times* said the worm was the most sophisticated cyber-weapon ever deployed and appeared to have slowed Iran's nuclear ambitions.[7] We can see that the astrology was right, yet our interpretation of what would occur was not.

In summary, here is a small sampling of some of Alan's report on 2012 and the years that follow:

- The time period will contain international social, civil, political, and military unrest, after which the world will be a different place, much like the difference between the 1950s and 1970s.

- The period will be consciousness raising for some and hurtful to others, especially those who resist change.

- There is no way to know whether the paradigm shift will result from a period of long change or will be due to one large series of cataclysmic events.

- What you believe will affect your reality.

- If the past is a prologue, change will happen piecemeal as we respond to events.

- The *Finger of God* pushes people to become more effectively aligned with their inner spirit.

- Conflict between secular and religious elements will be reflected in international tension.

- There will be rebellion against organized religion due to a desire for the eternal inner fire.

- Each person will be asked: What is your unrecognized necessity; what owns you? What interests and habits must you give up? What new belief must you adopt?

The Precipice of the Paradigm

Personally, I was surprised that Ouimet's astrology agrees so completely with ancient prophecy. All reveal a perilous time with tremendous opportunity; we can self-destruct or expand beyond our present awareness. According to Hawkins, the scale and direction of mindsteps are never fully anticipated and are initially resisted. Yet there is always a vanguard of people who perceive change ahead of the masses and, as Einstein was, they are usually ridiculed and denounced. It is through the eyes of this vanguard of people that this book peeks beyond the veil to anticipate the change that lies ahead.

What is unmistakable is that as we approach the limits of our present paradigm, we realize with dismay that many pieces of this wonderfully interconnected reality are cascading toward ruin. We are nearing the point where the consequences of all of our actions meet. This is the crossroads at which we find ourselves: destruction or breakthrough. Something huge, new, and unforeseen must happen for survival, and it must happen within us. Each of us must now decide whether we will resist change and increase destructive pressure, or embrace a shift in consciousness, an awakening of perception that will expand and forever change our reality. Whether we find destruction or breakthrough depends on us. It depends on whether we care enough for our children, for the planet and for life itself to leap across the edge of reality.

Chapter 2:
The Point of
the Arrow

The year 2012 has come and gone and with it the induced hype. Shamefully, many people will never know the truth of the prophecy because the media created a myth of the end of the world, promoted the myth they created, and then dismissed the true Maya message when their distortion did not occur. We should not be surprised, and yet the brazen misrepresentation is shocking. Now we must ask where we are on this path to a new paradigm; do the predictions and prophecies still have validity after the highly publicized date has come and gone?

Let us be clear that there was never any claim by the Maya that there would be cataclysmic change on December 21, 2012. They do place importance on the period of time we are in. Determining whether this period is significant only requires looking at three arenas: stress in planetary life support systems, increased perceptive abilities in individuals along with increased high-strangeness events, and advances in science and new technology that expands beyond the mechanistic view of the universe.

To look at planetary systems, I created the Life Support Systems Index (LSSI), a series of trends that assesses changes in stress levels. I evaluate these in relation to the rising incidence of high-strangeness events that challenge our current mindset. As the trend lines of the LSSI indicate stressed systems are moving toward collapse, at the same time, a rise in high-strangeness events gives promise of breakthrough. New science and new technologies either sustain planetary life support systems and expand human potential, or, because there will always be those who resist change, seek to control populations for greed and power.

Stepping back, an unusual picture begins to form. Events seem to fall into patterns like an unfolding and enfolding fractal, revealing an underlying design in the change underway. Happenings appear linked through an interactive process with a conscious driving force underneath the changes we see.

. At this point, the magnitude of the discussion causes people to back away, questioning whether a paradigm shift is underway at all. Are conditions really that bad? Is the environment really struggling and is global climate change real? The picture crystalizes in the LSSI trends that includes both human-driven and nature-driven forces such as population growth, climate and weather change, geological stress, global politics and economics, social tension, religious discord, new diseases, and more. Each trend represents a natural or human cycle moving toward the same crash point of unsustainability. In the past, each arena had an in-built ability to absorb change, but that is no longer the case. The in-built self-correcting systems have been stretched beyond their recoil capacity. Consequently, we are executing the last move on the chessboard. While reading about the situation and how governments are responding to public need, keep in mind the descriptions in the prophecies.

Solar Activity

One factor playing into the boundaries of our current bottleneck is the activity of the Sun. A sunspot is a localized area of magnetic activity on the sun associated with secondary phenomena such as solar flares, eruptions of built-up magnetic energy that emits radiation in several bands of the electromagnetic spectrum (white light, ultraviolet, x-rays, gamma rays). Coronal mass ejections (CMEs) are solar eruptions emitted from large bubbles of magnetized gas or plasma that explode into space. When energized particles carried on solar wind from the Sun hit the Earth, they are distributed along the lines of the Van Allen Belt, colliding with magnetized particles already present and creating the Northern Light phenomenon.

The Sun undergoes cycles of activity with maximum occurrences happening approximately every 11 years. We are currently in the maximum part of Solar Cycle 24. In 2006, NASA predicted this cycle would bring extremely large solar flares and CMEs. So far the sun has been relatively quiet, but this could change at any moment. In January 2013, pictures from the sun showed a dramatic increase in activity, with 15 new spots appearing in a very short period and NASA is warning that electronics may be interrupted.[1]

There are two reasons for concern with excessive solar activity. First, solar ejections drive extreme weather and impact climate change as well as contribute to geological Earth changes (covered in upcoming sections). Second, solar activity can disrupt electric grids. In the last half-century we have increased our dependence on electricity to such a degree that all aspects of life are impacted when the grid goes down. Anyone who has lived through recent superstorms understands this well. According to a 2009 NASA report, for the last decade they have been warning governments to prepare infrastructure for CMEs that could seriously damage or collapse the national electrical grid, affecting power supply "for a period of years."[2]

In 1989, 6 million homes in Quebec experienced a blackout caused by a solar flare.[3] On June 9, 2011, the *New York Times* included an article about a House Energy Subcommittee hearing that took place in May 2011. The report cites Joseph McClelland, director of the Office of Electric Reliability at the Federal Energy Regulatory Commission, saying, "If the solar storm of 1921 [the largest actually measured], which has been termed a one-in-100-year event were to occur today, well over 300 extra-high-voltage transformers could be damaged or destroyed, thereby interrupting power to 130 million people for a period of years."[4]

The extent that GPS, communications satellites, and the national grid systems impact every facet of our lives can't be overstated. If the national grid system fails it means interference with computers, sewage treatment, elevators in high-rise buildings, medical devices, cars, food distribution, water treatment and supply, social media, cell phones, military command, control of nuclear weapons, and more. Consider the magnitude of disruption and also consider what type of plan you as an individual should have in place for your family.

Ecological Stress: Global Warming/Climate Change

The most significant ecological stress in our current bottleneck is climate change. Whether you believe that global warming is the result of human activity, a natural cycle involving solar activity, or some combination of both, there is no doubt that climate change is real. It is considered by thousands of scientists to be the single most important and serious planetary trend needing to be addressed. Global warming drives extreme weather; melts polar ice, causing rising ocean waters and related coastal destruction; warms the oceans, thereby disrupting food chains; increases methane release; and impacts innumerable life support functions of the Earth.

Simplified, the dynamics of global warming involve increasing concentrations of carbon dioxide that increase the greenhouse effect of the Earth's atmosphere. It's a "which came first: the chicken or the egg?" situation: Warming temperatures increase carbon levels and increased carbon levels increase temperatures. Past geological record show that solar activity warmed the atmosphere first, followed by increases in carbon dioxide. The debate is whether the current cycle has been preempted by human activity that is raising carbon levels in the atmosphere before solar activity, thus driving natural temperature increases past the point of return. Which came first may not seem to have any relevance, but if human activity is driving the speed of global warming, then modifying our carbon dioxide–producing activity may provide a means to slow the impact while we come to terms with the significant challenges climate change creates.

The Earth has mechanisms for maintaining homeostatic ranges and the conversion of carbon dioxide into oxygen through the action of plants, specifically trees, often called the lungs of the planet. The rainforest is one of the Earth's carbon-converting factories. We find ourselves in a situation where solar and human activity are driving carbon dioxide levels up at the same time that we are destroying one of the Earth's primary balancing mechanisms. Another mechanism through which the Earth can bring temperatures back down is volcanic activity. Ash spewed into the atmosphere provides reflective material that can direct solar radiation back into space. Some of the increased Earth changes may well be the activation of these mechanisms that are driven by the balancing of internal and external forces.

Impacts of climate change include:

♦ **Extreme weather.** Even without excess CME activity of the Sun, the arrival of extreme weather cannot be argued. If the strength of Hurricane Katrina wasn't enough to convince people that weather is changing, Superstorm Sandy revealed what we can anticipate as the jet stream is altered by the effects of global warming.

- **Seasons changing.** It's not just your imagination that the seasons are changing. We see leaves falling earlier and snow covering the hills weeks and sometimes months before we remember as kids. And in spring, the sun seems warmer than it should well before it is officially summer. A new study shows the trends are more modest, but definite evidence has been established that the seasons are indeed shifting. Earth's seasons have shifted; the hottest and coldest days of the year now occur almost two days earlier. Scientists at the University of California, Berkeley and Harvard say the shift could be the work of global warming. To figure this out, the scientists studied temperature data from 1850 to 2007 compiled by the University of East Anglia's Climate Research Unit in the United Kingdom.[5]

- **Wildfires.** The occurrences of vast wildfires are escalating as the warming climate produces a longer fire season combined with greater incidences of extreme drought. The fire season today is two and a half months longer than it was 30 years ago, and we are experiencing record-breaking wildfires that have consumed large areas of land in several countries, destroyed thousands of homes, and killed massive numbers of wildlife. Big fires are four times more common than they used to be, and the biggest fires are six and a half times larger than the monster fires of yesteryear.[6]

- **Droughts.** Increased droughts are impacting food production. During July 2012, a state of emergency was announced in 1,369 counties across the United States as drought conditions worsened.[7] More than 3,200 record high temperatures were in North America the month before and, to make matters worse, certain regions experienced the worst drought ever recorded. Climatologists are warning that much of the western United States is on the verge of downshifting to a new, perilous level of aridity.[8] Droughts like those that shaped the Dust Bowl in the 1930s and the even drier 1950s will soon be the new climatology of the region—not passing phenomena, but normal day-to-day weather.

- **Elevated temperatures.** Summer 2012 saw a warming trend with thousands of record temperatures across the United States, United Kingdom, Australia, and many other countries. The elevated temperatures of seawater impacted the cooling of nuclear power reactors. This was driven home for me in August 2012 when the seawater used to cool reactors at the Millstone Nuclear Power Plant in Waterford, Connecticut, exceeded 75 degrees, forcing a shutdown of one of the two reactors. Millstone supplies 500,000 homes with electrical energy. It doesn't take much imagination to see the scale of the problems we face if this trend continues across the planet.[9]

- **Methane.** On June 28, 2012, large tubes of methane gas escaped into the atmosphere from under melting ice caps in the Arctic. "Giant fountains/torches/plumes of methane entering the atmosphere up to 1 km across have been seen on the East Siberian Shelf," writes Malcolm Light, retired climate scientist.[10] The consequence of this is an uncontrollable escalation in climate change.

Despite the overwhelming evidence that climate change is real, opposition to addressing the issues, through ignorance or greed, continues. The deliberations at the 2009 United Nations Climate Change Conference in Copenhagen were overshadowed by claims that the findings of leading climatologists based at University of East Anglia, Norfolk, England, were falsified as part of a scientific conspiracy. The claims were based on hacked e-mails and were later revealed as incomplete and false; however, the damage to the conference and public perception was established. The purposeful attempt to derail world action and ensure corporate profit was successful, at least temporarily. It is notable that this serious topic was not mentioned once in the U.S. presidential debates before the 2012 elections.

Geological Forces/Earth Changes

The term *Earth changes* refers to changes in the geology of the planet that are marked by events such as earthquakes, volcanoes, and tsunamis, all different aspects of the same internal forces. The Earth's crust is composed of tectonic plates that move in response to internal pressure derived from the Earth's molten core. The smoldering core produces heat and pressure that cause the plates to move in order to release energy. Earthquakes occur as plates grind against each other. Volcanoes provide an escape for hot molten rock, ash, and gas. Volcanoes and earthquakes that occur in the oceans result in tsunami waves, the size of which relates to the magnitude of the disruption.

Activity in the molten core produces the Earth's magnetic field, or magnetosphere, that protects the Earth from solar radiation and electrified particles. *National Geographic Magazine* reports: "Earth's magnetic field is fading. Today it is about 10 percent weaker than it was when German mathematician Carl Friedrich Gauss started keeping tabs on it in 1845. If the trend continues, the field may collapse altogether and then reverse. Compasses would point south instead of north."[11] A decrease in magnetic protection will allow increased solar radiation into the Earth's atmosphere causing the problems discussed in the "Solar Activity" section. It will also widen the atmospheric ozone holes, which will further global warming.

Although the idea of flipping the Earth's magnetic field seems like science fiction, it has happened many times. Magnetic traces in the Earth's geologic record show that the Earth's magnetic field flips approximately once every 200,000 years. The last time Earth's magnetic field flipped was about 780,000 years ago. *National Geographic* reports, "The magnetic north pole had moved little from the time scientists first located it in 1831. Then in 1904, the pole began shifting northeastward at a steady pace of about 9 miles (15 kilometers) a year. In 1989 it sped up again, and in 2007 scientists confirmed that the pole is now galloping toward Siberia at 34 to 37 miles (55 to 60 kilometers) a year."[12] Consequently, the Federal Aviation Administration (FAA) is requiring many airports to realign runway markers with bearings that reflect the new magnetic north. Though experts are fast to say that life will go on after a pole reversal, no one knows what the transition will be like.

Volcanic Activity

In order to have an increase in volcanic activity, there has to be an increase in pressure deep inside the Earth—enough pressure to force an eruption. Right now scientists are wondering if the weakening of the Earth's magnetosphere represents a change in dynamics at the Earth's core, changing internal pressure and increasing volcanic activity.

The largest study of volcanoes, conducted as the Smithsonian Volcanism Project, shows a steady increase in volcanic activity, although they are fast to say this increase is only related to reporting and does not confirm an actual increase in events. In 1914 there were about 35 volcano eruptions each year; by 1990 there were approximately 50. According to the Smithsonian there are about 1511 active volcanoes.[13] This doesn't mean they are actively erupting; it means they have the potential to erupt. Volcanoes can sleep for hundreds of years before erupting.

The impact of volcanic eruption on modern life was clearly seen on April 14, 2012. An explosion from the *Eyjafjallajökull* volcano in Iceland sent clouds of ash soaring 12 miles (20 kilometers) into the sky. The event disrupted air traffic in Northern Europe, with ripple effects far beyond. Travel chaos across the globe deepened as the vast, high-altitude plume of volcanic ash spread farther across northern and central Europe, forcing aviation authorities to close more airspace and ground more airplanes to forestall damage to jet engines.

Earthquakes

Earthquakes are measured on the Richter scale, with up to a 3 being a small earthquake and more than 7 a large one. Small earthquakes happen constantly around the world, especially along what is called the Pacific Rim of Fire. The U.S. Geological Survey (USGS) estimates there are several million little earthquakes happening all over the planet each year.

A new NASA study conducted with the USGS predicts that earthquake activity may be increasing due to global warming. According to a USGS study, retreating glaciers are changing external versus internal pressures in the Earth's crust. Rapid ice cap melting is shifting weight distribution and is increasing the likelihood of earthquakes.

Here are some recent events:

- 87,000 people perished in Sichuan Province, southwest China on May 12, 2008, when an 8.0 magnitude earthquake quickly followed a 6.2 magnitude earthquake.

- 316,000 perished and 300,000 were injured in January 12, 2010, in Haiti with a 7 magnitude earthquake centering in the town of Leogane. The town was virtually wiped off the map, and an estimated 1,000,000 people lost their homes. As of September 1, 2012, around 40,000 still live in tents.

- On February 27, 2010, a massive 8.8 earthquake, the seventh-strongest in history, struck Chile with such an impact that it changed the Earth's rotation, shortening the length of days by 1.26 millisecond, and shifting the axis of the planet by 3 inches according to scientist Richard Gross at NASA's Jet Propulsion Laboratory in Pasadena, California.[14]

- On March 11, 2011, a huge 8.9 magnitude earthquake occurred off the coast of Honshu, Japan, unleashing an enormous tsunami that leveled everything in its path. According to the National Police Agency of Japan, as of September 11, 2011, a total of 15,861 were killed, 6,107 injured, and 3,018 people were missing. The main Island of Japan was moved 8 feet by this incredible quake, and the Earth's axis was shifted a full 10 inches.[15] The damage to the nuclear reactors in the four power plants made this the worst planetary disaster in history (see the next section on nuclear technology).

Tsunamis

A tsunami is a series of waves resulting from underwater earthquakes, landslides, or volcanoes, and sometimes by meteor and asteroid impacts in the ocean. Surveys of the ocean floor and examination of shoreline sediment reveal that every few thousand years an asteroid or meteor hits the ocean, causing a large tsunami.

Historically, about 1,000 tsunamis have been documented, with only about 100 being large enough to cause damage and loss of life. The three most recent tsunamis, excluding the Japanese tragedy of 2011 reported in the previous section, were:

- August 17, 1999: Northwest Turkey was struck with a large earthquake, generating a local tsunami in which approximately 17,000 people lost their lives and thousands more were injured.

- December 26, 2004: A 9.3 Richter scale earthquake off the island of Sumatra in the Indian Ocean created a horrifying tsunami that killed more than 300,000 people in eight Asiatic countries including Sumatra, Sri Lanka, India, Thailand, Malaysia, and Bangladesh. The flood wave even reached East and Southeast Africa, with the height of the largest wave reaching about 100 feet. The tsunami caused nearly $10 billion in damage and more casualties than any other tsunami in history, according to the United Nations.

- July 17, 2006: An earthquake south of Java, Indonesia, caused a tsunami that killed 700 people.

(To see the record of tsunamis over the last 1,000 years, check out *www.tsunami-alarm-system.com.*)

New Patterns of Disease

There are three main disease concerns in the bottleneck: the change in distribution and prevalence of insect-born infectious disease, the mutation of old diseases into new variants, and the arrival of entirely new diseases.

The first concern is linked to changing weather patterns. As cold temperatures recede, cold-controlled insect-born disease can travel farther north and live for longer periods of time. Malaria, West Nile Virus, and Lyme disease are a few that fit this category. The *New York Times* reported on September 6, 2012, that meteorological and ecological shifts driven by climate change are creating a slow and unpredictable bloom of public health challenges.(14)[16] The American Public Health Association has declared climate change "one of the most serious public health threats facing our nation."[17]

In the same light, extreme weather and natural disasters increase the spread of infectious disease. Storms arriving with high floodwaters can override sewage control systems and contaminate local water supplies. The reduced hygiene of large numbers of people in the cramped quarters of storm shelters allows disease to spread more easily. Even wildfires and drought contribute to the picture by changing the predator-prey balance, allowing unusual diseases such as the hantavirus to flourish.

The second concern of mutations in existing strains of virus has raised fears of erupting pandemics. The popularly termed swine flu and avian flu are two examples that brought public awareness to the vulnerability of populations to the spread of such diseases.

Of greatest interest, however, is the advent of new and baffling illnesses such as Morgellons disease. The Mayo Clinic describes Morgellons as an unexplained skin disorder containing five distinguishing characteristics: disfiguring, itchy skin rashes and sores, crawling sensations on and under the skin that feel like worms, severe fatigue, short-term memory loss with an inability to concentrate, and the appearance of fibers or solid material that emerge from the sores.[18]

Studies conducted by the Center of Disease Control (CDC) revealed no parasitic or infectious origin.[19] Current health professionals are divided in their thoughts: Some believe it is a specific condition that needs further research, some believe it as type of mental illness known as delusional parasitosis, and others don't acknowledge the disease at all.

The most distinguishing feature of Morgellons is the appearance of unusual fibers that seem to be produced under the skin. Synthia and I have met people with this condition and have seen pictures of the material. The fibers were segmented and in some cases were several inches long. The disease provokes extreme anxiety and fear in those who suffer with it. However, what is not reported by the Mayo Clinic, CDC, or other investigative bodies, is that most of those who have the disease have no prior history of anxiety disorders.

People with Morgellons come from all walks of life and professions. Many are medical doctors. Theories abound, but there is little evidence to support any one cause. Thoughts include affects from genetically modified food, nano-virus technology gone awry, and extraterrestrial contamination.

Population and Food Supply

The majority of human-driven stressors in the LSSI model are motivated by the need to feed and support the exponentially growing population. According to the United Nations, on October 31, 2011, the human population reached seven billion. By September 2012, more than 65,000,000 more had been born.[20] It is obvious that supporting an escalating population requires an escalating amount of natural resources, energy production, and food and water. As the world's population grows, improving living standards without destroying the environment is a global challenge. The Action Bio Science Organization (ABSO) says that in 64 of 105 developing countries studied by the UN Food and Agriculture Organization, the population has been growing faster than food supplies.[21] Water and food shortages are further challenged by climate change.

To increase food production many countries are allowing the use of genetically modified foods (GMO). To be clear, these genetic modifications are not refinements of natural genetic strains. They consist of splicing the genes of different types of life-forms together, such as splicing pig genes into apples for better shipping, or splicing pesticides such as Roundup directly into plant genes. Pesticides used in this manner cannot be washed off, and because GMO foods are often unlabeled, the public has little protection from this massive experiment. French studies reveal that exposure to pesticides in every mouthful of food is causing an increase in severe forms of cancer.[22] Other effects, such as increases in the incidence of food allergies, endocrine disorders, and asthma, are also suspected to be linked to pesticides found in drinking water.[23]

Pollution

Increasing population automatically creates increases in pollution in all forms including from energy production and consumption, industrial and chemical waste, and, in some regards worst of all, the amount of plastic waste products dumped into the ocean each year. The World Health Organization reports that 3 million people now die each year from the effects of air pollution alone.[24] In the past decade, in every environmental sector, conditions have either failed to improve or are worsening.

Legislative steps taken to alleviate pollution often are devoid of common sense and science. For example, consider the legislation to remove all regular tungsten light bulbs for energy-efficient florescent light bulbs. Compact fluorescent, high-intensity discharge lamps are more efficient when it comes to light output per unit of energy required, but at what cost? The bulbs are made with toxic mercury that is considered an extreme environmental hazard. Breaking a bulb in the house requires special clean-up procedures, and breaking multiple bulbs may require the enlistment of a hazmat team! When burned out, bulbs must be disposed of at special hazardous waste disposal centers.[25] There are an estimated 110 million homes in the United States, and each has between 50 and 100 light sockets.[26] During one year, U.S. consumers purchase 2 billion light bulbs at the rate of 5.5 million every day. That is a lot of mercury.

Nuclear Technology

Nuclear technology is a cataclysmic time bomb. One act of war (the U.S. bombing of Japan at the end of World War II) and two terrible accidents (Chernobyl in Russia and Fukushima in Japan) have already occurred. The effects have not been fully determined or communicated. With the rising temperatures of seawater impacting the ability to cool reactor cores, climate change may play the final card with regard to nuclear technology.

Two old-fashioned atomic bombs killed an estimated 246,000 inhabitants of Japan in the final stages of World War II in 1945. The cities of Hiroshima and Nagasaki in Japan were destroyed. These bombs represent the only use of nuclear weapons to date. Today's modern bombs are capable of many more-fold destruction.

The accident in Russia at the Chernobyl Nuclear Power Plant occurred due to human error. On April 16, 1986, operators in the control room of Reactor #4 bungled a routine safety test, resulting in an explosion that ignited a fire that burned for 10 days. The radioactive fallout spread over large parts of Europe and western Russia, driving more than a quarter of a million people permanently from their homes. Asked when the reactor site would again become inhabitable, Ihor Gramotkin, director of the Chernobyl Nuclear Power Plant, replied, "At least 20,000 years."[27]

The publication *Chernobyl: Consequences of the Catastrophe for People and the Environment* (available through the Annals of the New York Academy of Sciences), states that among the billions of people worldwide who were exposed to radioactive contamination from the disaster, nearly a million premature cancer deaths occurred between

1986 and 2004. The publication has received criticism for its methodology and sourcing.[28]

The accident at the Fukushima plant in Japan that occurred after the 9.0 earthquake on March 11, 2011, caused a massive tsunami that crippled the cooling systems at the Tokyo Electric Power Company's (TEPCO) nuclear plant. The loss of cooling led to hydrogen explosions and reactor meltdowns that forced evacuations of those living within a 20-kilometer radius (about 12.4 miles) of the plant. The radiation was released into the air and is now encompassing the entire planet. On April 4, 2011, the Tokyo Electric Power Company dumped 11,500 tons of radioactive water into the Pacific Ocean in a last-ditch attempt to contain damage at the Fukushima Daiichi Nuclear Power Plant. Arnold Gundersen, a former nuclear industry senior vice president, told Al Jazeera, "Fukushima is the biggest industrial catastrophe in the history of mankind."[29] The extent of the damage and the full release of radiation are yet to be disclosed publically. A very poignant moment in the drama occurred before the Tokyo Electric Power Company started releasing radioactive water into the ocean on that evening: A power company official grew very emotional at the press conference announcing the intent to start dumping the water, apologizing to the Japanese people for the failure of the company.

The Fukushima Daiichi Nuclear Power Plant is one of the 15 largest in the world. As of this writing (2012), several reactor cores are still burning their way into the Earth as radiation continues to be expelled into the atmosphere and into the Pacific Ocean. Despite the extraordinary destruction, the nuclear industry and the International Atomic Energy Agency (IAEA) quickly relinquished their obligations to keep the international community fully informed about the ongoing crisis. As of this writing, the last public IAEA briefing on the Fukushima Nuclear Accident was June 2, 2011. During the first days of this horrible disaster, which is still unfolding and is estimated to do so for the next 20 years, the nuclear industry stood one expert after another in front of the TV cameras to convince us that Japan was unique and no such accident could ever occur in another country. Their real concern was obvious: protect the multi-billion-dollar industry, not the public or the planet. Is this the type of corruption referred to in the prophecy?

Global Economic Collapse

The collapse of the world economy in 2008 occurred after a period of frantic financial spending and uncontrolled debt. "Bankers, economists and politicians displayed the same kind of manic behavior as psychologically disturbed individuals in the years running up to the 2008 financial collapse," says a new study by Dr. Mark Stein, an award-winning scholar from the University of Leicester School of Management and published at PsychCentral.com.[30]

In the United States, through the first decade of the 21st century, federal government spending, overseen by President George W. Bush, increased dramatically, while revenues declined. The last two years of the Bush presidency saw the subprime mortgage crisis. With no money, never mind gold, backing up leveraged assets, the house of cards collapsed, and as the housing bubble burst, the stock market plunged and large financial institutions tottered on the brink of collapse. National governments bailed out banks and insurance companies that were supposedly too big to fail. The effects are still playing out in the worst economic disaster since the Great Depression. Economists warn that another crash is likely.

Needless to say, U.S. national debt grew significantly from 2001 to 2008, both in dollar terms and relative to the size of the economy (GDP). Proportionally, Bush increased government spending more than any predecessor.[31] National debt has continued to soar under the Obama administration. U.S. national debt as of November 2011 (posted on my Website November 30, 2011) was $15,054,163,621,371.29—that's 15 trillion, 54 billion, 163 million, 621 thousand, 371 hundred dollars and 29 cents. This figure exists as words only: No gold backs up the amount and no paper money has been printed to represent it.

The economic system is in chaos and hides behind a smoke screen of technical jargon and formulas. The cause of the financial collapse and the handling of the crisis are two of the biggest crimes of all times. As of this writing, U.S. debt has now exceeded the number in the previous paragraph by more than a further one trillion, 10 billion dollars— and counting. As one can imagine, big money equals big politics. China tops the list of U.S. creditors, holding more than $1 trillion in Treasury debt as of March 2012.

These numbers are words on paper to governments, but to the average person they represent real changes in lifestyle. Many people have lost jobs, homes, retirement funds, college savings accounts, and a lifetime of hard-earned assets. Some are living in their cars, on the streets, and in the extra rooms of family members' homes. Although the media enjoys portraying these people as having taken on more debt than they could pay back, most were hardworking people who had the rug pulled out from under them when their jobs suddenly disappeared, pension plans failed, and investments in the stock market crashed. Overnight, the middle class was virtually cut in half.

The cost of living is expected to continue to rise as drought destroys crops and oil prices continue to be unstable. In short, the economic part of the bottleneck is not going away anytime soon.

Religious Unrest

There is nothing new about religious zealotry being the cause of war. It is an age-old tension. Looking around the planet right now we can see most geopolitical unrest has religious overtones, along with the desire to control land and resources. There is also nothing new about friction between denominations within religions, or with people abandoning religious belief. Predictions that foresee these things have a pretty good probability of coming true. On the other hand, when religious factions such as the Fundamentalist Christian movement can drive politics in a country with clear separation between church and state such as the United States, and when religious institutions as large as the Vatican are in danger, prophecy seems a little more impressive.

Nothing needs to be said about the impact of religious momentum in American politics right now; anyone who has watched the last four presidential elections is well aware of the conflict. Also well publicized is the notable problem with pedophilia and the hiding of predatory priests that is undermining the moral and spiritual authority of the Vatican. Less well known is the Pope's attack on U.S. nuns, labeling them radical feminists. The nuns' transgressions appear to be the observance of love as their prime directive as opposed to church doctrine.[32]

Not to be minimized is the Vatican's 2008 declaration of life on other planets—not only life, but the possibility of extraterrestrial "brothers" possibly more evolved than humans. On May 5, 2008, in a

New York Times report, the head of the Vatican Observatory and scientific advisor to Pope Benedict XVI, Rev. José Gabriel Funes, is quoted as saying, "How can we exclude that life has developed elsewhere," noting that there is no contradiction between this belief and the belief in God.[33] Though this is not the same as an admission from the Pope, it may well indicate that the Vatican is preparing the ground for the paradigm shift necessary to accept interaction with extraterrestrials.

Whatever one thinks about these issues, or whatever side one comes out on, it can't be denied that they represent unprecedented tension and change.

Social and Civil Unrest

The level of civil unrest over the last two years hasn't been seen in the United States since the anti-war movement of the 1960s or the environmental movement of the '70s. The Tea Party mobilized massive political agendas on the political right, and Occupy Wall Street became an international movement on the political left.

Internationally, "Arab Spring" began on December 18, 2010, when large populations rose against governments in a wave of revolutionary demonstrations against government suppression. Large-scale protests escalated through Tunisia, Egypt, Libya, Yemen, Bahrain, Syria, Algeria, Iraq, Jordan, Kuwait, Morocco, Sudan, Lebanon, Mauritania, Oman, Saudi Arabia, Djibouti, and Western Sahara. Less than two years later, rulers were forced from power in Tunisia, Egypt, Libya, and Yemen.[34] In addition, the worsening financial situation gave rise to riots in Europe, most noticeably in Greece. As food and water supplies become more endangered and increasing superstorms like Sandy cause greater disruption, uncertainty and social anxiety will continue to rise.

Accelerating change fuels social unrest. Events happen so fast there is no separation between cause and effect, allowing situations to spiral out of control with frightening speed. The Internet is an excellent example: Although it allows instant access of information across the Earth, disputes are magnified into untangled webs, lies are written into history as fact, and truth is permanently distorted. It becomes increasingly difficult to weigh the truth of information and understand the motives behind government, corporate, and individual action. Though it is easy to retreat into self-protective isolation, each of us is being asked to step up and evaluate information against our inner sense of truth. The difficulties of accelerated change are pushing us into greater awareness. It is up to us to meet the challenge and open our minds to the expansion of consciousness that will light the way.

In fact, this push to paradigm shift can already be felt. The Vatican is not the only institution accepting the possibility of life on other planets and inevitability of contact. In 2012 the *Huffington Post* reported that, according to a UK poll conducted by Opinion Matters, "More than 33 million UK citizens believe in extraterrestrial life compared to just over 27 million—less than half the country—who believe in God."[35] A paradigm shift indeed! Similar polls in the United States suggest the same trend exists here.

Government Corruption

According to the Federal Bureau of Investigation (FBI), "Public corruption poses a fundamental threat to our national security and way of life. It impacts everything from how well our borders are secured and our neighborhoods protected...to verdicts handed down in courts... to the quality of our roads, schools, and other government services. And it takes a significant toll on our pocketbooks, wasting billions in tax dollars every year."[36] What happens, however, when government corruption is as engrained as public corruption?

Truthfully, no government has ever been or ever will be free of corruption. The problem is one of degree and perception. We are at a moment when international distrust of governments is at an all-time high, in many cases for very real reasons. In the United States, opponents have strongly questioned the legitimacy of the elections of the last two presidents, George W. Bush and Barack Obama. Public perception of government conspiracy is fueled by reality and imagination. Scandals such as the financial collapse and Wall Street, Halliburton's role in Iraq, Enron's manipulation of energy prices, and the loss of all financial papers in Building #7 after 9/11, raise valid questions—and these are only the tip of a very large iceberg!

The corruption in all world governments precipitates public distrust and unrest. The current feeling is one of a powder keg getting ready to explode. If the economy turns around and people are able to return to the pursuit of personal goals, the volatility will subside. However, the trend lines of the LSSI indicate more stress is on the way, rather than less. The question becomes whether our government institutions can respond by initiating real change, or whether they will waste energy and resource trying to hold together a dying system.

The transparency and integrity required to create something new and better are sadly missing in today's political scene. A new caliber of person is required who can move into legislative position with the intent to serve and lead, rather than gain personal power and influence. Public and government corruption become the same thing as we understand that we are the pool from which politicians are chosen. The bottom line is that we as individuals are being called to a higher level of integrity and action. When each of us steps forward, we create the leaders we need for the changes to come.

Stepping Up

The LSSI trends are the consequences of past choices. These consequences are pushing us toward needed change, yet they represent only one side of the equation of the current paradigm shift. Equal to the challenges we face are the concurrent development of inner resources to overcome them and the change in consciousness needed to sustain them. There is a clarion call for individuals to step up, learn from the past, and become the embodiment of higher consciousness. As we do, attitudes and how we conduct our activities will be transformed. Change will happen because we open to our power as spiritual beings, consciously interacting with deeper layers of reality.

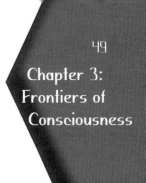

The LSSI trends account for only half of the force that is hastening change. The other half comes from our innate desire to grow. We are compelled toward taking a mindstep by our desire to experience more. Fulfilling the desire requires an expansion. Maya scholars say a shift in consciousness is a natural outcome of entering a new cycle of Long Count calendars. Describing consciousness and changes in consciousness is difficult however, because we have no clear definition or understanding of what it is.

Consciousness is considered synonymous with awareness, the ability to perceive one's surroundings. Self-awareness is the ability to perceive our impact and place in our surroundings. The idea of an expansion in consciousness is the ability to perceive more of what is present and to understand in greater depth our place within it. The question arises: Is consciousness merely a function of the mind, or is it something larger? Is it the substance of the universe, a self-organizing, energy-based continuum in which all intelligence is anchored? Early philosophers considered the ability to be self-aware what made humans different from all other life on the planet. Today's science considers consciousness the primary force within life. So, what is consciousness: a substance or a force, a particle or a wave? Is consciousness a field of energy that intelligently organizes the particles within?

Reality is often discussed in terms of frequency and vibration. Science teaches us to question the solidity with which our senses experience reality. Thanks to Einstein's famous equation $E=MC^2$, we understand that matter and energy are the same substance only vibrating at different speeds. This alone represents a shift in paradigm from Newtonian physics, and technology was fast to utilize the door that was opened. We know from our technology that frequency is linked to information: Information is transmitted on carrier waves encoded as frequency.

Frequency within an energy field organizes the particles it houses. This implies an intelligent universe and even imbues it with consciousness. The implications are vast.

In whatever manner we define consciousness, there are many indications that our awareness and our ability to perceive are changing. Where this will lead—what new reality is being bridged—is unknown. As we straddle the edge, however, we are interacting with mysterious phenomena that may always have been present but that we were unable to identify. Our changing ability to perceive provides an indication of whom we are becoming, the phenomena we experience provide a glimpse into what the new reality might look like, and new science provides context.

High Strangeness on the Rise

An increased ability to perceive different aspects of reality may seem a strange concept, yet across the board more people are having this experience. A 2002 poll conducted by the National Opinion Research Center at the University of Chicago revealed that 72 percent of those polled believed in life after death, 17 percent did not, and 11 percent were undecided.[1] The poll revealed a steady rise in the number of people believing in life after death over the past 40 years.

My sense is that the rise in openness to the paranormal is due to more people experiencing unusual phenomena such as having visions, dreams, and other types of interactions with deceased loved ones, having UFO sightings, and more. Rather than being ridiculed when they share their experiences, people are finding support within their community of friends and neighbors. Readers may have seen the newscast when the mother of one of the children killed at the Sandy Hook Elementary School in Newtown, Connecticut, in December 2012 reported being visited by her dead son several days after the shooting. Her declaration was treated with respect by a media used to ridiculing anything out of the norm. Another mother of the Sandy Hook disaster reported that her son asked her the day before he was killed what it was like to die, as if he could feel the bow-wave of what was coming. The frequency of such events and their impact on the experiencers are indications of the immensity of the change underway. Ultimately, the mindstep in which we are engaged is not happening to societies and institutions; it is happening to individuals who are then driving change in society and institutions.

The type of phenomena under discussion used to be called paranormal, meaning beyond our normal awareness or understanding, yet this definition is no longer accurate. Unusual phenomena have become common. Now they are termed high-strangeness events, and people of all walks of life are coming into contact with them. According to a 2005 Gallop Poll, three in four Americans have at least one paranormal belief.[2] Here are examples:

- **Precognition:** knowing who is on the phone when it rings, thinking of someone you haven't seen in years and then meeting them unexpectedly, having a sense of imminent future tragedies, and so forth.

- **Telepathy:** receiving a transmission from another person so that you know what he or she is about to say, sending someone a mental warning and having the person receive it.

- **Sending and receiving healing energy:** using prayer, mental telepathy, and/or energy healing techniques to send and receive vital life force with the intent of helping the healing process.

- **Mediumship:** receiving messages from people who are dead through images and thoughts, synchronicity and dreams, or having visions of the deceased with direct communication.

- **Awareness of synchronicity:** events lose randomness and are connected through synchronized happening that often appear coincidental.

- **Awareness of other entities:** angels, aliens, deceased people, spirits, and other beings commonly experienced as influencing human affairs.

We wonder: Are these experiences becoming more prevalent because reality is changing or because we are changing? Change becomes real the moment it is acknowledged, and I believe both reality and perceptions are undergoing rapid change (as we will see in future chapters).

Also impressive are the mass witnessing of unusual events. In the past, one or two people had experiences that most others did not believe occurred. Now groups of people are having experiences, and many are recorded on electronic devices. Here are some examples we will look at more closely later:

- Orbs of light appearing on photographs with no physical reason.
- Mass sightings of interactive, unidentified lights in the sky.
- Entire communities hearing unusual hums that seem to come from underground and/or the sky.
- Unusual explosions in the sky, such as the Norway Spiral on December 9, 2009.
- The uncanny sensation that there is an intelligent interaction between the phenomena and the witnesses.

Importantly, when people experience high-strangeness events, they receive authentication of their reality through their body. The body is constantly receiving information from the environment and sending the impressions to the brain forming our perceptions. This means that our body understands before our mind the significance of an event. Emotions, physical sensations such as tingling, goose bumps, and hot and cold flashes, along with gut feelings, alert us of the reality of events.

Another aspect of the paradigm shift, perhaps in response to the trends revealed in LSSI or the desire to maintain the old status quo, is a concurrent rise in covert technologies. Here are some examples that are explored in this book:

- Chemtrails (chemical contrails from aircraft that are seen over most of the United States and now acknowledged as a government program).
- Unexplained and new weather radar anomalies in Australia that may relate to weather modification experiments.
- The government initiated High-Frequency Active Auroral Research Program (H.A.A.R.P.) manipulating elements of the ionosphere.
- Mind control as part of military weaponry.

- The engineering of robotic insects both for spying and for delivering lethal injections.

It is easy to think these technologies and covert government activities are unrelated to the paradigm shift; however, I do not think so. It seems that the changes underway are being monitored and responded to by those who would direct, control, and manipulate them. However, what is occurring is bigger than our institutions or technology. Consider the advent of the computer. It has become a staple in every aspect of life, a development that required multi-disciplinary coordination and planning at all levels of society. What hidden controller of operations is at work? The totality of what we are experiencing represents the interconnection that organizes individuals within the design of reality

Inattentional Blindness

High-strangeness events indicate there are other layers of reality existing alongside us that we have been unaware of in the past. You may be wondering why we were unable to sense their presence earlier. It is similar to being unaware of radio waves or microwaves until we had a context to put them in, which allowed us to create technology to interact with them. In addition, aspects of our consciousness are changing, and thus our ability to perceive.

Have you ever slowed for a yield sign, looked for cars and trucks, then pulled out in front of a motorcycle you never saw? Or gone into a crowded room looking for your spouse and looked right at an old friend, yet never saw him or her? These are examples of inattentional blindness, the failure to notice a fully visible, but unexpected object. It occurs when our attention is engaged so fully in one direction that we overlook, or look through, anything else that is out of context. Although the term *blindness* implies that the object isn't seen, some research indicates that the object is seen, but dismissed as unimportant and then not remembered. In other words, the inability to perceive something for which we do not have a context is related to how we process information.

Being unable to perceive what we don't expect may be one reason why, in the past, people didn't experience as many high-strangeness events as today. Our cultural beliefs have changed, making those experiences less unexpected. At first this might seem at odds with the earlier statement that cultural beliefs are changing because of an increase in individual experiences. However, there is an interesting twist to the studies: It appears that although an object is not seen or remembered, its presence is processed by the brain, and does impact our perceptions and actions in a subliminal or subconscious manner.[3] In other words, although we don't see the event, we do perceive it on some level and it stimulates a reaction.

Imagine this scenario: You are driving along a country lane and, as you crest a hill, you see an unusual light in the sky emerging through the trees. Although the light is at tree level, makes no sound, and turns at a 90-degree angle—something an aircraft could not do—rather than stopping, you continue driving. Your mind dismisses the light as impossible and categorizes it as an airplane. Within minutes you have forgotten that you saw anything; however, your body did record the event. For years after, without making any conscious decisions, you avoid driving that particular stretch of road or alternately become obsessed with UFOs although you will swear that you have never had an encounter.

In this way, as more and more people have had such encounters with the unknown, they have been subconsciously influenced to seek and provide context for them. This opened the door for additional experiences, ones that are now engaged with a greater level of awareness. We can see the circular nature of how our perceptions are developed and how subtle interactions are driving us forward into a design we are not yet able to see.

Interestingly, although we may practice our observational skills or develop a meditation practice to become more aware, it seems we cannot increase our ability to perceive the unusual. According to research, we cannot train ourselves to see something we can't imagine. Chabris and Simons report: "If an object is truly unexpected, people are unlikely to notice it no matter how good (or bad) they are at focusing attention."[4] In other words, the only way to see the unexpected is for it to become expected.

Physical and Emotional Perception

High-strangeness events bring us into contact with non-ordinary reality. We focus on the mind as being our primary organ of perception. However, as discussed earlier, the body receives impulses from the environment and sends the information to the brain to help form perceptions that become part of our decision-making process. It is through the body that these realms have access to stimulate our awareness.

Emotions provide communication between the body and the mind.[5] Dr. Candace Pert explains that the neuropeptides that carry emotion convey information between the mind and the body. Much of the information received by the body is translated into emotions and conveyed to the mind through feelings. In high-strangeness events, emotions are heightened and the mind is often overloaded with stimuli. To control the overwhelm, emotions are suppressed and stored in the body as muscle memory, and details of the event are often not sorted until years later when the emotional content of the event is processed.

Another area of interest is the role of mirror motor neurons in creating behavior. Mirror motor neurons, originally discovered in the brains of macaque monkeys, exist in the neuro-circuitry of all mammals. They fire when we perform highly specific actions; different neurons fire in response to different actions. Whereas motor neurons fire as they command a muscle to perform an action, mirror motor neurons fire when we perform an action and also when we observe someone else performing an action. In fact, they fire even when we hear only the sounds of someone else performing an action.

In an article with Edge.org, neuroscientist Dr. V.S. Ramachandran, author of *Phantoms in the Brain* (1998), states:

> With knowledge of these neurons, you have the basis for understanding a host of very enigmatic aspects of the human mind: "mind reading" empathy, imitation learning, and even the evolution of language. Anytime you watch someone else doing something (or even starting to do something), the corresponding mirror neuron might fire in your brain thereby allowing you to "read" and understand another's intentions and thus to develop a sophisticated "theory of other minds."[6]

One of the effects of mirror motor neurons is that they create connection between people; they give an internal reality to an external event. When two people sit together drinking wine, as one person raises his glass, the other person's neurons fire as though he or she, too, were raising a glass, creating a shared experience. We wonder: Because mirror neurons are tuned to the environment, might they also respond to paranormal events? Might they react to an unseen external presence, for example, or other high-strangeness events that cause a corresponding physical or emotional sensation? If so, in addition to being important in forming our impressions and driving us forward, these experiences may also be the first step for another realm to teach us how to communicate with our emotional energy.

Increasing awareness of our body and emotions is a primary tool for us to investigate non-ordinary realms. With the advent of mind-body medicine, body awareness has become a mainstream skill for ensuring better health. As we become more connected to our body and the wisdom it contains, we may also be better able to communicate with other realms.

The Context of New Science

Science often provides context for changing paradigms. Quantum mechanics is the field of physics that resulted from observations of light and the extraordinary interactions among subatomic particles. What was witnessed forever changed physics. Wave-particle duality result-ing from Young's double slit experiments with light explains that all particles have the properties of both a wave and a particle. Although there are alternate interpretations, the standard interpretation of quantum mechanics considers this duality a fundamental property of the universe.

Young's experiments resulted in theories regarding the role of the observer in determining whether a quanta shows itself in a given moment in its particle state or in its wave state. Apparently, the observer or the fact of being observed is the causal factor. This makes conscious-ness a determining force of reality, supporting the metaphysical idea that thoughts create reality. A further question arises: What connects the observer to the observed? Is it a flow of energy, a field effect, or something else?

Strange occurrences between subatomic particles also reveal the concepts of non-locality and entanglement. Non-locality is the observa-tion that two particles can interact instantaneously while at a distance without any intervening force. To date, non-locality has only been wit-nessed when two particles have already established a relationship with each other, an event that is termed *entanglement*. When two particles, such as photons, quanta of light, electrons, or subatomic particles, interact physically with each other, they become entangled. When they are separated, they continue to interact as though they are still connected. Altering the physicality of one automatically causes an alteration in the entangled other no matter how far away. In addition to becoming the source of the next big technology shift, that of quantum computers, this finding provides a theoretical foundation for telepathy and other paranormal abilities.

We cannot assume that micro reality revealed by the actions of subatomic particles has a correlation with macro reality. However, it does form the science behind the World Wide Web and the assumption is fueling research and technological development around the world. This is seen with the Large Hadron Collider, a particle accelerator near Geneva that is run by CERN, the European Organization for Nuclear Research. CERN is one of two facilities that have been looking for something they call the God particle.

The standard theory of quantum mechanics incorporates the idea of a quantum field. Wave-particle duality asserts that all quantum fields have a fundamental particle associated with them. Particles carry the force of the field. For example, photons of light carry the force of the electromagnetic field and can express as either a particle or wave. The quantum field and particle that explain how matter obtains mass was theorized in the 1960s by Peter Higgs. His idea was that the universe is bathed in an invisible field now called the Higgs field. Every particle feels this field to varying degrees; the degree to which a particle is impacted determines the particle's mass.

The presence of a quantum field was also proposed by physicist David Bohm, who called it a subtle energy field existing beneath electromagnetism. In fact, the Higgs field is analogous to the electromagnetic field, but with different properties. The particle that would be associated with this field, the Higgs boson, is called the God particle since the property of mass is what allows physical reality.[7] An article in *Scientific American* states that without the Higgs field, "all elementary forms of matter would zoom around at the speed of light, flowing through our hands like moonlight. There would be neither atoms nor life."[8] Experimenters at CERN announced they had found the Higgs boson on July 4, 2012.

Discovering the Higgs boson provides another avenue to explore concepts such as the creation of the Universe. It may also allow us to understand new features of time. Time is the fourth dimension of the material world as described in Einstein's space-time continuum. Space and time are relative, depending on movement. However, everyone traveling together in the same space-time bubble is subject to the same laws, which allow Newton's physics to prevail in our material world. Some current scientists are putting forward extraordinary new theories. Dr. Wubbo Ockels, a Dutch physicist and former astronaut in the European Space Program states, "Time is the creation of life in response to gravity."[9]

The implications of this statement are incomprehensible, yet they bring forward the question: If time is a function of gravity, and gravity interacts with the field-particle that imparts mass, will the discovery of the Higgs boson allow us to bend or otherwise interact with time?

There is an interesting parallel between scientific discoveries of such mind-boggling implications with experiencing and being altered by high-strangeness events. Both change reality; both are part of an evolutionary mindstep.

It is a long-held metaphysical concept that energy and matter interact in a field matrix that organizes matter into life. The field is said to be formative and to provide the force that motivates, animates, and energizes life. Like current ideas of consciousness, this field is also thought to be holographic in nature, and through it all of life is interconnected and all actions are recorded. Is it possible that the Higgs field is a step closer to identifying a scientific counterpart to this metaphysical precept? As a particle zooms through the Higgs field obtaining mass, might an impression of its presence be made on the field and transmitted to all other particles within the field? Might the Higgs field provide the organizing matrix for these particles? If so, CERN may have provided the medium that explains high-strangeness events.

Science of the Future

Breakthroughs in science provide the framework for ongoing research into high-strangeness events. Non-locality and entanglement, wave-particle duality, the importance of the observer, and other aspects of quantum mechanics afford a means to create meaningful experimentation. Experiments conducted over the past 20 years reveal startling implications that pave the way to understand the anomalies explored in this book. There are no concrete answers, only more focused questions in a better developed construct.

Here is a small sampling of the type of research currently underway:

- Dean Radin, head of research at the Institute of Noetic Sciences, provides insights into the energy-field effects of our awareness and the importance of our emotions in understanding anomalies in his book *Entangled Minds: Extrasensory Experiences in a Quantum Reality.*[10] As stated in Synthia's book *The Path of Emotions*:

> Over the past two decades, he [Radin] has conducted experiments into presentiment, the ability to sense that something is about to happen. In a series of double-blind, controlled studies using heart-rate and skin-conductance monitors along with other physiological indicators, he measured people's responses as they were exposed to a wide variety of photographs. Some were calm pictures, others contained highly emotional pictures, both happy and sad.
>
> It was expected that subjects would have physical changes immediately upon seeing an upsetting or exciting picture, an effect that was well documented. However, the experiments showed that participants were having physiological changes three to six seconds *before* they were confronted with impactful pictures. The participants themselves had no premonition of what type of picture was coming, yet their bodies did. The repeatable results of four separate experiments demonstrated that the odds against chance were 125,000 to one. The studies also revealed that the strength of the response was proportional to the intensity of emotion in the event. Radin describes the three to six second interval as the "bow wave" of an approaching future event.[11]

- A research study published in 1999 by Russek and Schwartz validates the ability we have to feel the presence of another or to sense when someone is looking at us, even when we can't see the other person. Subjects in the Russek and Schwarts study demonstrated a 57.6 percent positive performance in knowing when they were being looked at from behind for an extended period of time. This ability increases when the subjects believe in some form of spiritual reality.[12]

- Research by Rollins McCraty published through HeartMath Institute cites experiments that show "a subtle, yet influential electromagnetic or energetic communication system operates just below our conscious level of awareness."[13]

- Some studies reveal the areas of the brain that are involved in high-strangeness events. *Brain Cognition* published a paper demonstrating that experiences of intense meaningfulness, including sensing a spiritual presence correlate with increased burst-firing in the hippocampus-amygdala complex of the brain.[14] Additional studies indicate the hippocampus is also involved in experiences of déjà vu, the strange and eerie feeling of recognizing something despite encountering it for the first time.[15]

- The Global Consciousness Project (*www.noosphere.princeton.edu*), the Global Coherence Initiative (*www.glcoherence.org*), and the Intention Experiment (*www.theintentionexperiment.com*) are all research-oriented institutes that promote global change through focused intent. The research produced by such groups indicates field-effects of thought that can be harnessed through focused intention to create positive world change.

- Extensive research exists on the healing power of prayer, focused intent, and energy medicine.[16]

All the current research moves in one overwhelming direction: to the conclusions that we are powerful spiritual beings and that focused, heart-centered intent is the most powerful tool we have. This is the tool we are developing as we move into hidden realms that reveal our interconnectedness. There are many wild cards, and I'm certain some completely unexpected new players will arrive and change the pace of change, enticing our spiritual wisdom to compete with our inner demons. These final days of the old ways are not going out without a struggle. Adjustments this large and profound electrify every tether of the life force. Another mind is interacting with us through the events that we are living and we can be sure of one thing: *Nothing is quite the way it appears.* What is required of us all right now is truth. As we put truth forward, respect and love will be the requisites for the cycle we are entering.

I began my involvement in the study of unusual phenomena in the early 1980s with research into the strange swirled patterns found in cereal grains for which I coined the term *crop circles*. At the time, I believed it was essential as a researcher to be an objective, neutral observer and collector of data. I studied the strange designs occurring in crops by recording dates and events, taking measurements, analyzing the soil and plants, and interviewing witnesses, all the while believing that the events I studied were somehow separate from me. I believed that doing the job right meant being invisible. Over time and after many odd occurrences, I came to a different conclusion. We cannot understand the types of events described in this book without taking into account the individuals involved. There is an interaction that occurs between people and events that makes individuals as vital a part of the mystery as the unexplained phenomena.

As one of the first to study crop circles, I realized early on that there was an intelligent design to what we were witnessing and experiencing. I made myself very unpopular by saying as much to the press, opening the door to derision. The main theory at that time, promoted by meteorologist Dr. Terence Meaden, was that crop circles were the result of weather actions. My observations brought about uncomfortable questions. At the time, I had no idea how uncomfortable these questions would become.

Nearly 30 years later, in 2009, I was asked by Stephen Bassett to speak at the Exopolitics USA Conference in Washington, DC, to refute former British Ministry of Defense spokesperson Nick Pope's statement that the government and Royalty of England had never been interested in crop circles. Not only, Pope said, was the government totally uninterested, but I was lying in my assertion that I supplied Margaret Thatcher's cabinet with reports on the phenomenon. Because I keep meticulous records and copies of all correspondence, I had ample evidence that Pope's statements were patently untrue. (See my book *Government Circles* [2009].) He attended my presentation, publicly conceded the truth of my assertion, and apologized.

On the morning Synthia and I were to leave for Washington, DC, I had an unusual experience. I was enjoying a shower and was in a relaxed meditative state as I reviewed the points I wanted to make in the lecture. Suddenly, I was overwhelmed with the realization that the key to the mystery I had spent 30 years of my life studying was to be found in personal stories. Each story held a unique piece to the puzzle, and the whole would not be understood until everyone put forward their personal piece. The realization was accompanied by a strong compulsion to share at the conference information about my childhood that I had never before told.

I did not succumb to the impulse and gave the lecture as originally designed. Afterward, as I provided interviews with different magazines and radio programs, I was approached by a media person I did not know. As I turned to him, I knew before he spoke what he was going to say. Looking directly into my eyes, he said, "It is time for us all to put forward our stories so we can move forward." There was a strange look of knowing in his eyes, and I felt he was validating my earlier message and impulse.

The next time I gave a presentation was at Dr. Steven Greer's Center for the Search for Extra-Terrestrial Intelligence (CSETI) conference at Rio Rica, Arizona. There I revealed my childhood story. Surprisingly, each of the presenters did the same and, in turn, each of us was brought to tears. In addition, both Dr. Greer and Dr. Lynne Kitei expressed that they, too, had instinctively felt now was the time to state these private experiences publicly. I find it hard to believe this was mere coincidence. In ways I can't explain, but that we explore in this book, these events felt orchestrated. I do not pretend to know how the personal information I provide in this and upcoming chapters fit into the larger whole. As people read and add their own piece of experience, however, I suspect a picture will begin to emerge.

Some of my personal story is public knowledge; some is not. Many know that I saw my first crop circle on June 30, 1983. I was driving along the A272 between Winchester and Petersfield, England. At the time I worked for the local government of Test Valley in Hampshire County managing the electrical engineering department. The A272 is a busy road, and the heavy rush hour traffic was moving quickly. Rounding a corner, I glanced to my left, looking down into the natural amphitheater of Cheesefoot Head. In the wheat field nestled into the hills, I was startled to see indentations in the crop forming five perfect circles. Together the five circles formed a cross. Transfixed by the perfect symmetry and unable to see any tracks into or out of the field, I felt compelled to pull over.

I was one of several thousand people to drive the road that day. I was surely one of hundreds who looked to the side and saw the formation, yet I was the only one to stop, walk down into the field, and examine the crop. I was the only one who returned that evening to talk with the farmer, Peveral Bruce. Because I did, everything in my life changed. One has to ask: Why did I do that? What force was already operating within me that caused me to react differently from the thousands of others who drove by? Was I preprogrammed for the events to come? As I said, I don't have the answers to these questions, but I am willing to share my story.

My parents were Elsie Lorraine Waite and Gordon Roy Andrews. I am the third child in a family of four. My older brother, David, was born before the start of World War II and passed away in 2012; my sister, Valerie, was born during the war in 1944 and currently lives in Wales; and my younger brother, Peter, was born in 1948 in Andover, England, where he still lives.

I was an end-of-the-war celebration baby, born on March, 7, 1946, in a 17th-century thatch cottage in the small village of Enham Alamein, England. The village is located in the heart of central southern England, 2 1/2 miles from Andover. My mother's family lived in the village. While Dad fought in the War, Mum worked in a local factory building equipment to support the British troops, plus looked after David. During the height of the War, after Valerie was born, while Dad was once again overseas, 7-year-old David took on the role of head of family. My mother and David told harrowing stories of hiding in hedgerows during air raids, biking for miles to obtain milk for the baby, and scrambling to keep Valerie safe from falling debris.

After the war my parents ended up in Enham because the village was home to one of the best rehabilitation centers in England. Enham Village, originally called Knights Enham, has a recorded history back to 1398. In 1918, a charity supported by King George V and Queen Mary, purchased 1,000 acres of land in the village and built a center to rehabilitate and employ disabled soldiers returning from World War I. The tradition continued, and in World War II my father was one of many who were invalided out of the armed services during the period of the Battle of El Alamein in Egypt and brought to the facility to recover.

My father, an officer in the Royal Navy, was involved in special operations that he spoke about very little. After the war, our home was visited by several dignitaries to show gratitude for the service of the wounded serviceman and see firsthand the help they were receiving. One of the people who visited my parents was Princess Mary, the only daughter of King George V and Queen Mary (she also held the titles of Princess Royal and Countess of Harewood). The second visitor, who shocked my mother by unexpectedly staying for tea, was Britain's most senior soldier, Field Marshall Bernard Montgomery, known affectionately as Monty. It is odd to remember my mother's recollection of him arriving straight from debriefings with Prime Minister Winston Churchill and President Eisenhower, and sinking into the quiet and relaxed environment of her modest front parlor. (A photograph of us kids with Mum, Dad, and Monty can be seen on my Website.)

In 1951, just two years after the excitement of Monty's visit, I experienced my first high-strangeness event. At the time, I had no idea that my experience was anything more than a child's dream. By this time our family had moved from the thatch cottage to a semi-attached brick house about a quarter-mile away. I was 5 years old. In this new location I had two odd dreams. I seemed to wake from sleep with a wrenching feeling in my lower stomach, as if I was hurtling along a fast-moving roller coaster. Then, after a strong tug in my solar plexus, I found myself floating across the bedroom ceiling, face-down, seeing Peter and Valerie in their beds as I glided over them, before floating through the wall. Both dreams ended when I reached the community field behind our housing complex.

After these two dreams I became terrified to enter our house. I repeatedly told my father that there were small men inside. I often saw the men inside the empty house next door. Convinced I was suffering from the same post-war trauma reflected throughout England, my father patiently walked me through the house to demonstrate that there were no small people hiding under the bed or in the closets. On one occasion, he even took me into the house next door to show me it was empty. Nonetheless, my terror continued and I often refused to come into the house at all. My mother would become furious with me; considering the horrors she lived through, one can understand why the groundless fears of a child were incomprehensible to her.

Around the same time, I developed an unexplained rash. My body erupted in large blisters, which were full of clear yellow liquid and hurt tremendously. I was wrapped with white bandages from head to toe and suffered great discomfort. None of the many doctors who looked at the blisters could explain what caused them. Today they would be likened to radiation or chemical burns. The burns remained with varying degrees of severity for several years. (All of this is written in my medical records which can be viewed on my Website.)

It is interesting to note that since birth I have been part of a long-term research study conducted by the National Health Service. This might be why my childhood medical records were not destroyed after the requisite amount of time, as happened with most people from that time period. The study consisted of all children born during one cold March week in 1946. There were 16,695 of us who automatically entered the medical scrutiny of the study, which eventually became a project of the National Survey of Health and Development. Throughout my childhood, doctors and nurses arrived at our house to subject me to tests and ask my mother and me endless questions about physical and psychological health, education, emotions, and all aspects of development. Today just 5,000 of us remain in the study. Although I still receive a postcard asking basic health questions every year, the doctors and nurses are no longer in evidence. The stated mission of the study is to "realize the scientific potential of the NSHD as a world class, interdisciplinary life course study of aging by: Scientific discovery of life course influences on normal and healthy aging; transfer of knowledge to policymakers, health practitioners, and other research users; and promotion of healthy aging."[1]

Until recently, I did not consider any of these events to be noteworthy. Unexplained childhood illnesses were commonplace, as were frightening childhood dreams. Health studies were being conducted all the time. Because there was no significance to these events, they did not play a conscious role explaining why I stopped that day on the A 272 to look at something odd in a field. By the time I was fully engaged in crop circle research, I barely even remembered these events and certainly did not consider them important. It was not until a spontaneous regression with Doctor James Harder that these childhood memories took on greater significance.

It is not true, however, to say that there was no awareness of the paranormal in our household. My father had a keen interest in the mysterious and for good reason. He often referred to a déjà-vu type of experience he had when the war ship he served on docked in the Grand Harbor of Malta. Although he had never been to Malta, he had the distinct impression he had been there previously and often exclaimed how strange it felt. Beyond the typical déjà-vu experience, where one feels as though events have happened before, Dad had detailed memories of the layout of the streets, even knowing where certain cafés were located. When the ship's crew learned of his apparent familiarity with the surroundings, they often consulted him about where they should go during shore leave. Dad said it was as though he had lived there before; he could not explain it.

Then, in 1957, when I was 11 years old, my family, minus me, had a UFO encounter. It occurred during a family outing on a typical Sunday afternoon. Mum and Dad asked Peter and me if we wanted to take a drive around the country. This was an enjoyable Sunday outing for us; Mum would make sandwiches and bring a flask of tea. We often finished our drive at Stonehenge, laying down a ground blanket next to the famous Altar stone and using it as our table. No fences or security guards then, and not many cars either; we loved and respected the Stones just as others had for well more than 2,500 years.

That Sunday was not the same as others. For some reason that I don't recall, I didn't want to go. Mum, Dad, and Peter headed off without me. It was late afternoon when they reached a small hamlet called Faccombe about 8 miles north of our house. They drove up a small, sloping country lane and near the top caught sight of a silvery, disc-shaped object hovering just above tree level. My dad estimated it was around 200 feet away. Stopping the car, Dad and Peter got out in order to see better. They watched the disc, reporting that it swayed slightly from side to side and rose higher, like a spinning top, as a bright narrow beam of light emanated from the center of it onto the pine trees below. Remembering this event now, I am struck by how similar the description is to that of Travis Walton's experience on November 5, 1975, recorded in his book, *Fire in the Sky: The Walton Experience* (1978). Travis has become a good friend over the years, and the similarity makes me wonder what deeper connections there are between us.

Figure 4.1: Members of the author's family at Stonehenge.

My mother responded much as Travis Walton's workmates did in his recounting: She was furious with my father and brother for getting out of the car, shouting at them to get back in. Suddenly, as though aware of the commotion its presence made, the object quickly rose and, faster than lightning, shot away and was gone, leaving my family awestruck and somewhat frightened. Mum and Dad often talked about this event; however, to this day Peter doesn't remember anything about it, including the many discussions we had about it as a family. His only memory is of my mother talking about it after I began my research into crop circles. In recent discussions my brother raised an interesting fact: Our entire family and our children have always been drawn to the area of Faccombe. Even before the event it held a strong attraction to us that was not destroyed by a frightening, and fascinating, experience.

None of these events seemed in any way related to the crop circle research I began in 1983, and when I quit a high-paying government job to bring the world's attention to the phenomenon in 1991 I did not need any explanation as to why. My fascination was enough of an answer; if I needed more, I looked to my father's unusual experiences as my inspiration. All this changed in 1997 when Dr. James Harder visited my wife and me at our home in Branford, Connecticut.

Dr. James Harder (1926–2006) was a professor of civil and hydraulic engineering at the University of California in Berkeley. He was a major player in UFO research, working with Professor Allen Hynek during the U.S. government's official investigation into the UFO, known as Operation Blue Book. He was extremely proficient in the skill of hypnosis and worked extensively with UFO abductee cases. He was the hypnotist who regressed Travis Walton and his workmates, as well as Barney and Betty Hill, the first two people to claim to have been abducted during a close encounter with a UFO, in New Hampshire on September 19, 1961.

I met Harder during a press conference in 1991 at the USSR Consulate in San Francisco. Harder, Russian pilot/cosmonaut Marina Popovich, and I were providing research findings to a riveted press corps. In the following years, Harder became interested in me because of his investigations into the second marriages of UFO researchers. He believed these second marriages were arranged, presumably by extraterrestrials. The details of how Synthia and I met and what happened to us afterward fit his theory. He had been asking to meet with me for some time before he called on October, 17, 1997, saying he was in the neighborhood and asking if he and his wife, Rose, could stop by to talk.

Figure 4.2: Dr. James Harder, Marina Popovich, and the author, USSR Consulate, San Francisco, 1991.

They arrived and, as they sat down, let us know they had very little time, as they had a plane to catch. Synthia put on a kettle for tea and within minutes Harder was asking if I wanted to be hypnotized. I said no, explaining that I wanted my memories to be free of any possibility of having been influenced through a process I didn't understand. He agreed with my concerns and changed the question, asking me if I wanted to learn a method to be able to retrieve answers myself. I said yes, and Harder explained a simple kinesiology-type method of asking questions and letting my fingers move to give me answers.

"Do you want to continue?" he asked after a few minutes of using the technique. I nodded. The tea kettle sang, and Synthia got up to get us tea. By the time she returned—no longer than five minutes—I was in a deep hypnotic trance. Synthia's work brings her into contact with many professional hypnotherapists. She later remarked that she had never seen anyone work that quickly and effectively. Despite my protestations, the hypnosis had been framed in such a way that my objections were bypassed.

The trance lasted approximately 45 minutes. I sat alongside Dr. Harder, and the proceedings were witnessed by his wife, Cedar, and by Synthia. I had not spoken to Harder or anyone outside of my family about my childhood dreams. In fact, I had only mentioned it in passing to Synthia during a discussion about astral projection and the Monroe Institute. Harder had no way of knowing my past and could not have planted the events in my mind.

As soon as Dr. Harder asked me to go in my mind to a significant event in my life, I saw a very bright, white light emanating from the field behind my childhood home in Enham. I then relived my dream: floating from my bed across the ceiling and out of the bedroom into the field. This time, instead of waking up, I went toward the bright light, where I saw two American-style military men in uniforms standing on either side of an opening. It seemed to be the entrance into the uncomfortably bright light. The men looked very serious; they did not move or say a thing.

I floated inside the opening and was drawn toward a table that looked a bit like an upside-down cobbler's shoe-hob: smooth with rounded edges, silver in color, with the appearance of a continuously solid piece. There didn't seem to be any screws, rivets, or joints. Inside, the light became more pleasant and easier to deal with. As I approached the table, I was flipped face-up and slowly lowered onto it. I was not in control of any part of what was happening; my movements were involuntary and the experience was without my permission. I was not afraid; rather I was numb and disconnected from any feeling at all. On the other hand, from the time of these dreams as a child, I was terrified.

As the hypnosis continued, I saw a being with large, almond-shaped eyes. In my head I heard words that I knew were a direct communication from this being: "We are sorry to be doing this, but it is for a future time." He seemed to be referring to the burn-type rash that later appeared on my arms, legs, and torso. During the regression, I asked the entity a number of questions and was given direct answers. I was provided with details of future events that included declines in environmental health. I was shown a location on the edge of the field behind my childhood house where a single oak tree was located in a wooded area in the company of two plants: a bluebell and a primrose. I heard in my head that when these plants grew together, scientists could monitor their condition as a measure of the Earth's health.

As I relayed the information to Dr. Harder, he suggested that if I wished, I could connect directly with the entity and see through its eyes. I agreed. Immediately I felt myself merge with the being. I opened my eyes and the being looked out of my eyes at the room. We focused our gaze on Synthia, and I was suddenly terrified that Synthia wouldn't understand what was happening and that she would reject me and this being who felt like another aspect of me. I saw Dr. Harder motion to Synthia and quite suddenly she flashed a beautiful, warm, and welcoming smile. I was immediately flooded with a feeling of love so profound and all-encompassing that I never wanted to leave it. It flowed in palpable streams between Synthia and me, linking us together in the truth of the experience.

After the session ended, the Harders immediately left to catch their plane. I must admit that I was confused and angry, feeling as manipulated by the regression as I had at the manner in which I was handled by the entity. I also knew I had passed a marker that could not be withdrawn. Once an event is experienced through hypnosis, it is impossible to remove the experience; it becomes a new overlay on top of the original memory and can never be removed. In addition, believing the information was an enormous leap of faith. Although the imagery was vivid and the details very exact, the idea that these were actual memories of an event that occurred 46 years earlier, stretched my trust. I needed proof.

Synthia and I flew to England to check the details of the regression in February 1998. It was dark when we arrived at my daughter's house, and we were tired, but I was too impatient to wait until the next day. We immediately drove to Enham and found the house in which I grew up. We parked in a lot alongside the field that ran behind the housing complex. The moon was full so that I could easily see the surroundings, and I led the way to the spot where I saw the light in my regression. Once there, I turned in a circle, looking back at the lights coming from my old bedroom window. A flood of feelings washed through me along with a knowing sense of truth. The emotions were overwhelming, and I knew the information from the regression was true. Synthia, however, had no such measure for validation. We stood back to back in the field and meditated. A satellite flew in a straight line overhead. "If the regression was real," Synthia thought, "that satellite will be a UFO and change direction." Immediately the light made a 90-degree turn, startling Synthia into the recognition that something unusual truly was going on.

The next day we returned to the field to find that where we had stood the night before—the place where I remembered the bright light coming from—was the center of a dark green ring approximately 35 feet in diameter. The grass forming this ring was greener and longer than that of the rest of the field. A few feet away, in the hedgerow at the back of the field, just as I had seen, there was indeed the only oak tree growing in the area. It was winter and the vegetation around the tree was unrecognizable; however, when we visited months later with my brother Peter and sister-in-law, Jean, we found bluebell and primrose growing around the base of the tree. The grass ring was still present as well. After hiring a plane, we flew over and took pictures.

*Figure 4.3: Grass circle outside the author's childhood
home in Enham.*

The regression experience is still difficult for me to take at face value. There are layers and layers of feelings and implications associated with it. I have become more open to unusual stories and ultra-careful about not judging other people's regression accounts or unusual memories. I deliberately did not mention anything about these events during the hundreds of television and radio interviews I took part in since 1997 until the Rio Ricco conference. It was important to me and my credibility as a researcher to be neutral, and I felt the integrity of everything I worked for was at risk by becoming personally involved. However, we are now entering a new time and the ground is shifting. I now believe the things we have kept secret will make the most significant difference to the expansion of consciousness.

The situations discussed in this chapter and throughout the book open more questions than answers. They demonstrate an interactive connection to something larger than us, existing on levels we do not see or understand. How can a thought in someone's head be heard and responded to by a light hundreds of feet in the sky? Are we interacting with another species, or a larger aspect of ourselves? Are some of the urges and spontaneous, intuitive thoughts we generate coming from outside of ourselves and transmitted to us? And what is this incredible force we call love?

The truth that nothing is quite what it appears is becoming more apparent. A larger design is being executed, and we are each playing our part in bringing new realities into being. Sometimes we act knowingly; sometimes we are influenced by a larger mind that interacts with us in the nebulous region of our brain where the subconscious mind meets conscious awareness. We are on a journey with a time line, and we are being interacted with to meet our deadlines. In the pages to come, consider that there are no accidents. Each person and every event has a force running through it that is part of a design. That force is consciousness.

PART
II

Conscious Circles

Circle Creations *by Wayne Mason.*

Crop circles are indentations in fields of crop made by plants bent into swirled patterns. Although there is a 400-year record of such events, the modern-day phenomenon began as simple circles in England in the late 1970s. Through time, the circles evolved into intricate and precise designs. Most people believe that they are made either by people or are a mysterious phenomenon created by an unknown force. My take is different: I see an interface taking place in the fields among crop artists, researchers, and experiencers, all orchestrated by a higher intelligence that is pulling the strings.

Part II details the non-ordinary events and personal stories that form the foundation of my conclusions. For the first time, readers will be introduced to the world of crop art from all perspectives. It quickly becomes clear that there is something much larger going on—something we can all learn from as we examine consciousness through human interaction with a more expanded reality.

From the moment I saw my first crop circle, an element of destiny entered my life. As described in Chapter 4, I was rushing to a meeting, yet the attraction was so strong I pulled to side of the road and parked my car. In suit and tie, I struggled over a barbed wire fence and negotiated a path through the briar on the steep embankment toward the circular arrangement. Once in the field, it was impossible to see the indentations that were so clear from above. Following my instincts, eventually I stumbled out of the waist-high crop into the hollow formed by a circle. I stood in stunned silence, unable to fully comprehend the bent plants that seemed to flow into a cookie-cutter perfect pattern. A strong feeling enveloped me of another presence, watching. The feeling was so uncanny that several times I almost rushed out of the field.

Although late to my appointment, I quickly examined the construction. I studied the edges of the formation, looking for tracks into and out of it and found none but my own. I lifted plants and looked at the soil underneath. It was undisturbed. No weight had crushed the small nodules of dirt. The plants lying flat in swirled symmetry were most mysterious of all. They were bent at a 90-degree angle, seemingly placed in perfect position to create the eddying flow that formed the circles. Feeling the pressure of work, I left the field long before my curiosity was satisfied. Something within me was activated and I could not leave the mystery alone. During my subsequent three decades of crop circle research, the awe and sense of an invisible observer has never left. This is a constant reminder that we are dealing with non-ordinary reality.

The impression this first circle made on me was profound. I started spending all of my free time looking for of them. I soon met Pat Delgado, a former NASA electro-mechanical design engineer who was also looking at the circles. Together we founded the first research group,

Circles Phenomenon Research (CPR). By summer 1986, a small team had formed to investigate the increasing reports of circles throughout south-central England. It consisted of Pat, Fredrick (Busty) Taylor, a light aircraft pilot and driving instructor, and me. We also worked with Dr. Terence Meaden, head of the British-based Tornado and Storm Research Organization, and were assisted by many friends and interested people. Eventually other research organizations formed and many people were involved with the mystery.

I coined the term *crop circle*, which the media eagerly latched on to, and our team catalogued the features that became the foundation of what is known about the phenomenon today. Over the years, the formations evolved from simple circles to elaborate, complex designs, all of which we photographed, measured, and analyzed as we compiled our data base. However, most of what we needed to know existed within the simple circles of the early days. The importance wasn't necessarily the physical evidence we collected; it was what happened during the investigations—the energy we were exposed to—and the ways in which we were changed. The evolution of complexity and design in the circles was like a mechanism that kept us interested while our consciousness evolved. In some ways it formed a mirror for what was happening to us inside.

The fact that we were involved in intelligent interactions with a mysterious force was evident from the very beginning of our investigations. It took many years to piece together and acknowledge the pervasiveness and importance. This chapter offers, essentially in chronological order, a small sampling of stories that demonstrate the high-strangeness events that drove us into new realms of exploration.

A Sense of Presence

At the start, indications of intelligence in the phenomena were obvious in the way the formations related to ground features. Rather than being randomly placed in the fields, the designs were correlated to human structures. They were aligned with field boundaries, roads, and topographies. As the phenomenon developed, the formations began to align with features in the landscape. Rather than paralleling the grid-like tram lines that offer tractor access to the fields, for example, the formations paralleled the lines of underground water courses or old

Roman roads. These features are not visible at the ground level; they are identifiable only from the air, yet the formations were consistently associated.

At first the evolution of design seemed to be driven by the phenomenon's own mechanisms. Over time it became apparent that the phenomenon was responding to the researchers and people visiting the fields. As soon as a feature was noted and labeled as distinctive, the feature would change in the next set of circles. Our statement that the designs aligned to human structures, for example, seemed to propel the phenomenon to start aligning with landscape features. Noting that all clockwise circles had counterclockwise rings, we ventured to create a theorem. And the next formation displayed a clockwise rotation with a clockwise ring. When we noted that all circles maintained a specific ratio of rotations to diameter, the next circle was made to a strikingly different ratio. It seemed as though the phenomenon seemed to be listening to our conversations and challenging us.

The interaction became more personal when I heard a disembodied voice. I was working in my office, a converted outbuilding in the backyard of our home, inputting data into my Commodore computer (very high tech at the time!). Every detail of every crop circle our team investigated was added to the growing database. All the data was cross-referenced, which amounted to hundreds of hours of work, most of it tedious.

This evening as I put data into my computer, I was barely paying attention: my fingers hitting the keyboard as if by remote control; my mind almost in a meditative state. Suddenly, a male voice echoed out of thin air saying, "What are you doing?" The voice came from in front of me to the right. I pushed back my chair and wheeled around. No one was there. The door and windows were closed. I went inside and asked my then-wife, Wendy, if she had heard or seen anyone; she had not.

Back in the office I sat thinking about what had been said and how I felt when hearing, "What are you doing?" The emphasis was on the word *are* and the inflection seemed to infer that I was wasting my time. I felt admonished and knew exactly why: We were not going to find answers in the arena where we were looking. The voice hadn't offered an alternative, and so I continued, recording all the details as though stamp collecting. Several years later, the interaction with this mysterious force offered more direction.

An Alarming Response

The years between June 1983 and July 1986 were filled with continual excursions into the fields. With the exception of the disembodied voice in my office, the phenomenon existed in the countryside and we traveled to interact with it there. It didn't follow us home. The first indication that we were dealing with an aspect of non-ordinary reality that might not only follow us home, but physically interfere with our lives, began on a weekday afternoon in July 1986.

I was investigating a particularly interesting formation near the Oxfordshire town of Wantage. The formation ended with a pathway leading from the circle out into the standing crop, stopping at a 2-foot hole. The soil had not been removed from the hole and left in a pile; it was completely gone. A policeman had discovered the unique crop circle and stopped to inform the farmer, James Mathews, who subsequently called me.

At that point, I still worked for local government and had to find a slot of time to slip into the field. My work involved access to radiation-detecting equipment and, when possible, I took it with me as part of a new circle examination. After inspecting the circle, I measured it for radioactive emissions; no radiation was detected. Surveying the hole, I saw a stone resting at the bottom of a small depression. I picked it up to take home for study, placing it in a packet and labeling it to send for soil analysis. I checked my watch so can say with certainty that I left the site at exactly 4:15 p.m., a time that would be ingrained into my mind by events to come.

Once home, I placed the packet with the stone in my office, locked the door, and turned on the intricate intruder alarm that protected the property. The sensors included radar, infra-red, and microwave technology so that movement and heat both could be detected. The system, called the Treble-A Alarm, was one I had invented and patented so I knew the design inside and out. The alarms were controlled by a timer that permitted an early-morning milk deliveryman to enter the driveway and then re-activated after he left. The timer ran on the electric supply from the grid system.

That night—early the next morning, really—at 4:15, all hell broke loose. Alarms screamed and lights flashed. The control panel was in the office, and I had to go out there to see what was going on. Knowing the police were on the way, I asked Wendy to stand at the upstairs window overlooking the office while I went with a large, bat-sized stick to investigate. The office door and windows were secure. The infra-red heat detector was flashing, indicating someone was present. A search revealed that no one was there, and there was no evidence that anyone ever had been.

I spent hours the next day overhauling the system to determine why it activated. There was no reason for the false alarm, and I speculated a heat bubble from the heating system. However, the next morning was the same. At exactly 4:15, Wendy and I were jolted awake by screaming alarms and flashing lights. Once again I went to the office to check the control panel. This time, instead of the infra-red detector being activated, it was the radar technology indicating that someone was present, throwing my heat bubble theory out the window.

As I looked in astonishment at the control panel, I had the distinct feeling of being watched. Hairs stood up on my arms. As before, no one was there nor was there any indication anyone had been. In addition, the battery-operated office clock on the wall had stopped working; the hands were fixed at 4:15. The clock had no connection with the alarm system. Back in the house, I noticed the electric timer on the control panel was not working; the rotating plate showing the time had stopped at 4:15 a.m.

I must be a slow learner, because the alarm activations continued for 12 consecutive nights with no discernible reason. Eventually the local police withdrew response cover. Nothing made sense. Different types of detectors sensed a presence that wasn't there. Battery-operated clocks and electric timers were stopping at 4:15. The only thing that had changed since this began was the introduction of the stone, still waiting for mailing. I speculated that the stone must be the culprit—another false direction.

Finally, in a flash of understanding, the meaning became clear. I was sitting in my office pondering events, my eyes wandering over the office décor. On one wall I had a large map of southern England where I had placed colored pins for every crop circle found. I used a different color for each year and, in the three years I had been studying the phenomenon, the map had in-filled significantly. As I looked at it, an overall pattern emerged that I had not registered before: The bound-ary around the cluster of color pins on the map formed an equilateral triangle.

I could not quite believe what I was looking at and was surprised that this pattern had not screamed out to me before. I picked up a measuring tape in disbelief and measured the leg from a field near Winchester up to the Wantage field from which the stone sample had come. It scaled to 41.5 miles. The next leg from Wantage to an active site just outside Warminster also measured 41.5 miles. Finally, the fields in Warminster back to those in Winchester—another 41.5 miles.

The alarm activations stopped immediately, although the stone never left for analysis. The equilateral triangle was what my attention was meant to be drawn to; somehow not only had the alarms been geared to the numbers that would be revealed in the field, but synchro-nicity had also sent me out of the field at 4:15. I thought I had received the entire message—the importance of the triangle and significance in the numbers 415—but I had not. More was to come, but not for another six years, after my first marriage had collapsed and I was living in America with my second wife, Synthia.

The Dialogue Continues

Any doubt that the phenomenon was responding to us was resolved with the events of August 23 and 24, 1986, during two routine, aerial surveillance flights. In the early days we found new circles either through farmers who called to alert us to formations on their land or through aircraft flights over the fields. On August 23rd, Busty, his son Nigel, and I were out looking for new circles. We flew by known circles in the Cheesefoot Head area, taking more pictures as we searched for new events. We were flying over Longwood Estate when Busty banked the plane to avoid the flight path for aircraft approaching Southamp-ton airport. Dipping his wing and looking down into the field, Busty turned to say, "All we want now is to find all the formations we have seen to date wrapped into one, like the Celtic Cross."[1] Up to that point, the phenomenon was comprised of simple circles, circles with annular rings, two to three circles in a straight line, and several sets of five cir-cles forming a cross such as the one I had seen in 1983.

The next day Busty was flying with another researcher, Omar Fowler. As they flew past Cheesefoot head and over Longwood Estate, at exactly the spot where Busty had dipped his wing and made his comment the day before, Omar called Busty's attention to a new formation below. It was an overlay of each of the crop patterns that had arrived to date. The sense of disbelief quickly gave way to the realization that this was not coincidence. Busty's request had been heard and responded to. The eerie sensation of being observed seemed to be confirmed as the phenomenon responded to our conversations.

Mental Interface

Interaction went a step further when the phenomenon began interfacing with our thoughts. Although there are innumerable examples of events that have happened over the years, two were most impactful to me. The first happened in 1987 and occurred at the site of a single oval ring, about 10 meters in diameter, in Kimpton, Hampshire. The ring was in the field for several days before additional small circles arrived in other parts of the field. Pat, Busty, and I, along with fellow researchers Don Tuersley and Terence Meaden, and a few others, spent a day fully measuring and analyzing the events. I even took my parents, asking them to bring the family dog to see how she responded to the circle. The dog became ill on entering the circle and we decided to leave. Afterward, I went back alone for a measurement that had been missed. We always tried to research in pairs in order to verify events, and I could have waited to go back the next day with Pat or Busty. However, I felt compelled to return.

The sun was dropping in the sky and getting ready to set across Salisbury Plain. It was a calm night, and I was engulfed in peace as I stood near the ring, overcome with awe at the mystery we faced. It was a profound moment of reverence and in response to the feeling, I asked in my head, "Please, God, give me a clue to help solve this mystery." Of course, I never expected an answer—at least, nothing more than a thought in my head.

Immediately on completing my prayer a strange sound began to emerge from the ground near the ring, around 7 feet away. At first it was soft, and I thought it was some kind of grasshopper, but it sounded more like an electronic chirping, similar to the sound of a mounting electrical charge. The sound got louder and louder, reminding me of the sound that occurs when high voltage is applied across an anode and cathode, just prior to the snap and flash of discharge. The sound continued to grow in intensity, becoming terrifyingly loud. I could feel the air pulsating as it hit my cheek. The air itself felt ready to discharge, and if a discharge happened, I feared an enormous energy would be released or a portal opened from which something would materialize.

I am not proud of what happened next: I panicked. All I could think was that I had to get out of the field before the discharge occurred. Immediately upon my feeling of panic, the sound stopped. The stillness of the air was almost as frightening as the disturbance. I had not expected to receive an answer to my prayer, and I was equally shocked that it responded to my emotions, but I did not doubt that it had. The phenomenon seemed to have made a huge leap forward—or, alternately, had I? For the next weeks I could not get this event out of my mind, referring to it daily and feeling deeply impacted. The fear of that moment did not stop my research. If anything, the respect the phenomenon seemed to have for my emotional state made me more confident.

The second direct interaction with my thoughts didn't occur until more than a year later at a place called Charity Down Farm. A team of us were there investigating a circle that the farmer, Geoff Smith, had reported. It was a circle with two rings around it. After taking measurements, I returned to my home in Andover.

That night (September, 9, 1988) I decided to initiate a direct interaction. I lay on my bed and prayed for a specific symbol to arrive in a field that night. I visualized a traditional Celtic Cross, a circle surrounded with four satellite circles. It was an advancement on Busty's design in that the satellites were bound together with a ring. I asked for the design to be constructed in the closest possible field to my home. I chose this symbol because it was unique; it had not already arrived as a crop circle.

On the morning of the 10th the telephone rang. Geoff Smith was calling to report another circle. His team was harvesting the field with the circle and rings that we had visited the day before and discovered a second formation. He let me know that he could only let the design remain intact for a short time; he needed to harvest because rain was forecast for later in the day. I telephoned Busty, who met me at the airfield, and within half an hour we were flying over the field to take pictures. When I looked down out of the aircraft window, I choked with emotion as I viewed the Celtic Cross laid out in the crop below.

Looking at the patchwork of fields and towns, I realized that this field was the closest unharvested field to my house. No other field between the countryside and my house had crop left to receive a circle. It appeared my request was heard and answered on all counts. Features of this circle became critical to our research, and we used it as the cover of the book Pat Delgado and I co-authored, *Circular Evidence* (Bloomsbury, 1989). This was the first book written on crop circles and it became an international best-seller. It was posted on the Queen's elite Summer Reading list and contains the information that provided the foundation of crop circle research.

The Growing Phenomenon

The types of events our team was having were by no means unique; every research team reported such events. Researchers' experiences were almost eclipsed by those of crop circle enthusiasts visiting the fields in droves every year. Many who become involved with crop circles report events; it is the prime reason people have difficulty believing any crop circles are man-made. Some of the anomalies experienced around the crop circles include:

- Equipment failures: Cameras stopped working and electrical equipment failed inside circles and while flying overhead.

- Electromagnetic and electrostatic anomalies: Compasses rotated wildly and magnetometers recorded small variations in magnetic fields.

- Odd animal behavior: Geese broke formation to fly around formations, dogs became ill, horses bolted.

- Physiological reactions: Many people reported miraculous healings while inside some circles whereas other circles caused people to have extreme headaches or nausea.

- Some researchers experienced missing time or time distortions.

- Interactions with, or witnessing of orbs, beams, and flashes of light, UFO, or other strange lights in the sky. (This is covered more fully in upcoming chapters.)

- Shadowy figures have been seen in the fields.

- Many people experienced a type of déjà vu reaction upon seeing crop circles, evoking strong emotion and a sense of remembrance.

- Spiritual awakenings: Intensity of emotion, familiarity, and sense of presence reportedly awakened people's sense of spiritual connection.

Those who report such experiences range from individuals to groups, from energy intuitives to skeptics, and from researchers to hoaxers. The events occur spontaneously and also in response to prayer and request. Following are some additional instances of interaction.

Receiving the CSETI Logo

The first publically reported incident of an interactive group event occurred in 1992 on the night of July 23rd, when a group assembled on Woodborough Hill in Wiltshire, England. The group was brought together to work with UFO researcher Dr. Steven Greer, founder of the CSETI (Center for the Study of Extraterrestrial Intelligence) research organization. Present were Dr. Steven Greer, his colleague Sheri Adamiak, and a team of CSETI members. I invited fellow crop circle researchers Busty Taylor, Paul Anderson, and Reg Presley, lead singer of the popular '60s band The Troggs. Many others joined us, including UFO researcher Linda Moutlon Howe. At one point we totaled around 50 people, although many left before the project began. The intent was to initiate an interaction with the phenomenon using the mind-protocols developed by CSETI.

Woodborough Hill is one of the highest peaks in central-southern England and overlooks the spectacular Wiltshire landscape. I suggested this site to Steven not only because crop circles had arrived abundantly in the fields over the years, but also because it was an area of frequent UFO sightings. On this July evening, as Steven led the group through his protocol, nothing was pre-planned; events evolved with input from the group. At some point it was suggested that we attempt to transmit an image and request that it appear in the fields as a crop circle. It was agreed, and we proceeded.

No common agreement on the design ensued, so we decided to spend a few minutes in a group meditation asking that an appropriate image emerge. At the end of the meditation, Steven went around the group asking each person what image he or she saw during the five to 10 minutes of focus. Shockingly, everyone saw the same thing: some type of triangle. Then we continued with the CSETI protocol, which consisted of focusing on the image intending that it be received and a crop circle be created. We also attempted to transmit the image by scribing it in the sky with a high-powered laser. As Sheri reported, "We went into a CTS (Coherent Thought Sequence) and we projected and connected our minds with the minds of the circle-makers and just held that image as long as we could sustain it. I think we did it for at least 20 minutes. When we finished, we used the big lights to also draw that pattern in the sky."[2]

Although the group didn't learn of it until two days later, the next morning, on July 24th, in a field 5–6 miles away at a place called Roundway, a formation arrived that seemed to be a direct response to the group meditation. It consisted of three circles connected by three lines to form an equilateral triangle.

Sheri Adamaski reports. "There it was, glistening in the sun and it was exactly what we had projected, exactly. I can't tell you the feeling. I have never had a sensation like that in my life. It was the most joyous, wonderful sense of connection and unity consciousness that I had ever experienced up until that point. We were in tears, tears of joy, just beside ourselves. So that has become the CSETI logo."[3]

A Reverse Blind Test

Another strange incident occurred with a group of researchers who collected plants for analysis by a biologist in the United States. On July 6, 1995, they decided to conduct a blind test by making a crop circle and sending the plants for analysis without declaring the circle was man-made. This created a controlled blind test, considered a scientific standard of research.

The team constructed two different-sized circles connected with a looping pathway in a field near their home in Whitchurch. The next morning they called to let me in on their plan, and I flew over the formation to take pictures before the formation was disturbed by the plants being collected. The photos revealed a challenge for the testers.

The simple design the team constructed in the empty field wasn't the only event to happen there that night. Two additional circles appeared that the team had no knowledge of. Fascinatingly, these circles were not made of flattened plants: The plants remained standing but were white instead of green, as though all chlorophyll had been removed. Also, the unusual circles were not randomly placed in the field; they were positioned at a right angle to the axis of the man-made circles, forming a triangle with the larger of the two man-made circles as the apex.

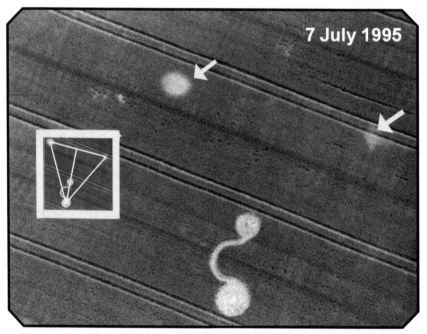

Figure 5.1: The Whitchurch test circle with mysterious additions.

Measurements revealed additional correlations. The diameters of the two new circles were the same. When the diameters of the two man-made circles were added together and divided by two, their mean value turned out to be the same as the diameter of the two new circles. The significance of this combined design wasn't fully appreciated until many years later and only because of another nudge.

The Flower of Life—July 27, 2003

Another example happened in 2003 with Graham Pritchard, a middle-aged tai chi instructor. His interest in crop circles was inspired through his understanding of chi, or life force, and the manner in which it runs through the body in channels called meridians. The effect of chi on vitality and health was reminiscent of the many stories people reported of miraculous health benefits received while visiting crop circles. The healing attribute of crop circles was a key element that convinced many people that they could not have been made by people. Other people believed the sacred geometry of the patterns created the healing force. Graham wondered which theory was true.

On July 27, 2003, Graham Pritchard and his younger brother planned to make a crop circle at a field near Barbury Castle, an Iron Age fort in Wiltshire on the Oxfordshire border. This spot had seen many crop formations through the years. They planned to construct the design known as the Flower of Life, an ancient geometry dating back to at least 635 BCE as seen in a display in the Assyrian Rooms of Le Louvre in Paris. The design forms a flower-like arrangement of seven or more overlapping circles within the symmetrical structure of a hexagon. This image is considered by many to be a sacred geometry with healing effects.

Graham and his brother designed the image and worked out the construct steps, but on the night they intended to create it, Graham's brother became ill. Disappointed, they abandoned their plans. The next day Graham received the shock of his life when, checking the Crop Circle Connector Website, he saw the Flower of Life design placed in the field they had chosen at Barbury Castle. The design in the field had 12 petals in the flower, a more elaborate version than the seven he intended. The circle-makers had one-upped his intention!

Interactions Continue

These types of experiences still happen to those visiting the circles today and are a primary reason why believers will not consider the possibility that humans construct crop circles. A YouTube presentation describes the experiences of Klaas van Egmond, professor of geosciences at the Utrecht University in The Netherlands. I met Professor van Egmond in 1996 at a meeting at the Institute of Resonance Therapy in Cappenberg, Germany, where I was speaking to a group of scientists and government officials.

In the YouTube video, van Egmond discusses two events that occurred in recent years during research in which he was participating. The first involved discussions around a dinner table about the features of the Maltese Cross. The next day, a design appeared in the circles resembling the Maltese Cross and contained specific features they had discussed. The second event involved a discussion the professor had with the research group involving the Earth's magnetic field. In the early morning of the next day, he reported that a huge replica of the magnetic field around our planet appeared in the field outside the bed and breakfast where he and the group were staying.[4]

Direction Received

I wish to conclude this chapter slightly out of time order to relate an event that proved to be crucial in advancing our understanding. One of the interesting aspects of the crop circle puzzle is the way one event or stream of events seem to drop out and then continue years later. Looking at time as a fixed linear scale, this seems very disjointed. However, if time is viewed as cyclical, synchronicity with other events becomes the integrating factor. After Synthia and I met and fell in love, it became clear that each of us saw and understood a different part of the same picture. Together, each of us had greater access to the whole. The next event anchored this conviction and furthered the information received by the 4:15 alarms. It also set the stage for an event yet to come.

This incident occurred in 1992, although I have incorrectly stated publicly that it occurred in 1994. People often ask why I never spoke of this before 2009. I can only say it seemed too personal and I did not fully understand what it meant. In writing this book, I looked at the notes in my archives that we wrote after the event. The event occurred on December 9, 1992. I was shocked to read details that I had forgotten and that now make more sense than ever.

Figure 5.2: 1991 Barbury Castle formation and 1992 Oliver's Castle triangle.

Synthia and I were fast asleep in her parents' home in Branford, Connecticut. According to my notes, at 3:05 a.m. I awoke from a dream in which Synthia was applying crystals to my body to heal my back. I woke as if a switch had been thrown and sat upright in bed. Unbeknown to me, Synthia was awakened at the same instant. She saw me sit up and witnessed me stay unmoving for several minutes. I felt immobilized, although I don't know if I couldn't move or if the information was so intense that I didn't want to.

During that time my mind was filled with the image of the triangle at Oliver's Castle, the one that had appeared five months earlier during the CSETI protocol on Woodborough Hill (1992). I distinctly understood that the purpose and function of the triangle was decidedly important, especially when applied across the landscape. I saw the triangle on the map on my wall that existed between Wantage, Winchester, and Warminster, and saw the triangle formation known as Barbury Castle (1991). I had the fleeting sense of the formation interacting with unknown energy related to healing disturbances within the Earth. I saw that all things are connected and alignments activate a flow of energy. I also received information about time and distance that I could not fully retrieve.

As quickly as the download started, it ended. This experience and the information it contained were way out of my league. I wasn't a healer; I was an electrical engineer. I started across the bed to write it all down but was interrupted. The event wasn't finished; the download continued through Synthia. I watched as she received information. Here is what happened in her words:

> "I was awakened out of a deep sleep and was aware that Colin was also awake. Suddenly, he sat bolt upright as a beam of bluc light entered the room. I did not see the light with my physical eyes; rather I saw it in my mind's eye and felt its effect. The light was living and the room was vitalized in a manner I had only experienced twice before. The beam hit Colin and he seemed to expand and fill with energy. I felt unable to move as I witnessed this light interacting with Colin, although to be honest, I think if I could have formed the intention to move, I would have been able to; I simply couldn't form the

intention. Suddenly, the beam moved off Colin and he deflated in much the same way as an old balloon, slumping beside me in the bed.

"I was now able to move and started to reach toward him, but things weren't over. The beam swept across the bed and the light now entered me. I felt myself physically expand and immediately began receiving information about triangles within the human body. I saw a human figure with their hands slightly extended away from their side with their palms facing outward. A triangle of energy existed between the Third Eye in the forehead and the palms of the hand. The degree that the hands were raised was essential as it opened a portal that brought energy into the base and/or second chakra and increased healing energy within the body. At the same time, it activated the Third Eye. In this position, with the Third Eye as the apex, the central line of the body which contained the chakras bisected the base of the triangle. The second chakra was approximately one third of the distance upward toward the Third Eye. I did not understand the significance of all this, but knew it was important. Immediately the light just turned off and, like Colin, I deflated. The room felt very empty and dead without the living quality of the light."

After Synthia was released from her experience, we compared notes and were astonished to discover that we received essentially the same information: mine related to the Earth, hers to the human body. (You can see a visual of this in the illustration in Chapter 7.) Synthia used the information she received in the system she shares in her book *The Path of Energy* (New Page Books, 2010). However, the full extent of the experience and how it fits together with other pieces of the puzzle is still unfolding.

Shifting Reality

When all of these events are compiled in a chapter such as this, two things happen. First, they seem totally unbelievable. Also unbelievable is that such events could happen without us making connections and huge leaps of understanding. Time itself is the reason connections are so hard to make. The time between these events was filled with details, measurements, and theories. These events seemed to be small moments outside of reality. In fact, they were outside of reality as we knew it; they were indications of the reality our mindstep is taking us toward. At the time, we had no context in which to put them. One more piece of the puzzle had to arrive before we could create context. Fully seeing and appreciating the picture couldn't happen until we faced the hardest aspect of the phenomenon. We had to wrestle with the one aspect no one could internally accept was real: We had to tackle the issue of hoaxing.

Throughout the 1980s and 1990s, researchers were aware that some crop formations were made by people, but we didn't believe that man-made circles explained the mystery. The experiences we were having, the complexity of the geometries, the impossible-to-reproduce characteristic features, the magnetic anomalies, odd animal behavior around the circles—all combined to create the mindset that we were locked into. Human involvement was not part of the real phenomenon and had nothing to offer to our understanding.

On the other hand, there was no litmus test for determining a "real" crop circle, and the phenomenon had grabbed the public's imagination. Once *Circular Evidence* was published (1989) and the Alton Barnes agri-glyph of 1991 appeared on the cover of a Led Zepplin album, people flocked to the fields to see and experience the magic for themselves. Research organizations multiplied in number, and leading experts competed with each other to be the foremost authority. The result was that people doing true research were rarely the first to enter a circle. Often it was well after the evidence was destroyed, because once one person walked inside the formation, it was impossible to know whether the tracks, broken plants, and compressed soil occurred from the visitors or the makers.

Another problem was that we honestly could not imagine what would motivate someone to make crop circles. Who would willingly get up in the middle of the night and traipse across the countryside in all types of weather to create a design in a dark field? The only possibility that made sense was that they were being paid to disrupt the magic that was happening. There was plenty of evidence that the government had an agenda to derail the research—more than enough to fuel the assumption that crop artists were government agents.

By the late 1990s, researchers and human circle-makers were diametrically opposed as the subject took on religious fanaticism. The tension between believers and non-believers was high, and progress was at a standstill. Everything seemed to revolve around whether we could categorically prove that crop circles were real. As it turned out, we were asking the wrong question.

Blinded by the Light

In 1996, Synthia and I went to Finland, where I was speaking at a conference in Helsinki. In the audience was crop artist Robert Irving. Knowing he was there to hear what the researchers were thinking and suspecting he intended to disrupt the event, I was less than enthusiastic when he asked Synthia and me to meet for a cup of coffee. Despite my reservations, we agreed and met in the conference cafeteria. The conversation went in many directions and led to a further meeting later in the week in a café in downtown Helsinki.

Our dialogue was intense and occasionally antagonistic as we discussed different aspects of the phenomenon. Synthia began the conversation feeling quite hostile to Robert, but as she listened to and assessed him, she decided that he was being honest. We didn't agree with what we heard, but it was clear to us both that he wasn't lying. This significantly challenged our beliefs about the intention of hoaxers. At one point, Robert leaned in to say that the circle-making community was convinced that I and others knew the entire phenomenon was man-made: "We thought for sure you would call us out after finding all our stuff in a circle. We were nearly discovered and ran from the field, leaving behind our equipment. We were shocked when none of you even mentioned that it was there!"

The conversation moved on and covered many other points. Several hours later, we departed. After Robert left, Synthia fixed me with an appraising gaze.

"Did you?" she asked.

"Did I what?" At this point the conversation had moved well past what Synthia was referring to.

"Did you find their circle-making equipment in that formation?"

I shrugged and nodded uncomfortably. "Yes, but we thought someone had planted it there to throw us off track, and I'm still not convinced that wasn't the case."

"Why wasn't it included in your reports?"

"It was. It's in the internal field reports and in the computer data base. We just never released it to the public. We didn't believe the formation was man-made and didn't want to give the hoaxers any air time. The more attention we gave them, the more they distorted events."

This conversation revealed the crux of the research problem: Researchers by and large didn't believe man-made circles could explain the phenomenon. Therefore, we had no context in which to see the fingerprints that the crop artists left. We could not see because of our own inattentional blindness. We needed an expansion of consciousness and as in such things, mine occurred cataclysmically.

Hoaxing Front and Center

Relegating man-made circles to an unimportant minority of cases ended when I wrote a grant and submitted it to Lawrence Rockefeller, who was funding research. One part of the study included an investigation into the prevalence of hoaxing, proposing to hire a private investigator and thoroughly research the claims. I was convinced this might provide the breakthrough we needed to put the hoaxing dilemma to rest. It was never my intention to convey this information to the police and have anyone arrested, but the possible fallout of this course of action could have resulted in exactly that.

I announced my intentions in 1998 when the grant was approved, a year before the project began. The impact produced stunning and unexpected results. I expected crop artists might try to convince me not to arrest anyone; I did not expect that researchers would. For the first time I began to suspect that Robert Irving was right: Although most researchers were honest, some did know the extent of human involvement in making circles and were complicit. Supporting this, I received a picture taken with a night-equipped camera of a very high-profile researcher in a field with circle-makers as they created a formation. This person never admitted that the involved circle was man-made even though she was present during its construction.

Another researcher said in conversation, "Yeah, come on, we know they're man-made, but so what? Why spoil everyone's fun?"

At the end of the summer, crop circle photographer Steven Alexander and Karen Douglas asked me to meet with them at a restaurant in Southsea, Portsmouth, with a few other researchers. They wanted to discuss their concerns. Paraphrasing, they said: *Crop circles are unique pieces of landscape art that promote spiritual upliftment. If you start arresting the makers, you will be doing a grave disservice to the subject and impinging on people's spiritual journey.* Hearing this, I knew the subject was in deep trouble and made a 180-degree turn in my approach. Rather than trying to prove that humans could not make circles, I determined to find out how they could. This was still not the crux of the matter. I had to be pushed quite a lot further before I understood the true quest.

With eyes freed from a constrained mindset, the human fingerprint was everywhere. Cataloguing the details, I assessed all the circles that arrived in England during the two year study (1999–2000) and determined that 80 percent of them were made by humans.[1] That left 20 percent where human involvement was unable to be detected. Twenty percent left a huge amount of the mystery unexplained. The problem was that many of the man-made formations in that two-year time period were elaborate, were beautiful, and had anomalous phenomena associated with them. Nobody was prepared to believe they were man-made. In fact, for the crop circle believers, the litmus test for whether a crop circle was made by a mysterious force or by humans seemed to rely on the presence of anomalous phenomena and an emotional response. If it made them feel good or evoked spiritual meaning, it could not be man-made.

After the announcement of my 80/20 findings, I became an instant pariah. Researchers flocked to denounce my report and my integrity. I received screws in the mail and was publicly accused, even by very good friends, of being bought off by the CIA. Steps were taken to remove me from the history of the subject; to this day, Wikipedia refuses to include my name on the crop circle page. They use my research findings, but when people around the world try to add details of my involvement with the subject, the editors of Wikipedia immediately remove it. The saddest denouncement came from a woman who considers herself to be a proponent of the spiritual side of crop circles. When I was diagnosed with squamous cell cancer, she wrote me a letter stating that "cancer was God's way of punishing me for discrediting the subject." It was a new low, even for the most extreme fanatics.

For me, this response meant it was time to reach deeper. Why was it that dissenting opinions could not be tolerated? What was everyone so afraid of?

Breaking Free

Many prominent researchers before me had undergone a change of opinion on the prevalence of hoaxing, such as Pat Delgado, George Wingfield, documentary producer John Macnish, Dr. Simeon Hein, Ron Russell, and Peter Sorenson. Pat simply withdrew after an embarrassing exposé with a hoaxed circle; George and John both publicly declared their change of view and remained in the debate before moving on to new vistas; Peter became a circle-maker; Simeon, Ron, and I continued researching. The biggest issue for me was that too many truly odd experiences had occurred to be able to say that the phenomenon wasn't "real." I needed to understand my experiences.

How was it possible that man-made circles have the same anomalous phenomena associated with them as the "genuine" circles? The question— "Are they real or man-made?" —was no longer relevant; they were both real and man-made simultaneously. Now the question became: "How and why do circles in the field, no matter how they got there, cause high-strangeness events?" Moving forward with this question lifted the veil into non-ordinary reality. It revealed the missing piece of the puzzle: human consciousness.

Exploring this new vista required two actions. First, it was vital to speak with the circle-makers. John Macnish was a former BBC producer and owner of a production company called Circlevision, and produced many of the best crop circle documentaries. In the final years of his involvement with crop circles he wrote a book, *Crop Circle Apocalypse: A Personal Investigation into the Crop Circle Controversy,* in which he describes an interview conducted with the first publically proclaimed team of circle-makers, Doug Bower and Dave Chorley (commonly referred to as Doug and Dave). Macnish reports these words of Doug Bower:

> *"I can't explain it. Dave can't explain it either, but when we're sitting in the field and looking at the whole thing, that feeling comes through to us, that feeling of mystery, that feeling of why are we here at all?"*

There was a long silence as Doug sat staring at me, then Dave picked up, "Doug used to say to me sometimes, while we were out and we'd just done one, (meaning made a circle) why do we do it? And we could never explain that certain thing. And Doug used to say, 'Do you think there's something that makes us?' And that did and still does really get to us. Were we being told, almost, to go out and do them? I know it sounds crazy."[2]

Oddly enough, it didn't sound crazy to me. In fact, I couldn't think of any other reason why two elderly gentlemen might be coerced out of a comfortable pub late in the night to slosh around a field. John Macnish gave me the lead I needed to pursue.

Secondly, I had to re-examine two decades worth of data. The years of data collecting, cross-referencing them, and the huge archive I had compiled turned out to be needed after all. My new non-gratis status in the crop circle community gave me all the time I needed. The material in this book is the result of taking up the challenge.

Dialogue With Circle-Makers

Talking with the circle-makers was much more difficult than one might imagine. They truly do not want to be known. They don't claim specific circles as their handiwork and seldom make public appearances. In a rare video interview, John Lundberg, one of the circle-makers from London, explains that the power of their artwork is in the mystery it evokes in viewers. The circle-makers seem to enjoy that people have spiritual experiences interacting with their handiwork. Taking credit for specific circles, Lundberg explains, would diminish the effect.[3] This is similar to what Robert Irving said to Synthia and me over coffee. However, there are two additional reasons I can think of. Lawsuits could result from such proclamations as many farmers feel the circles are vandalism. Likewise, many crop circle enthusiasts are angry and vengeful toward crop artists. Making a claim against a favorite formation could be dangerous.

To talk with circle-makers I had to overcome the divide between researchers and crop artists that I had been instrumental in creating. Because researchers did not believe man-made crop circles were legitimate, we characterized circle-makers as deceivers, and I was initially one of the loudest voices decrying them. Consequently, none of the circle-makers were happy to talk with me. The irony was not lost that I had become the focus of the same anger I had helped generate as I expanded beyond the entrenched position of real versus hoax.

The exception to the no-talk imperative was circle-maker Matthew Williams, the only person in England to have been arrested and charged with making crop circles. His willingness to share information made him an essential bridge between the two camps. Matthew is direct, is irreverent, and uses bad language. Consequently, many people write him and his information off as tainted. That is a mistake. Matthew's information is first rate. I have appreciated his help and humor very much.

One would expect that if anyone was to blast the idea of non-human intelligence being involved with the making of crop circles, it would be a crop artist like Matthew. Not so. Instead he tells illuminating stories of high-strangeness events that happened to circle-makers as they constructed their elaborate designs, starting with why they go out in the field at all. In these stories we find that artists, researchers, and experiencers are all connected through the high-strangeness experiences we share. It becomes very clear that something bigger is going on.

A Strange Compulsion

Shortly after 11 p.m. on Saturday, July 30, 1999, Matthew was sitting at home watching television when suddenly he felt a strong urge to go out and make a crop circle. Although this wasn't unusual, he was alone and typically made circles with other people. In his mind was impressed the image of a flower design. He considered the design, determined the construction steps involved, and decided he could make it alone. The now-familiar rush of adrenalin set in and he was psyched to make the pattern he saw in his mind. Gathering his equipment, he set off into the countryside.

Matthew drove down the country lanes past several fields before he found one near Avebury that "felt right."[4] Leaving the car in the lay-by (an area for cars to pull off the road), he trekked to the edge of the field with his equipment. Making a circle was a sacred rite for Matthew, and he performed a short ceremony before entering the field. As he walked out into the crop, he was immediately worried, as he heard voices and someone playing the guitar in the distance. He wondered if he should continue, then quickly felt safe as it suddenly became very cold and he was surrounded in misty fog. He made the circle and returned home.

Over the next few days he inquired about the people who had been in the field talking and playing the guitar while he had been making the circle. Matthew found a woman who said she was there with a group of women, although no one was playing the guitar. She said that those present meditated on a flower design asking that it be created for them. Shortly into their meditation, a bank of fog formed over the field below. The next day the women were delighted to find that the pattern they had visualized was manifested. Of course, they didn't know at the time that Matthew made it, just as he didn't know they were requesting the design he saw in his head.[5]

Apparently this compulsion to make circles is not unique. Doug and Dave experienced it, Matthew Williams does, and so do many others as well. In an interview with On the Edge Media, Matthew describes the role that "feeling" had in whether his team made or did not make a circle. If the idea felt right, they made it; if it didn't feel right, they held off. They used that criterion to choose fields, plan designs, determine timing and most everything else related to making circles.[6] It sounded eerily familiar to the way that many researchers found circles in the early days: We felt compelled to follow our sense that a circle was just around the corner.

I see no difference in Matthew's story with my own prayer for a Celtic Cross. Did human circle-makers pick up my request the night that I asked for a Celtic Cross? Did Busty Taylor's request, the CSETI logo, and Graham Pritchard's Flower of Life arrive the same way? It is clear that we are all connected in this phenomenon in ways we do not understand. Whose plan is at work and what forces are involved?

Encountering the Presence

I was prepared to hear that man-made circles produced anomalous effects for experiencers; I did not expect the extent to which crop artists reported strange events while making circles. It seems circle-making lore is as full of unexpected phenomena as that of the researchers and enthusiasts. Peter Sorensen reports that many crop artists talk about the odd and often frightening experiences they've had. In the afore-mentioned video interviews of John Lundberg and Matthew Williams, both describe unusual events.[7]

Here are two incidents that are well recorded with witnesses:

The first occurred while a group of crop artists made the formation known as The Spider's Web, which appeared in a field at Avebury in 1994. The circle-making team was joined by a radio journalist, Ned Pamphilion, who wanted to document that crop circles are man-made and observe firsthand how they could be made at night. Everyone present witnessed flashes of light coming from unexplained sources within the field. The sound track that was recorded and aired on a hospital-based radio station, Hampstead Royal Free, can be heard at *www.circlemakers.org/ra.html.*

Another documented event occurred during the 1999 making of the 3-D cube formation, also in a field at Avebury. This design was commissioned by the *Daily Mail* newspaper and made by a group of four artists from London who called themselves the Circle Makers. The farmer, Mr. Farthing, was paid by the newspaper to place the design in his field. Reporters from the *Daily Mail* recorded the creation of the circle, which took place on a full moon night during the height of the crop circle tourist season. Although many people were outside watching the fields that night, no one saw the formation being made, including researcher Chad Deetkin, who was watching for circle activities until 1 a.m.[8]

The next day the *Daily Mail* interviewed people who were visiting the formation. Most were adamant that it could not have been made by human hand. More interesting was the interview of the circle-makers. The artists revealed that they occasionally saw strange lights in the fields while making circles and once encountered a bright light that lit up the formation they were making, causing them to lie on the ground in fear of being caught, except the light wasn't coming from a human source.[9]

If crop circle adherents believe that high-strangeness events are indicators of a real phenomenon, then it appears that circle-makers are part of the magic. High-strangeness events happen to everyone, no matter what camp you are in. Here are some of the reports from circle-makers:

- Mysterious orbs moving around the fields as the circle-makers execute their designs.

- Encounters with dark shadowy forms that have sent more than one circle-maker running from the field in fear.

- Unexplained urges to make certain designs, even down to a specific field and position in the field, finding later that the positioning related to other events they knew nothing about.

- Unexplained flashes of white light and beams of light flashing in the field as the circles were being made.

- Time anomalies; elasticity of time to allow the completion of circles.

- Fog banks protecting circle-makers from being seen by watchers on the hillsides.

- Unknown interactions with other circle-makers creating formations that relate to each other in ways neither planned.

- Weather changes over the circles; reports that raining over the circle stopped as they made it while raining continued outside the circle.

- Going to the field intending to make one design, but suddenly altering it and creating something different— something with meaning to other unrelated people.

- Designs that one group of artists worked on showing up through another group.

This is just a small sampling of the stories that exist. For more information, here are some Websites to check out: *www.circlemakers.org, www.circlemakerstv.org,* and *otherworldyencounters.wordpress.com/2010/08/27/a-brilliant-expose-on-crop-circles-by-the-notorious-matthew-williams/.* Time-lapsed photography of people making circles can also be seen on the Circle Makers' Website.

Julian Richardson is by all standards one of the most preeminent crop artists. In a private video interview with a fellow circle-maker, he describes his own involvement with mysterious happenings while making crop art. He has kindly granted me permission to view and quote from the video. The information attributed to Julian is taken from this source. I was surprised to find how similar his thoughts and experiences were to my own and how interwoven our lives have been.

Julian says, "I first became aware of crop circles in 1989 at 15 years of age. I saw them on television, and felt instantly attracted to them." I was fascinated to hear Julian say this. Whereas my attraction took me into a lifelong passion to study the mysterious effects of crop circles, Julian's attraction led him into a lifelong passion for creating them. I have been researching crop circles for 30 years. Julian has been making them for 22. It struck me that we are two people who have committed enormous effort from two very different perspectives and arrived at the same conclusion: There are deep, unanswered mysteries involved with crop circles that are best understood through an exploration of consciousness. Extrasensory perception is at work on both sides of the crop circle subject. A researcher is more than an investigator, and a crop circle-maker is more than an artist. They are counterparts in an intuitive exchange and the interaction between them is where truth lies.

It is apparent in the video that Julian is a sophisticated and thoughtful person. He is not malicious or antagonistic. He speaks of feeling a resonance with the plants and allows intuition to guide him to fields and designs.

Julian described many happenings while making crop circles, including two teams showing up at the same remote field where circles rarely were made and unbeknownst to each other, constructing very similar designs, and two crop circle enthusiasts staying in a bed and breakfast and, before going to sleep, looking out the window at the field alongside the place and asking for a crop circle to appear. Julian says, *"That same evening, my team specifically chose that field and made them one. Only thing is, we didn't know them and never met them!"*

He also says:

One night, making a circle, we all saw what is referred to as an Amber Gambler, an orange light above the neighboring crop field. It looked to be about 50 feet in the air. It remained stationary for about one minute before it faded, dropped down and was gone. It was about the size of a Beach ball and was not a military flare, which we regularly witness around the Salisbury Plain training area. There was also another occasion when we saw white lights in the sky above us which suddenly disappeared. A green light came on where they had been, before zipping off and leaving a trail.

One of the most meaningful moments for me as I watched the video happened when Julian discussed a formation I had researched extensively. This crop design was made in the geometry of a pentagon. After it was made, a friend sent me several rolls of film containing a series of aerial photographs of the complex design. Placing the photographs from different angles together, I soon saw that the formation was placed in a field that itself was a perfect pentagon. The field was bounded on all five sides by hedgerows separating it from additional fields beyond. Not only was the pentagon geometry of the formation proportional to the pentagon shape of the field, they were also perfectly aligned side for side. I used this formation extensively in my lectures to demonstrate that an intelligent hand was involved in positioning and constructing the circles.

At the time I did not believe crop circles were made by people, and if Julian Richardson had told me that he made the pentagon, I would not have believed him. The formation was purposefully and perfectly aligned; what person could manage such a flawless job?

Julian Richardson did, in fact, make the circle. Of greater interest is this: Julian went into a field to make a pentagon formation. It was dark, he didn't have an aerial view, and he had no idea what the shape of the field was. He created the formation in that particular field because it "felt right." He did not purposefully pick the shape to match the field or align the sides, yet there it was. Julian says, *"I would have been hard pushed to have actually placed it [the pentagon] there by design. I was shocked to say the least when I saw the aerial images!"*

If Julian didn't align the formation to the field, then how did it happen? How was it that his affinity for this field matched the geometry of his design? And why would crop circle-makers end up in fields making designs that others asked for? In discovering the world of hoaxers I found my belief in a higher guiding force was stronger than ever. How this force used our own thoughts, compulsions, and passion to synchronize and orchestrate events was the real mystery.

When asked if he believed something was guiding events, Julian's unequivocal response was *"Yes, yes I do. There may well be far more to this than we realize."*

It doesn't take much to see the similarity between the experiences of circle-makers, researchers, and crop circle enthusiasts. The same synchronistic force that draws researchers and enthusiasts into the fields and that compels them to meditate, to sit all night in eager anticipation, also draws circle-makers out in the middle of the night, compelling them to express their artistic prowess in a craft that defies understanding. The result is synergy: two disparate groups generating something greater together than either would or could produce alone.

Welcoming Expansion

Until we embrace the act of circle-making, we are passive observers of a mysterious phenomenon. When we welcome the input of crop artists into the magic, we complete a circle; we come face to face with a deeper dialogue. At that moment we accept the power of human consciousness to create and influence reality.

I was propelled to embrace the act of circle-making because the circle-makers' artwork, sprawled across fields and eliciting deep emotions, inspired, uplifted, and changed my life. It doesn't mean the crop artists are all wonderful people with spiritual understanding or that we would be great friends. In fact, the humanness of the phenomena might be the most astounding part of the whole dance. The people involved—researchers, enthusiasts, and circle-makers alike—are real people, flawed each in his or her own way. We have bias, tempers, jealousy, limitation, and fear. Even so, we are capable of creating magic.

At one point, when the anger of crop circle researchers and enthusiasts at circle-makers was at its height, I wondered why everyone was so afraid. Synthia wrote in my 2003 book, *Crop Circles: Signs of Contact,* "It is interesting that the circles are perceived as valuable only if they are made by a non-human source. It is as if we are afraid to be powerful, co-creative, spiritual beings."[10] Would we rather give our power away to an outside force than take responsibility for the condition of the world around us? The inattentional blindness that keeps us from seeing the obvious saves us from confronting the result of our own fears, limiting beliefs, and lack of imagination. In the final analysis, what we embrace when we close the circle is our own evolution.

Encounters with high-strangeness events provide clues about the mindstep we are experiencing. The ways in which we are touched and changed hint at developing aspects of humanity. The crop circle enigma emerges as a huge experiment that we are stumbling our way through. On the journey we are offered glimpses into the future.

The last two chapters make it abundantly clear that something bigger than individuals is at work in the fields. Humans may make crop circles, but they don't set off alarms, wake people from a sound sleep with an information exchange, or choreograph the circle players in the dance they are engaged in. A higher force or intelligence is at work. Whether this intelligence is our own higher or collective consciousness, a yet unknown universal force, or an off-planet life form remains to be discovered.

Examining the types of interactions and how they impact us helps us know what is being awakened and who we are becoming. However, exploring unknown reality requires that we move beyond our rigid ideas of what is possible, let go of our expectations and not be put off by the foibles of being human. We will make mistakes, succumb to the needs of our egos, and often act out of limitation and fear. It doesn't make the journey any less important or the road we walk any less valuable.

I don't know what inspired the early circle-makers to go into the fields. Doug and Dave said it started as a desire to trick UFOlogists by making a "landing nest."[1] Yet farmers report seeing the circles in their childhoods in the 1920s and a 17th-century newspaper reported a "devil's circle" with an artistic rendition reminiscent of crop circles.[2, 3] The same manner in which we must acknowledge that man-made circles can and do create anomalies, we must also acknowledge that some circles cannot be explained as human-made. Some formations defy explanation and indicate that a foundational phenomenon formed the template for what followed.

One formation that defies the man-made explanation appeared as a triple circle in a field in Westbury on Salisbury Plain on August 4, 1987. Salisbury Plain is a large military area where high-level maneuvers are carried out. On Tuesday, August 4th, I took pictures of the triple circle formation. A military helicopter that was conducting aerial maneuvers can be seen in several shots. The helicopter was piloted by Captain D.F. Borrill of the 658 Squadron, who saw the formation and photographed it from the helicopter. His photographs were part of a military report submitted to Command several days later.

In my pictures the southernmost of the three circles can be seen to be neatly swirled in an anti-clockwise direction, which is as I observed it. Due to my job and the number of circles arriving daily, I wasn't able to return to measure the triple circle formation and take samples until the weekend. When I returned with Pat Delgado and Busty Taylor four days later, we were startled to see that something had changed. The southernmost circle had been disturbed; plants stood up in tufts and the entire direction of the lay was now clockwise![4]

In order to confirm my own photograph, I contacted the military base on Salisbury Plain and was given a copy of a photograph taken from the helicopter. It confirmed that the original direction of the swirled crop in the southernmost circle was anti-clockwise on the 4th of August, but clockwise on the 7th. To my knowledge there is no human explanation for this, as has been agreed upon by several circle-makers. A simple reversal of the photographic negative does not explain the features. For one thing, the background is not reversed. For another, two separate cameras were involved. Inattentional blindness also cannot explain this, because the images were captured on film. It is this type of event that convinces me there are many unknown elements in the mystery before us.

Rather than worry about whether the circles are man-made or not, looking at the experiences people have is infinitely more revealing. This chapter examines four categories of experience: the personal interaction that engages our minds and emotions; the many ways the phenomenon interacts with the physical world, such as equipment failures and changes in compass bearings; time anomalies that a few people have experienced; and the orchestration of events. There is another element not discussed here: the prevalence of sightings of UFO-type lights and orbs over and around crop circles. This aspect is discussed as part of a larger phenomenon in upcoming chapters. This chapter creates context for crop circle experiences through the scientific breakthroughs discussed in Chapter 3.

Interactions With Consciousness: Mind and Emotions

There is no question that the first interaction people have with a crop circles is emotional. The designs elicit strong feelings as they reflect the sun in the pristine countryside. They seem familiar and tug at something within us that is just out of reach. They excite our mind, instantly freeing our imagination from imposed constraints of what we believe is possible. They compel us to come forward and get involved. Crop circle artists describe the same feelings. Even when they first came forward to prove crop circles can be made by people, they quickly describe being drawn in by the elevated emotion that occurs from creating the designs.

Whether we speak of an artist compelled to use the fields as canvas, a researcher ignited with inspiration, or an enthusiast using designs for meditation and healing, emotions inspire our actions. I once considered the emotional reaction a side effect of the circles; I now consider emotions to be an important feature of interaction. People rarely take action based on mental impulse alone; an idea has to be infused with emotion to provide the energy for action. In addition, as Synthia describes in her book *The Path of Emotion* (New Page Books, 2013), emotion provides information, communicating between the mind and the body.

Dean Radin's telepathy experiment conducted under the auspices of the Institute of Noetic Science, published in 1999, reveals two essential features of telepathic exchange. First, the body receives information before the mind as seen by the physiological reactions that were recorded prior to cards being turned over. Second, emotion plays a large role in the mechanism of telepathy. The greater the emotion evoked from the picture shown, the more dramatic the physiological response.[5] In essence, emotion provides the carrier wave for information. Consequently, the intensity of our emotions relating to crop circles may be an important part of the telepathic-type interactions reported, such as that between researchers and circle-makers.

The physiological component of telepathy is also interesting. When people feel compelled to make a circle, or compelled to say a prayer, the mind is pushed forward by a physical desire. In episodes of inattentional blindness, information we don't "see" is processed by the body and drives behavior without our conscious awareness. In addition, mirror neurons, which can be activated without visual contact with another, can create the perception of experience. There is much to be learned in these areas, yet even now they help provide context for high-strangeness interactions. Even more important than the mechanisms of how the phenomenon impacts us, is the issue of what is changed in us when it does.

Interactions With the Material World

Physical interference with equipment is one of the most frequently occurring crop circle anomalies. Like the alarms set off in my house in 1986, reports cannot be explained as a human hoax; they represent the interaction of an intelligent force with the physical world. In reviewing my database, I realized that when researching these events, focus was on the equipment rather than on personal response. We looked to what happened to the equipment for clues about how the crop circles were made and what type of force might be involved. The goings-on were cited as validation of the importance of a specific formation, especially as we sought to identify the "genuine" circles. In taking a second look, I threw out those assumptions and asked: If the items being interfered with were secondary, what information was being relayed?

A good example is seen in the sequence of events around the activation of my house alarm. What was significant wasn't the physical interaction of a force with the alarms, but that they were used to attract attention to information we were not seeing. The alarms stopped after my focus was drawn to the significance of a particular geometry: the triangle in the landscape. In 1996, the information continued in the download that occurred to Synthia and me. We were shown that, when the triangle was applied to the land, the geometry created healing effects for the Earth. When applied to people, it created healing in the body and enlightening of the mind. In reviewing the data, I noticed something else that I had missed.

In our shared experience, Synthia saw that the triangular arrangement of the palms of the hands and with the Third Eye opened the two lower chakras and energized the body. A line drawn from the Third Eye straight down the body to bisect the base line that ran from palm to palm, traveled through the rest of the chakras. It was impressed on Synthia that the second chakra was approximately a third of the way up this center line. I looked at the triangular arrangement in the landscape among Winchester, Wantage, and Warminster, and realized that when Wantage served as the apex, a line drawn to bisect the line of the base revealed that Stonehenge was also approximately a third of the way up this central line, a near match to the position of the second chakra.

I remembered the test circle at Whitchurch and looked again at the triangle it created with the two mysterious additions. The second part of the man-made formation fell on the center line approximately one third of the way up, as can be seen in the inset of the image on page 90. I knew immediately that this ratio was clearly important. Stonehenge has a long history as a healing site. Recent archeological excavations reveal that sick or injured people made pilgrimages to the stones from all across Europe to partake of its healing powers.[6] If the information was congruent to Synthia's human triangle, the triangular arrangement in the landscape might activate Stonehenge as a power generator for the Earth. The circles at Whitchurch seemed to be a reminder not to overlook the importance of this arrangement.

Electromagnetic Possibilities

Now I wondered what the failure of equipment, rotation of compass needles within circles, and the odd behavior of geese revealed. If physical interactions were attention-getters to direct our awareness, where was our focus being drawn? In the 1990s, these events gave birth to speculation that the force making the circles caused a fluctuation in the Earth's electromagnetic field thereby causing these effects. Accordingly, my main research focus in 1998 was to take magnetometer readings within crop circles. Findings revealed a slight shift in the electromagnetic readings around some crop circles that corresponded to the shape of the formation. Not all crop circles demonstrated this effect. At the time, I was still looking for a litmus test to determine "real" crop circles. Consequently no further readings were undertaken.

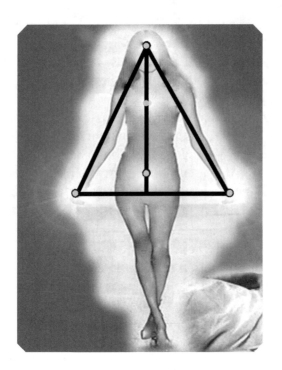

Figure 7.1: Human and landscape triangles.

Could the interaction with our electrical equipment have been an attempt to draw our attention to the Earth's electromagnetic field? Certainly we have seen major changes in the Earth's electromagnetic field in the past few decades, such as the hole in the magnetosphere over the South Atlantic Ocean called the South Atlantic Anomaly. However, if people are making the circles, might our attention be drawn to something else entirely? Could the intelligence within the phenomenon be demonstrating that intention combined with geometry can interact with and alter electromagnetism?

The ability of sacred geometry to shift consciousness is part of many systems of ancient spirituality. The sand paintings of both the Native American Zuni Tribe and Tibetan Monks, yantras, and mandalas are all examples of patterns and geometric structures made with the intent to shift consciousness and move energy. As Paul Devereux writes in his book *Secrets of Ancient and Sacred Places*:

> Sacred geometry is the geometry inherent in all nature, whether it be the energy dance of atoms and molecules, the formation of a crystal, the growth of a plant or human skeleton, the motion of weather systems or galaxies. Certain patterns and ratios are used by nature in the formation of the manifest universe: the process of becoming is governed by the implied geometry. Such geometry is used in magical invocation for the same reasons. The builders of the ancient sacred monuments closely observed the ways of nature and encoded its architecture into their structures so that the holy places would act as microcosms of the whole universe.[7]

Crop circles might further empower intentional geometry through the entrainment of emotional energy. The intention of groups of people is magnified by the emotional response to the mystery. A grant proposal is underway for funding to further study the electromagnetic effects of intentional geometry enlisting the help of circle-makers in the experiment.

Sound Vibration

The mysterious sound is another instance of an interaction of some force with physical reality. The sound I heard at Kimpton when I prayed for an answer to the mystery was intense, interactive, and never forgotten. For many months my account was all that existed; there was no other evidence of sound anomalies produced within the circles. That changed when the sound was heard during a surveillance operation called White Crow, which took place overlooking Cheesefoot Head near Winchester, England.

The surveillance operation hoped to film a crop circle being made. We enlisted special low-light image-intensifier cameras that were focused on a field at Cheesefoot head 24 hours a day for one week. The field was chosen as a likely spot for an event due to the number of crop formations that had previously occurred here. No crop circles arrived during the week of the surveillance operation. However, 200 yards from the control caravan, a team of 11 people underwent an extremely bizarre experience in a crop circle involving the same sound heard at Kimpton.

We were sitting in a circle during the early hours of the morning meditating and inviting an interaction. Suddenly, we heard the sound approaching us from the East. We drew together in concern as it swiftly rotated counter-clockwise around the crop circle where we were. It rotated for several minutes before becoming stationary a few feet away from our position. Pat Delgado felt he was being asked to walk toward it. We were excited that we were able to record the sound and now had proof of its existence. (The full details of what happened can be read on my Website.)

Skeptics immediately claimed the sound was that of the grasshopper warbler bird even though the recording was taken in the dark of night. The sound arrived again, this time interacting with cameras during the filming of a BBC television program on crop circles with Pat and me. It was 1989 and we were in a circle in Beckhampton. Silbury Hill, the largest man-made ancient mound in Europe, loomed in the background.

The sound arrived as we filmed. It increased in volume and intensity every time Pat stepped into the center of the circle and decreased when he stepped away. The TV camera was running and the sound was recorded and shown nationally on the BBC program *Country File* aired in Great Britain. In the film, I am shown standing next to the sound engineer telling him that I can hear "our sound" at the same time that the engineer reports hearing loud bursts of the sound in his headset. Simultaneously, Pat is complaining of a static feeling on his arms and his head, and confirms he also hears the sound. It then became so loud the engineer tears off his headset as red fault-lights flash on one of the TV cameras, destroying it.

The strange saga doesn't end there. So impressed was the program director, John Macnish, that we were invited to the BBC Pebble Mill studios in Birmingham to comment live as the program was transmitted. We were wearing microphones and listening to the countdown to the program in our ear pieces. Exactly when we heard "Four, three, two, one; on air," the lights dipped and power to the studio was lost. Standby generators kicked in quickly and power was re-established so that the show went on. Whatever the sound is, a grasshopper warbler bird could not produce such effects!

The high-quality recording of the sound allowed us to analyze it. In real time, it sounded like an electro-static chirping. Slowed down, it broke into two components that sounded similar to the pinging of sonar equipment or the sonar sounds of dolphin. I began to play the sound at my lectures in both real time and then slowed speed. More important than what we learned in the analysis was what happened to people when they heard it: It elicited extremely strong emotions, often causing people to cry. Synthia experienced it interacting with her energy field, causing it to expand and contract with the changing tones.

Initially we investigated whether the sound provided clues to how the circles were made. In actuality, every time the sound arose we were in a circle that already existed. Examining our reactions made us realize that the sound changed how we felt and thought. Vibration can be used to transmit information as our electronic age demonstrates. Consider the way technology encodes information on vibration, which is then sent via radio or microwave to produce radio, television, and cell phone transmissions. Perhaps the sound we heard was vibration coded with information. As Dean Radin's experiments indicate, emotions support the transfer of telepathic information. One wonders whether the activation of emotions forms the connection that compels people around the fields and orchestrates their actions as part of the telepathic link between people and events. Vibration and entrainment of emotion might also be involved in creating the healing effects and the promoting of spiritual upliftment that many people experience.

Time Anomalies

In 1994, at a formation called the Scorpion, located between the megalithic stone circle of Avebury and the mound of Silbury Hill, crop circle investigators from the same team that set up the blind testing of plants in 1995 experienced one of the strangest, most unusual encounters to date. They were in the formation collecting plants for analysis when they observed Army helicopters maneuvering overhead, one landing on Silbury Hill. There was a sense that they were being observed.

The group left the formation and, as they were driving toward Avebury saw, a black car approaching from the opposite direction. It was mid-day. With no recollection of any event in between, they suddenly found themselves a half-mile down the road alongside a second formation known as the Galaxy. They had no idea how they got there. The black car was nowhere to be seen. Confused, they pulled to the side of the road and then, after a moment, continued on. Once again, with no memory of what occurred or knowledge of how they got there, they found themselves 35 miles down the road near Andover, traveling in the wrong direction. Their confusion was not alleviated when they noted that the time on the dashboard was two hours later than it had been mere minutes earlier. Strange marks were later found on their necks and other places on their body. Although this has all the hallmarks of a typical alien abduction scenario, could it also have been directing our attention to time?

Matthew Williams reports another type of time anomaly. Rather than missing time, his experience seems suspend or reverse it. His story can be heard in an interview with *On the Edge TV,* where he reports being with a team of people creating a crop circle in the night. Asking for a time check, he is told that it's five minutes past one. With the design well underway, he figures they will have time to finish. They work until he sees the sky beginning to turn red and realizes the sun will be up in an hour and that they will not have sufficient time to complete the design. Looking into the sky he says, "God, I really, really need some more time for this." He then asks his teammates for a time check. Looking at their watches, Matthew is once again told that it's one o'clock. Startled, he looks back into the sky to see that the cloud bank has returned to where it was at one o'clock and that it is again dark. They continue and finish the circle before light.[8]

Events such as these seem so impossible that we immediately think they are untrue. Until something like this happens to you, there will always be an element of doubt, because the stories are difficult to verify. People can be honest and still be deceived or mistaken. When trying to understand the significance of the event, we tend to put the importance on the act being undertaken. We wonder if the people who lost time needed to be adjusted or were part of an alien experiment; we ask if the design in the circle Matthew and his team were making was critically important to some plan.

Could these events be drawing our attention to properties of time? The alarm events in my house were only important in getting my attention so that I could be directed to other information. Equipment failure and electromagnetic anomalies may be pointing us to a different understanding of the electromagnetic interaction of mind and matter. Perhaps time distortions are directing us to a different understanding of time. Science tells us that time is fluid; can time be influenced through conscious interaction?

Orchestrating the Larger Picture

One of the most prevalent experiences people have in relation to crop circles is synchronicity. They have an idea to visit a crop circle and doors start opening to make it happen. Money arrives, people appear to help, and the first circle that is visited has personal meaning. Strong emotions are evoked as the coordination goes well beyond chance, instilling significance to the event and providing a sense of personal importance. The world suddenly seems personal, warm, and friendly.

Over and over we see the coordination between individuals who are requesting circles and those making them. John Lundberg tells us in his interview with Matthew Williams of distortions that cause mistakes to be made in the construction of designs, which then prove to have greater significance. In one instance, Lundberg describes making a mistake in the execution of a design when, unbeknown to him and the team he was working with, another team was making a circle in an adjacent field. The mistake in the formation Lundberg was involved in corresponded directly to the other formation so that it seemed one was interacting with the other.[9] Matthew also talks of teams working in the fields unknowingly interacting with each other. In other instances, mistakes point to ancient sites in the landscape, some that were not visible from the ground but that could be seen in aerial photographs.

We have to wonder if the predominance of the crop circle phenomenon in England is also orchestrated. England has one of the most extensive networks of megalithic sites on the planet. Could the formations be directing our attention to the significance of these monuments? An understanding of Earth energy has been one of the outcomes of examining location of formations. Maybe our attention is being drawn to a deeper respect for the planet with an increased awareness of the Earth as a form of consciousness.

Over and over in crop circle lore, researchers, enthusiasts, and circle-makers express the feeling that another intelligence is present. In the first circle I visited, the sense of presence drew me forward and continues through the evolution of my 30 years of experience. I have no doubt that events are orchestrated; for whose purpose or benefit I cannot say.

As noted in Chapter 5, the evolution of designs from simple circles to elaborate renditions of fractals, three-dimensional figures, and Mayan motifs mirrors the evolution within our consciousness. Considering all the mysterious interactions, the phenomenon seems to be asking us to look at what is possible. Vibration, resonance, electromagnetic field effects, and sacred geometry seem to mix with our mind, emotions and intent. Combining these is taking the mindstep to the next level of reality.

All of our inquiries in this chapter are speculative supposition. The discovery of Higgs boson (discussed in Chapter 3) will most certainly galvanize a scientific revolution that could provide the medium for understanding the bigger picture this mystery is giving us. Right now, we are left to investigate the high-strangeness experiences and notice how they change us. This will provide a key to interacting with larger reality and unlocking the phenomena we are investigating.

Moving Forward Into Greater Reality

High-strangeness experiences with crop circle phenomena form the basis for moving forward to investigate more aspects of non-ordinary reality. What is learned can be applied to understanding the intelligence that we are interacting with and what that interaction holds for us. The crop circle phenomenon is an experiment in learning, a chessboard for a dynamic interaction that introduces us to ourselves.

Whether we make the circles, research them or experience them, they demonstrate that human consciousness has the power to interact in the physical universe in unimaginable ways. We are not there yet, but the experiences in the fields show us who we might become. Here are some key points to guide the way forward:

- High-strangeness events reflect back our own beliefs. Where we are limited, we will find limitation; where we are curious, we will find questions; where we are untruthful with our inner selves, we will find deception in the phenomena.

- Non-ordinary reality speaks to us in language and imagery that we can relate to. Anything outside our imagination is subject to inattentional blindness.

- Intention is our vehicle for acting in this realm. Energizing our thoughts with emotion and focusing the energy with intent opens the edge of reality. Here we might find that we can communicate telepathically, heal the physical body, alter electromagnetic fields, and even shift time. If we develop in this direction, we will be conscious co-creators of reality.

- The entrance to this realm comes out of genuine connection to our core self and the taking of heart-centered action. When we connect to the spirit of creative imagination within, we interact with layers of consciousness that compel us into the fulfillment of action.

- We are encouraged to follow our feelings, trust our emotions, and expand our limits. What stops us is lack of trust in each other, in ourselves and in the unknown.

The new era we are entering will have many surprises. The mysteries we encounter today are only the harbinger of higher strangeness yet to be experienced. How far we can move into this realm will depend on how much we are willing to challenge our view of what is possible while staying grounded in what is true.

Bridging the Edge: Non-Ordinary Reality in Ordinary Life

Stone Bridges into Mystery Phenomena *by Wayne Mason.*

Part III explores a variety of phenomena that challenge our view of reality. Whereas high-strangeness events are described in historical accounts for millennia, interactions with these events are suddenly advanced. Our connections with UFO, for example, have evolved, and new phenomena such as strange black-bag entities have arrived. What we believe is changing. Consequently, we are opening to new vistas that challenge the boundaries of what is real. As we approach the event horizon of a new awareness, interactions with non-ordinary reality will continue to increase. Engaging these phenomena is bridging the edge of reality; embracing the intelligence within the phenomena is the mindstep we are approaching.

Structured objects and lights in the sky earned the names flying saucer and UFO (unidentified flying object) in the 1940s. Sightings were frequent during aerial battles of WWII and reported by both sides of the war. So common were the small metallic spheres and colored balls of light that flew alongside bomber planes, they earned the name Foo Fighters by the crews who repeatedly saw them.[1]

By no means do the encounters of the 1940s represent the first time that unexplained lights and objects in the sky were seen and recorded. Roman armies wrote of strange, silvery "wine goblets" in the sky[2] and the Bible is replete with descriptions that sound strikingly similar to today's UFO encounters such as Ezekiel's wheels of fire (Ezekiel 1:4, 16–21). The Ancient Astronauts Society has accumulated numerous references to extraterrestrial visitors in ancient cultures from around the world.[3] For example: Sumer, the first organized civilization, has several representations in their art of aerial ships, some looking like rockets, others like airplanes with people inside. Pictures of these can be seen on many Websites.

Ancient descriptions of high strangeness events are very similar to those of today, and it seems likely that UFOs have always been part of Earth history. Although there are more reports of UFO sightings now than in the past, it is difficult to assess whether the UFO is actually more present, or whether we are more able to see it. The scientific age provided wonderful advancements in knowledge, but it also caused inattentional blindness in areas of high strangeness. Society in general has not been prepared to accept anything outside the scientific or religious paradigm. Even though religious stories are filled with high strangeness, the events are considered separate from reality, not an integral part of it.

We can only look to present-day phenomena and say with assuredness that the amount and type of UFO sightings reported since the

1940s have increased dramatically worldwide. In addition, technology increases what we are able to see, and media transmits events to more people. With the dramatic increase in awareness of the UFO comes a corresponding expansion of consciousness. What seems to have changed the most over time is our willingness to see and engage the phenomenon.

Interestingly, many mass sightings of UFO events are precipitated by people looking into the sky for other reasons. People are looking to see things like an eclipse of the sun or a comet when a strange object appears in the sky. One of the side effects of the crop circle phenomena has been the significant increase in UFO sightings in south-central England, which leads to two conclusions: More people are on the hillsides overlooking the fields to witness what is present, and the presence of crop circles has opened people to new possibilities. As we will see, there is also considerable evidence that the crop circles draw UFO activity. What we wonder is whether the UFO was drawn to crop circles by the designs or by the collective intent of people who gathered. Whatever the reason, people are looking to the skies and are being changed.

The recent UK poll Opinion Matters stated "More than 33 million U.K. citizens believe in extraterrestrial life compared to just over 27 million—less than half the country—who believe in God."[4] This represents a considerable shift. Mass sightings, video and photographic support of mass sightings, media-witnessed UFO events, interaction with electrical technology, pilot sightings and interaction, and military involvement in UFO events have made denial of their existence more difficult. In addition, UFO interference with technology such as the association of UFO sightings with power outages brings them front and center in civil emergency planning.

Here is a list of both well-known and little-published events that fit the criteria for a growing phenomenon over the last 50 years. There are many hundreds more sightings and some much higher profile cases; however, this list illustrates the trends.

▸ On November 9, 1965, the Northeast of North America underwent a large-scale blackout after a pulse of current tripped the relay at the Ontario Hydro Commission plant. Ontario, Canada, as well as Connecticut, Massachusetts, New Hampshire, Rhode Island,

Vermont, New York, and New Jersey in the United States were without power for up to 12 hours. The source of the pulse has never been identified, but tentative suspicion was centered on the Clay Substation of the Niagara Mohawk network. Several witnesses had UFO sightings in this area just before the blackout, including five witnesses near Syracuse, New York, who saw a glowing object ascending just before the event. Reports of unexplained sky-lights continued across New England during the 12-hour period. A woman in Seacliff, New York, saw a disc-shaped object hovering, popping up and down, and then shooting away just after the power outage and reports continued all through New England during the blackout.[5]

▸ On March 16, 1967, at the Malmstrom Air Force Base in Montana, Captain Robert Salas claims an object came over the site while he was on duty and shut down 10 minuteman missiles. He made his claim in Washington, DC, at a press conference at the National Press Club in September 2010. The press conference consisted of former senior military officers and U.S. government witnesses to UFO activity related to National Security and was reported on many news outlets, including FOX News.[6]

▸ On July 11, 1991, a solar eclipse over Mexico City had thousands of people looking at the sky. It was the perfect stage for a mass UFO sighting when a bright, metallic, solid-looking object appeared and hovered over the city. At least 15 separate video tapes were recorded of the event, making this the most documented UFO sighting in history. When journalist Jaime Maussan aired video on TV, thousands of people called in to report having seen the object. Skeptics claim the object was Venus, unmasked as the sun was eclipsed. This interpretation does not address what is seen on camera. The object was seen over many different cities during a 90-minute period.[7]

▸ I was present on August 18, 1991, in Wiltshire, England, as a Japanese film crew for Nippon TV was shooting an episode of *Thursday Night Mystery Circle* when a bright light appeared. Twenty-five people witnessed an interactive event described in more detail later. During the event, Air Traffic Control eliminated military or civilian aircraft as an explanation.

▸ On July 24, 1992, at 12: 33 a.m., approximately 30 people witnessed an interactive exchange initiated by Dr. Steven Greer and his CSETI group in Wiltshire, England. The interaction was significant for the differences in perceptions among the group.

▸ On March 13, 1997, a clear night, hundreds of people were looking to the sky for view of the Hale Bopp comet. Instead, hundreds more in a 300-mile swath from Nevada to Tucson were treated to a display of unusual objects in the sky. Phoenix, Arizona, was the first to make an official report of an array of lights and a v-shaped, solid craft. Photographs and videos were taken, becoming one of the most documented cases of a UFO sighting in history. Governor Fife Symington originally undermined reports, but eventually admitted to having seen the lights himself and agreed that they were not military craft.[8]

▸ On July 16, 2001, more than 75 people reported seeing 15 to 20 lights over the area in Carteret, New Jersey. The lights are said to have appeared at 12:29 a.m. and lasted for two minutes. Witnesses included police, reporters, and drivers, many of whom pulled to the side of the New Jersey Turnpike to watch.[9]

▸ Mass viewings of three silent, luminous objects occurred on several occasions: August 21, 2004; October 31, 2004; October 1, 2005; and October 31, 2006, in two suburbs of Chicago: Tinley Park and Oak Forest, Illinois. Witnesses describe the lights as red or red-orange, circular in shape, and moving slowly in formation for about 30 minutes on each occurrence.[10]

▸ At 12:40 a.m. on June 8, 2008, a South Wales police helicopter flew over an RAF base near Cardiff International Airport waiting for landing clearance. The helicopter was manned by three experienced crewmen who noticed a brightly lit saucer shaped object above them. The object suddenly dropped toward them at high speed, causing the pilot to take evasive action. The object sped away, and the helicopter chased after it at maximum speed until flying over the Bristol Channel then had to turn back due to low fuel. Hundreds of people across Wales reported seeing a UFO in the days around this event.[11]

▸ On January 8, 2008, in Stephenville, Texas, home of the George W. Bush ranch, hundreds of residents reported seeing several different types of UFO. Some saw triangular looking crafts, others disc-shaped. Most reported the crafts were the size of a football field or larger. Several people reported the presence of military aircraft that seemed to be in pursuit. The incident was covered extensively by news media including Larry King (CNN), the History Channel, *UFO Hunters*, and more. Pressed to making a statement, the U.S. Air Force claimed to be conducting training flights involving 10 F-16 fighter jets. A report by the Mutual UFO Network (MUFON) used FAA radar information that showed the F-16 flight paths and also that of an unknown object. The MUFON report states: "This object had no transponder and was tracked on radar for over an hour. Most of the time the object was either stationary or moving at speeds of less than 60 mph. At 7:32 pm the object was tracked accelerating to 532 mph in 30 seconds and then slowing to 49 mph only 10 seconds later."[12]

▸ On Tuesday, November 7, 2006, more than a dozen O'Hare International Airport employees witnessed a metallic, saucer-shaped craft in the air over Gate C-17. It was first spotted by a ramp employee working with United Airlines flight 446 to Charlotte, North Carolina. Most of the crew, along with several pilots and supervisors, are reported to have witnessed the event. According to the *Chicago Tribune,* witnesses reported the disc was clearly visible for two minutes then departed at high speed leaving a hole in the cloud cover. The event was published in the *Chicago Tribune* and reported on CNN, MSNBC, FOX News, and eventually aired on *UFO Hunters* on the History Channel in a February 11, 2009, episode entitled "Aliens at Airport."[13]

▸ A UFO was observed at a wind farm in Conisholme, Lincolnshire, England, on Sunday morning, January 4, 2009, by multiple witnesses. One turbine was broken off and another damaged. County councilor for the area, Robert Palmer, said he saw a "round, white light that seemed to be hovering over the wind farm". The wind farm is owned by Ecotricity. A spokesperson said the extent of damage was "unique."[14]

Interactions

Exchanges with inhabitants of craft from the sky are well documented from ancient times to modern abductions. Religious terms aside, biblical interactions with higher intelligences seem strikingly similar to modern day reports of exchanges with extraterrestrials. What has changed is the name we give these beings: angels, Elohim, Quetzalcoatl, extraterrestrials, or God. If we take the leap and accept for discussion purposes that biblical encounters are encounters with an alien intelligence, what can we learn from these events?

As with all aspects of the phenomena, interactions have evolved. In biblical stories, the beings are unable to act in this physical realm. Their vehicles become visible and they can communicate, but they seem unable to act and therefore engage humans to perform functions for them. The role is that of servant and master. In the Battle of Jericho for example, one might assume higher beings would have the power to destroy the city, yet God gave Joshua, his chosen leader, precise directions in how to use resonance to collapse the walls. The army was to march in unison around the city once each day for six days while blowing trumpets and carrying the Ark of the Covenant. The soldiers were to remain silent. On the seventh day, the army marched around the walls of the city seven times, then all gave one great shout and the walls fell flat. The story is eerily reminiscent of watching a bridge fall from the effects of vibrational resonance.

Also of interest is that God is unable to have direct contact with humans. Even looking at God caused instant death, as proclaimed in Exodus 33:20: "You cannot see My face, for no man can see Me and live!" The inability to sustain contact without harm seems paramount in the evolution of interaction. Present-day abduction cases seem bound by the same problem. Starting with the first abduction case of Barney and Betty Hill on September 19, 1961, abductions have been carried out in a manner that limits direct physical contact with the beings or their craft. Although assumed this was for their benefit, perhaps it was for ours. Instances where humans had unshielded contact with alien technology resulted in severe illness reminiscent of radiation sickness. Two important examples in this vein are the Cash-Landon case of 1980 and the Travis Walton abduction of 1976.

In the Cash-Landon case, two women, Betty Cash and Vicki Landron, had a direct encounter with a large craft. Close enough to feel the intensity of heat and hear a load roar, both women became ill. Within hours they developed symptoms of radiation exposure that included nausea, vomiting, diarrhea, weakness, a burning sensation in the eyes, and a feeling of sunburn. Days later they both started to lose their hair.[15]

The Travis Walton case is even more fascinating. Without going into the entire story, Travis was caught by a beam emitted from a UFO in the forests of Flagstaff, Arizona. He was thrown several feet in the air in full view of his coworkers. Terrified and not imagining he could have survived such an attack, his coworkers tore off, leaving him for dead. Later they returned to find Travis's body was gone. Five days later Travis reappeared outside of town with an incomplete memory of being abducted.[16]

The emotional toll this incident took on Travis and his family is great. Travis, Synthia, and I had breakfast in Portland, Oregon, at a conference we attended in 2010. I asked him what his current feelings were about the intent of his abduction. He surprised us by saying he suspects being hit by the beam was accidental and the abduction was an intervention to save his life.

Abduction stories frequently revolve around genetics programs commonly surmised being carried out by alien intelligence for their benefit. On the other hand, I suspect the genetics program may be aimed at our evolution, perhaps preparing us to sustain contact with other off-planet species.

One element that is changed in the present-day phenomenon is the role that we play in the encounters. In the past, interactions were initiated by the phenomena: UFOs showed up in the sky, and people had unexpected close encounters on the road or were stolen from bedrooms and returned altered. Humans were passive experiencers with no power to even fully remember events, never mind influence the direction they took. Today, humans are taking a more assertive role in interactions.

Japanese Film Crew (1991)

An interesting event occurred to a Nippon Television crew I was working with from Japan. They were in England to conduct a night watch, hoping to film a crop circle being made. The television cameras were positioned next to a caravan parked high on a remote hill overlooking the fields at Alton Barnes in Wiltshire, England. The footage was to be part of the Nippon program *The Thursday Night Mystery Circle Show.*

An overhead canopy protected their television cameras as they panned across the field below just after four in the morning. Out of the clear, dark sky appeared a bright, yellow-white light. Cameras were aimed to capture the unexplained luminosity hanging about 30 degrees above the horizon. The light in the sky slowly brightened and seemed to remain stationary. The camera was pointed in the direction of Heathrow Airport in London, about 80 miles east of our location, so at first we thought we were seeing the landing light from an aircraft heading directly toward us and thus appearing stationary.

One of the film crew grabbed a bright, handheld spotlight and flashed it at the sky-light. Incredibly, the light brightened, enlarged, and pulsed back. The effect on the people present was electric. Our bodies were immediately on high alert, with our observation skills sharpened. I had heard several stories of how quickly these balls could move, sometimes shifting from being a spot in the sky to being dangerously close to observers in a blink of the eye. The sense of connection with the light made such a shift seem entirely possible.

Afraid the light might not stay present long, I quickly darted into the caravan and telephoned West Drayton Flight Control Center near London. Working in local government and being well known to officials had advantages, as I realized when my call was put through. Explaining the situation to one of the flight controllers, I asked if there were aircraft currently in the air over the area where we were positioned. I was told there was not; there were only two aircraft overflying UK airspace at that moment and only one flying in our direction. Its call sign was VRBJD, traveling from Montreal to Paris at 45,000 feet.

Thinking I was putting forth an impossible request, I asked if the two aircrafts that were flying, even though not in our immediate area, might be able to extinguish all external lights for a brief moment. I wanted to categorically rule out that we weren't somehow watching one of them. Incredibly, the controller put our request to the aircraft. Of his own accord, he also asked the pilots to extinguish the cabin lights. Both pilots agreed and turned off all lights for 120 seconds. We then knew for certain that the light we were watching was not from an authorized aircraft.

Meanwhile, the light in the sky was still responding to the hand-held spotlight and continued to interact for several more minutes. The crew member flashed the spotlight toward the luminosity, turning it on and off in repetitive sequence. The sky-light not only pulsed the same sequence back, it dramatically increased in size with each pulsation. Everyone present felt the eerie sense of being perceived by the intelligence within the luminosity.

The film crew left without footage of a crop circle being made, but with footage that challenged their preconceived ideas of UFOs. Gone was the perception of the UFO as something remote, distant, and separate from us. Also gone was the concept that UFOs were somehow threatening. In its place was the realization of interconnection with an intelligence we don't comprehend.

Phoenix Lights (1997)

One of the most publicized and best investigated cases of a large-scale UFO event happened in Arizona on March 13, 1997. Many lives were changed after the mass sighting of unexplained phenomena in the sky. Two separate objects were seen by hundreds of people who were outside for a once-in-a-lifetime sighting of the Hale Bopp comet. One object was described as a V-shaped object, a delta-shaped object, and as a carpenter's square. Also associated with the object were several spherical lights. In addition to this triangular formation of lights passing over the state of Arizona, witnesses in Phoenix also saw a series of stationary lights. Footage can be seen on YouTube.[17]

The governor of Arizona, Fife Symington, made fun of the reports at the time of the incident but later admitted that he, too, had seen the huge object over the city and said it was "otherworldly."[18] He stated in a television documentary on the History Channel that he was aware of more than he said at the time. Apparently he was under orders to downplay the event.[19]

Phoenix councilwoman Frances Barwood demanded an explanation from the authorities. Not surprisingly, she was stonewalled. She telephoned Senator John McCain asking for answers. McCain made contact with the Air Force and was told that the incident was caused by flares dropped during a military exercise between 9:30 and 10 p.m. However, because the reports began at 8:15 p.m. in a different part of the city, it is widely believed that after the huge object passed over the city shortly after 8:00 p.m., the nearest air force base created a diversionary explanation by dropping phosphorus flares just before 10 p.m.

Councilwoman Barwood then interviewed more than 700 witnesses in an attempt to understand what happened. I met with Frances when she was in the midst of interviewing witnesses and was also able to speak with several people. Witnesses described driving on the freeway in downtown Phoenix under the enormous delta-shaped object. When it passed overhead, stars disappeared as the object moved slowly through the sky. All witnesses agree that there was no sound. Many said the sheer size was frightening.[20]

Since the event I have become friends with Frances and one of the main proponents of the mystery, medical doctor Lynne Kitei. Both women's lives were changed as a result of their encounter with the mystery. At the time of the Phoenix Lights occurrence, Dr. Kitei was an internationally acclaimed physician and health educator, and the chief clinical consultant of the Imaging-Prevention-Wellness Center at Arizona Heart Institute in Phoenix. Dr. Lynne, as she is known, worked on the cutting edge of early disease detection and prevention with an acclaimed background and promising future.[21] Seven years after witnessing the Phoenix Lights, and after repeated high strangeness events that began in 1995, Lynne Kitei broke her silence and ended her medical career. She put her extensive energy and intellect to work writing a book on the Phoenix Lights and producing an internationally award-winning documentary on the subject.

Dr. Lynne and I were both compelled to tell the personal side of our stories in 2009 at the Rio Rico conference. Why did we feel it necessary to do so; what did our stories have to impart? Lynne's house is high up in the hills overlooking Phoenix. Her view of the valley and the events of 1997 were unobstructed, yet she did not see all of the events others saw. In addition, earlier in March she saw orange lights she could not explain. Several times she was compelled to take pictures from her balcony that revealed objects not apparent to the naked eye.

On the first occasion that Lynne saw the lights, she described three amber spheres forming a stationary triangle in the sky, seemingly only a couple hundred feet away from her home. (The details of this are described in the next chapter.) As with the triangle in the fields that became the CSETI logo, the triangle formed the basis for the logo of the organization Lynne founded, The Phoenix Lights Network: Evolution to a New Consciousness. The logo is called a universal peace emblem. The significance of the triangle in the unfolding of consciousness continually recurs in high-strangeness accounts.

Clues to New Reality

One of the most striking indicators for me of how our perceptions are influenced in our interactions with high-strangeness phenomena occurred during a project I conducted with Dr. Steven Greer and CSETI. Most people have heard of Steven for two main accomplishments. His group, Center for the Search for Extra-terrestrial Intelligence (CSETI), was involved in working with protocols that Steven developed to initiate interaction with extraterrestrial intelligence. As mentioned in Chapter 5, his protocol involves using meditation to bring group brainwaves into coherence thus focusing the intent on making contact. Using remote viewing techniques, participants reach with their minds into space making contact with UFOs and "vector" them to the location of the project. When sky-lights appear, Steven uses a very strong laser to create visual interaction. As with the spontaneous actions of the Nippon Television crew member, the sky-lights typically interact with the sequencing of the laser.

This all seems incredible, yet there is not much difference in Steven's protocol to the natural efforts people made in connecting with crop circles to ask for design. What Steven did differently was to create a methodology. His protocol has been used extensively with reportedly good results.

The second thing Steven is well known for is bringing together high-ranking military personnel, pilots, and government agents in a disclosure initiative. His initiative means to disclose the facts about extraterrestrial intelligence by presenting the testimony of more than 500 government, military, and intelligence community witnesses with firsthand experience.

The event described here happened on July 24, 1992, at Wood-borough Hill in Wiltshire, England. It was a drizzly night with low hanging clouds. Around 30 people were gathered on the hillside to engage Steven's protocol. A bright orange light appeared to the west in the direction of Warminster. It remained stationary for several minutes, growing more brilliant as time went on. We suspected it was an aircraft coming toward us. After about five minutes an aircraft approached the sky-light and the sky-light noticeably dimmed, then moved off to the north. Watching through binoculars, I could see the sky-light as it moved away, quickly reaching a much higher rate of speed than the approaching aircraft.

Suddenly, we saw a white light darting at low level through the clouds, coming quickly toward us. The light moved overhead and Steven flashed his laser directly at it. The light immediately disappeared. What was interesting is that, though everyone saw something in the sky, not everyone saw the same thing. Half those present saw what I just described. The other half saw something completely different: They report seeing the light appear, dart around, and move overhead as the first group did. For them, however, the light was bright red. When Steven shone the laser and we saw the light disappear, the second group never saw his laser; they saw the light split in two, with each new light traveling away in divergent directions.

As we began excitedly talking about our experience, it became clear from the confusion that half were describing something different than the others. I interviewed everyone while taking careful notes and was shocked by several elements. There were not several different versions; there were only two. People fell in one camp or the other, and the division of perception was almost even. In addition, people seeing one thing were not standing apart from those seeing another. Everyone was standing together; people seeing different events were intermingled. More importantly, there didn't seem to be a difference in beliefs or expectations and almost everyone felt the sky-lights were consciously engaged.

This event seems to be directing our attention to an interaction with our perceptions. It might be teaching us that how things appear is not how things are. As said in Chapter 7, high-strangeness events appear in a context we can understand and therefore reflect back our own beliefs. Although the disparate accounts were not belief driven, the event demonstrated categorically that what we see is not necessarily what is happening. Many people present at the Woodborough event had the impression that both groups were seeing different aspects of the same happening, as if events were occurring in several dimensions at once and different people were tuned to different layers. Of course it is possible we were seeing two separate events in superimposed layers. I have often felt that humans are wired for certain experiences, and this seemed to demonstrate, or reflect, that observation.

Concluding Thoughts

I don't know what UFOs are or what alien intelligence is. What we call "off-planet intelligence" could be life forms sharing the Earth with us in different dimensional spaces such as visitors from our own future. Most likely the phenomenon is an out-picturing of our own consciousness. All things are possible because all things are equally impossible. And yet, the phenomena are here.

Noting the changes in social acceptance of UFOs, we wonder whether mass sightings are more than coincidental. Are appearances during astronomical events purposeful? Knowing that people will be looking skyward, is there an intention to engage us and prepare us for a paradigm shift? Long-term skeptics became believers in Phoenix after personal and direct experiences. Governments worldwide are participating in a disclosure process, revealing their investigations into the phenomena. The Vatican announced the possibility of life in other areas of the Universe. Clearly ideas about the phenomenon are changing.

We might wonder if the extraterrestrial (ET) mind is aware of our thoughts and seemingly influences them; if they can override our technology, are clearly interested in our war time efforts yet typically don't cause us harm. Why are we so afraid of this paradigm shift? What could we learn about our place in the Universe that causes us so much fear?

Working through our own inner fear and resistance is where change must occur now. Events from the fields of England show that humans have immense capability that we are only beginning to tap. Learning and using techniques such as remote viewing may be the next step forward. If we fear being powerless in the face of an advanced technological society, then let us advance our consciousness to become equals. What if open comings and goings of different life forms to this planet and contributions to our science and institutes of learning are the future? The paradigm shift may open the door for us to take our place in a universal community.

Orbs are a subset of the UFO phenomenon that appear in two very different aspects. The first are luminosities in the sky with unique features. They are typically seen at close range and can be quite small. They sometimes appear to have structure or at least substance, but most of the time appear as luminous spheres of various sizes. Their behavior exhibits intelligence, and they interact with elements of the environment. Consistent with Foo Fighters, the ones I have experienced in crop circles behave as though they are probes investigating people, places, and events. Having said that, nothing in the UFO realm is ever totally consistent!

The second type of orb is a relatively new phenomenon. This type shows up in photographs and is not seen with the naked eye when the picture is taken. They are of varying size and are often confused with the much more common artifact of a camera flash reflecting off dust or water droplets. This typically happens in low light when a flash is used, or when another light source creates a reflection off the dust mote or water droplet. The vast majority of photographs I have analyzed have turned out to be camera artifacts, yet this does not explain all of them.

The New Phenomena of Photographic Orbs

When I first began investigating photographic orbs, I honestly couldn't see what the fuss was all about. It seemed clear they were the artifacts of light reflection off objects that was interacting with the camera lens. However, a few pictures were taken in conditions that did not fit those needed to create such an effect. In addition, photos taken in quick succession often show an orb in one photo and not in other photos taken only fractions of a second before and after. This made me sit up and take notice.

The vast majorities of photographs that reveal orbs were shot in sacred spaces such as stone circles, temples, and ancient sites, or are taken during spiritual ceremony or special moments, or are related to exquisite nature sites. They are frequently seen in photos of pregnant women and in family photos in the weeks after someone has died. When my father-in-law died, my sister-in-law was pregnant. It was a wonderful confirmation of my father's-in-law presence when an orb showed up in pictures taken of my sister-in-law during this time.

Orbs are usually related to an elevation of spirit, and what sets them apart from camera artifacts are the stories people tell about the timing and what the orb meant to them when they saw it. The orbs usually arrive during highly significant moments for the photographer or people in the picture. Our friend Meg Blackburn Losey, bestselling author of *The Children of Now* series, describes feeling compelled to step away from a group she was part of to take pictures while in Christchurch, New Zealand. Later, she understood why, as she saw the array of meaningfully placed orbs in the photographs.[1]

Orbs may show up in pictures as a single entity or in large and small groups. They may appear randomly all over the photograph or in geometric arrays. They are often white but can be fringed with color or have rainbows going through them. They often appear as self-luminous spheres and may have structured geometric patterns. Although often appearing in low light conditions, I have seen them in photographs taken in full daylight as well.

Skeptics believe new phenomenon arrived with the onset of digital cameras, yet older cameras produce them as well. A significant encounter I had with photographic orbs occurred in 1990 at the International MUFON Conference held in Chicago and broke through my skeptical mindset. This was my first appearance at a conference in the United States where I was presenting alongside a number of well-known speakers. During the lecture several people took my picture from several different vantage points and at different times during the lecture.

After speaking, I was to meet Dr. Steven Greer for the first time. When we met he apologized, saying he wanted to attend my lecture but was physically exhausted and needed to lie down. He then added, "Don't worry, I didn't miss a thing. I astral projected into the room and heard it all."

At the time I laughed and didn't think anything more about it. When I returned to England after the conference, I was looking at photographs taken by my wife on our 35mm camera. One photograph in a series she took during my lecture showed a white, luminous transparent orb floating just behind my head as I stood at the podium. Shortly after, I received two more photographs from two attendees. Both pictures, taken at different times with different cameras from different positions, had captured what appeared to be the same orb. All were identical in size, shape, color, and transparency. If they were all camera artifacts I would expect different models of camera to produce different orbs. It must also be noted that this was well before digital cameras.

Figure 9.1: A photograph showing an orb taken during the 1990 International MUFON Conference in Chicago.

Dr. Steven Greer suggests they were pictures of his astral body. Many intuitives claim orbs are the vehicles of disembodied consciousness: the baby about to be born or the spirit leaving this world. Some people believe they are a vehicle for ghosts. I was surprised one day to catch a glimpse of an old Walt Disney cartoon with a ghost in it. When the ghost moved, it transformed into a ball of light and looked much like these orbs. I often thought Walt Disney was a visionary; I just didn't realize he might have interacted with this realm.

Many people believe the photographic orbs are depictions of high spiritual energy. As with the crop circles, it doesn't make sense to waste time on the question of whether the photographic orbs are produced by a mysterious phenomenon or are a camera artifact. It might be more important to ask if the arrival of the orb has significance. After all, if the force behind high-strangeness events can interact with us, could they not orchestrate images on camera lenses? The questions become: What synchronicity was in play and what sacred dance enacted?

Real-Time Orbs

Real-time orbs are sky-lights that are luminescent and usually white or reddish-orange, although they have occasionally been reported as metallic blue. They do not flicker, emit smoke trails, produce sound, or discharge flames. They are able to maneuver very close to the ground, hover motionless, and move at unimaginable speeds in an instant. People who see them typically report a sense of being perceived by the orb and interacted with. Though they do appear as single objects, they are most often seen in small groups. When in groups, they tend to fly in geometric formations. Many people feel orbs are spirits as opposed to a vehicle, though they sometimes seem to attach and detach from a larger craft and become part of the light arrangement of the structured UFO.

One of the main differences between orbs and other types of UFOs is the capacity in which they seem to function. Orbs come up close and personal, appearing to investigate humans and what we do. They are decidedly interactive and are able to produce thoughts in people's minds.

Phoenix, Arizona (1995)

Although Dr. Lynne Kitei's involvement with UFOs is often categorized as having begun on March 13, 1997, with the appearance of the Phoenix Lights, her actual experiences began with orbs in 1995.

Lynne was in the shower when she heard her husband, also a physician, call from the bedroom for her to come to and look out the window at what he was seeing. Their house is on a mountainside and the bedroom overlooks Phoenix; the wall is one big window. When she looked out, she saw three amber orbs forming a triangle less than

100 yards away. She particularly noticed that the light of the orbs did not glare like other city lights; they had a special quality. Lynne relates that the top orb began disappearing. She grabbed her camera and took photos of it while it was still very dim, just before it faded completely.

Even though the light was gone, Lynne somehow felt that it was still present. Moving outside, she took more photos while noticing an unusual silence: There were no birds, wind, or other typical noises. As she watched the two remaining orbs, she had the distinct feeling that they were aware of her watching them before they, too, dimmed and went out. At this time, Lynne knew nothing of such phenomena and never had an interest. When the photos she took were taken to be developed, the clerk gave her back the negatives with no prints; the negatives were blank. Instead of throwing out the negatives, Lynne saved them.

Lynne and her husband did not see the orbs again for two years. Then, on January 22, 1997, she again saw three amber orbs, this time equally spaced in a straight line. They were only visible for a short period before they imploded and disappeared. The next day, January 23rd, the three orbs returned, this time in front of South Mountain and below the red warning lights placed to guide air traffic away from the mountain. Once again, Lynne grabbed her camera. Although fully charged, it went dead.

When her husband came home half an hour later, Lynne pointed to where she saw the orbs, describing to her husband what she had seen. Immediately the orbs returned in the same spot, a line of six then slowly forming a V-shape that appeared to cover an area of about a mile. Lynne phoned the FAA and talked with one of the air traffic controllers. The controller became excited since he also had seen the lights. He stated that the orbs had not shown up on radar.

There were no more sightings of the orbs until March 1, 1997, when Lynne had another short sighting. On March 13th, when the mass Phoenix Lights sighting occurred, Lynne and her husband did not see the large craft that everyone else saw; they saw one light at about 8:20 p.m. At 9:20 they saw another lone light. As they watched the 10 p.m. news, another line of six lights appeared outside their window. Lynne grabbed the camera as three disappeared, leaving her to photograph the remaining three.

Another surprise awaited Lynne. After the March 13th sighting she started to feel compelled to take the negatives of the earlier pictures she took of the orbs that showed nothing back to the developer. She told me in a conversation that she actually heard a voice instructing her. She did take the negatives back and this time asked for prints to be developed even though the negatives were blank. The prints revealed four orbs hovering over the city.[2]

Stratford, England (July 14, 2007)

A set of five orbs brought the town of Stratford, England, to a halt on July 14, 2007, when hundreds stopped to watch what was happening above the town. Five orange orbs hovered in the sky for close to half an hour. It started with four; three formed a triangle, and the fourth was off to the side. After a short time they were joined by a fifth orb that arrived traveling toward the others at breakneck speed before slowing down and stopping a short distance away. At that point people had emptied out of pubs and area homes to watch. The orbs emitted no sound and were stationary for approximately a half hour before moving slowly beyond the horizon. Local resident Tom Hawkes states that there were no stars in the sky, only the lights.[3]

Castle Rock, Washington (November 10, 2012)

A recent report of an orb sighting is posted on the National UFO Reporting Center Website. The sighting was witnessed by a retired commercial pilot who has been flying since 1977. The event occurred three miles east of Castle Rock, Washington, between Castle Rock and Silver Lake. The sky was dark and clear with no cloud ceiling. The man was driving home when he encountered three reddish-orange glowing spheres arranged in an equilateral triangle and hovering at close range. The driver lost sight of the objects as they went behind trees, re-emerging within seconds. The objects were so close the driver almost stopped, fearing they would block the road. He continued driving and the three glowing orbs maintained distance.

The orbs were silent, and did not blink, rotate, or change color. They were very bright and were about the size of a dime held at arm's length. Initially he couldn't tell if the orbs were actually lights on the corners of a triangular craft. When he pulled into his driveway, the orbs maneuvered into a straight, equally spaced line. As if they had been escorting him home, they shot into the air and disappeared.

Calls to the Cowlitz County Sheriff and Castle Rock Police revealed that no one else had phoned in the sighting. Although the driver wishes to remain anonymous, his report was investigated and the pilot's integrity confirmed by former police officer James Clarkson. The pilot asserts that he is trained to be highly conversant with aircraft, and these were not aircraft navigation lights, emergency lights, landing lights, helicopters, lighter-than-air craft, weather balloons, flares, Chinese lanterns, or meteorological events.[4]

Orbs in Crop Circles

Some of the best photographic evidence of orbs has been shot within crop circles, probably because of their location in the English countryside. In England the phenomenon of orbs is ancient. They have been called Earth Lights, Amber Gamblers (orange globe), and Spirit Lights, to name a few. They are often associated with sacred sites such as Stonehenge, Avebury, and ancient burial mounds. One of the hills in Wiltshire is named Golden Ball Hill, a tribute to the number of orbs seen in the area for hundreds of years.

Reports of orbs in crop circles are described with various colors, but always exhibit behavior suggesting they are aware of their surroundings. From the earliest reports, it appeared evident they were purposeful. Remarkably, one film shows an 18-inch solid white orb seeming to separate the crop as it crossed the fields with an apparent interest in investigating a formation.

The best footage was shot by Steve Alexander, who was on Milk Hill in Wiltshire, England, with his wife, Jen, filming two crop circles. A farmhand, Mr. Leon Besant, was harvesting the adjacent field. In the film, Steve pans from one crop formation to the other. He was just getting ready to pack his video camera when he and Jen saw something flickering in the field. At first they thought it was a bird.

Steve zoomed in on the flickering to pick up an orb gliding over the crop toward one of the formations. The orb showed interest in an area of cereal crop within a few feet of one design, hovering about three feet above the ground. At times it actually moved into the tractor tire marks known as tramlines, almost touching the ground. Then it rose up a few feet and did a circuit that took it around the crop circle. Picking up speed, it headed toward the next field where Mr. Besant was driving his tractor.

It maneuvered over the hedgerow, lifting over the trees at the field's boundary to head directly at Besant. The orb approached the farmer's back and, as Besant turned the tractor to cross the field, he stopped short to watch the orb pass over his head and then continue toward the south. Besant had no idea that what he saw and reported to his boss was captured on Alexander's film.

Analysis of the video with light contrast showed that the orb was a solid object. After moving over the farmer, it suddenly rose at a sharp angle into the sky and disappeared from view. I interviewed Mr. Besant, and he confirmed that he saw the white orb traveling up and over his head. He was very excited to see the film that validated his experience. Steve Alexander's video can be seen on YouTube.[5]

On July 8, 2010, an excellent photograph was taken by Bob Schindler of a solid looking orb maneuvering above a field that has been involved in much crop circle activity. As Bob took the shot, the orb was stationary and floating just above ground level. When he and his friend first saw it, they thought it was on old helium balloon. Then it began to move, eventually out of sight across the field. This photograph is probably one of the best ever.

The British Military Film an Orb

Silbury Hill is an ancient, man-made pyramidal mound forming one of the sacred sites near the megalithic stone circle of Avebury. The hill and the immediate area around it have a long history of high-strangeness incidents that include tall white beings, unexplained engine and equipment failures, and sightings of unusual animals. A book should and will no doubt be written about this area as some sort of portal.

During July 21, 1990, to August 12, 1990, a covert military surveillance operation took place around Silbury Hill. It took place at the same time as a famous crop circle surveillance project known as Operation Blackbird, happening 19 miles away. In the early hours of one morning, two soldiers with image intensifier cameras and recording equipment observed a large, bright, white, self-luminous orb over the fields to the south of Silbury Hill. The orb was estimated to be around 25 feet in diameter and moved east at moderate speed. It was not seen again after it dropped behind a thick clump of trees. (I was given a copy of this fascinating footage and will make it available at the Website for this book.)

Concluding Thoughts

I am struck by the repetition in high-strangeness accounts involving the triangular geometry. The triangle has played a large role in my own evolution of thought. I believe it entrains energy; more information related to it is yet to come and may be related to a second repeating observation relating to the quality of light. Lynne Kitei noted that the quality of light coming from the orbs was very different than other light. Synthia noted in our joint experience related in Chapter 5 that the light in our room was alive and imbued with a quality outside of everyday reality. I suspect we will find this is important and related to the triangular geometry.

I feel a connection with Lynne, as though we are in the same experimental group. The voice Lynne heard that sent her in a direction she would not have otherwise taken was very much like the voice I heard 30 years ago sitting before my Commodore computer that sent me looking in other areas. That we were both compelled in 2009 at the Rio Rico conference to reveal for the first time very personal experiences feels like an orchestrated event.

I am also impressed by the fact that Lynne saw something very different on March 13th from others who witnessed the mass sighting. It is nearly identical to the experience of the CSETI group on Woodborough Hill in England. We know the phenomenon can reveal itself in specific ways to specific people. Is there a reason why it shows itself one way or the other? Does it depend on some quality within the person? The recurrence of incidents such as these indicates to me that we are involved in a process of integration with another mind. One wonders what is driving and integrating events.

I don't think photographic orbs are really very much different from real-time orbs. They may both be the same phenomenon at different levels of density or visual presence. Synthia feels the orbs are etheric vehicles that can be constructed, inhabited, and used by any consciousness to traverse this plane of existence. This can be astral bodies, discarnate beings, ETs, or higher mind. Events in Chapter 12 seem to support this concept, and I suspect this phenomenon has been present on Earth for millennia and has a large hand still to show.

Our capacity to emotionally and mentally engage non-ordinary reality is increasing. Although we proclaim that the phenomena are changing, in fact it may be us. Our body is the vehicle we use to interact with the world, including the realms of non-ordinary reality. Through the body we receive more information than we consciously engage. Much of that information is processed subconsciously, becoming the basis of gut feeling, instinct, and insight. If unusual phenomena have always been present, on some level the body has known it.

Often people who experience high-strangeness events have a sense of affinity with them. Even though the event is totally new and unexpected, it feels familiar. People say things such as "I felt like I was waiting for this all my life." Currently we are more able to process the information our body is receiving from non-ordinary reality. As we move forward in our ability, we encounter more new-to-us aspects of reality and, as the paradigm shifts, our job is to figure out how to engage and interact with these new elements.

The three items detailed in this chapter fall into the category of totally new and unique events. We are beginning to see signs of things that may always have been present but are only now losing the camouflage of our inability to perceive. We are left to question whether we are encountering the technology of a more advanced race or new life forms we have never seen.

The Black Bag Entity: Object or Creature?

A new type of phenomena is making a small but significant debut. Synthia and I encountered this entity in fall 2007. We had never heard of it or seen anything like it before. At first, we didn't know what we were looking at.

The encounter happened while Synthia and I were returning from my brother-in-law's funeral in Wales. We stopped at a café on the side of a small road along the border of Wales, a few miles before the entrance to the M4 motorway that would bring us back into England. We were drinking coffee while idly looking out the window, and both of us saw a black bag floating down the street and intermittently watched it waft along on the breeze as we talked. At first, neither of us commented on it as it billowed and rolled just below the tops of the trees. However, it began to seem unusual because it didn't drop to the ground or blow out of sight. We didn't say very much, but each of us watched it intently. It just didn't feel right.

It wasn't until we paid our bill and walked outside that the depth of the incongruence set in. There was not enough breeze to keep this object in the air for the lengthy 15 minutes that we had been observing it. There was certainly not enough movement of air to explain the magnitude of the bag's apparently random shifts and sways.

We stopped to look more closely, and the object immediately began to alter. It lifted up and flattened out. We still tried to convince ourselves that it was just a black plastic garbage bag caught in an unusual current of air, but both of us felt our attention was electrified. So engrossed were we that we didn't notice a clutch of rooks (crows) gathering in one of the pine trees across the street.

Suddenly, we were shocked when the birds took flight and the entire flock attacked the bag. They dove at it, pecked it, and pulled on it. With each assault, the object rolled, losing the bag-like contours that gave the rooks something to grab. Within a few seconds it was rolled into a tube shape with smooth, curved edges that looked like rubber. It was so black it felt as if it absorbed light and carried more density than a normal object.

What happened next was the biggest shock of all. It suddenly rose and shot off in a straight line at great speed. The rooks followed for a brief moment, then flew back to the trees. We watched until it disappeared over the horizon, which only took a few seconds. It traveled in the opposite direction to the movement of cumulus clouds higher up in the atmosphere.

We were shook, but immediately tried to remember everything we could about the encounter. We noted several things:

- Given its ability to move quickly and the amount of time it stayed over the road in front of us, it seemed to have been hanging around the café purposefully.

- It was relatively low to the ground, never lifting higher than a few feet above the trees until it took off after the rook attack.

- It changed shape as the features of the plastic bag morphed into new forms.

- Originally it was about four or five times greater in size than that of a rook with wings outstretched; once changed, it was about the diameter of one rook body and four or five bodies in length.

- The new tube-like form was sleek and appeared hard; it had a reflective sheen.

- It was silent; had no observable eyes, appendages, portals, or lights; and, once transformed, moved faster than any living thing we had ever seen.

- It was absolutely foreign, but in no way threatening. It did not seek to fight the rooks, only to escape.

- The writhing it went through during the rook attack transmitted a feeling of pain.

- At the beginning of the encounter we held the door open for it being a plastic bag; at the end there was no possible way that it was.

Despite being present together, Synthia and I recalled slightly different details. She saw the bag floating down the street from the left, while I remembered it floating down the street from the right. This was reminiscent of the duality of experience during Dr. Steven Greer's UFO encounter.

The biggest question we had was whether it was a living entity or a craft of some kind. At first we both voted in favor of a craft, though neither of us had ever seen a rook attack an object that way. The behavior of the rooks made it seem as though what we saw was some type of creature.

We searched the Internet and made a number of queries, but at that time no other reports of such an object existed. Since then we have found five other reports; all appear to be after ours. They span the globe, coming from England, Amsterdam, Illinois, Peru, and Texas.

England (August 2010)

Oddly, the first report we found came from a crop circle apprentice named Malcolm Treacher. In an interview on CirclemakersTV, Malcolm describes seeing the object with four other people: three circle-makers and another novice, who, like Malcolm, was being trained in the art of circle-making. The five were walking along a farm track into the field when they saw an object moving. It was 20 feet in the air and about 40 feet ahead of them, moving right to left.

The first thing that came to mind when Malcolm saw it was that it looked like a very large, black plastic bag, approximately eight feet long and three feet wide. He might have dismissed it as a bag floating on the breeze and changing shape as it moved except for several peculiarities. First were the odd curves and points as it moved, which could have been actual changes in shape or could have been changes in view as the object rotated. Also, the object maintained a constant height with a regular speed and flight path, something a bag doesn't do. The oddest aspect was the speed with which it disappeared. Flying behind a tree, it completely disappeared in the few short seconds it took the group to pass the tree. Based on its trajectory and speed, it should have been in the sky a few feet ahead of them, but it was completely gone.

No one in the group responded to the event, but everyone noted that something unusual had occurred. At one point in the interview, Malcolm said, "If you put a broom on the end and a witch on it, it would be about right"[1]—meaning, I suppose, that it was eerie in its strangeness.

We found an interesting parallel to our sighting when I exchanged e-mails with Julian Richardson, one of the circle-makers present. He agreed with Malcolm's general description. He said, "Five of us saw this black triangle about 30–50 feet above us. It started as a diamond shape. It had a flat appearance, seemed to me to be 2D. It glided over our heads before it went behind a tree, we all saw it. No sound, no lights. After going behind the tree in the direction we were heading, it disappeared.[2]

Instead of the three-dimensional object that Malcolm saw, Julian's perception was that it appeared to be two-dimensional. Also, as with

Synthia and me, Malcolm tells us there was a discrepancy among some as to the direction the object headed off in. It seems there were mirror image memories of the direction the object went as it glided over the trees.

Peru (Year Unknown, Believed to Be 2010)

An extraordinary video was posted on the Internet but unfortunately has been removed. It was recorded by Gladys Cordova on a very windy day. In the film, tree tops can be seen whipping wildly about. Along the hillside, three to four white and black plastic bag–looking objects are flitting about. Although they look like they are being tossed by the wind, the bags are moving irrespective of the wind. Gladys calls the bag entities creatures, and by the end of the video, it is hard not to agree.

Although at first they look like plastic bags flying purposefully through the sky or tumbling down the mountain cliff, at the end, one seems to grow appendages and run across the valley floor. These are true shape shifters, seemingly growing and absorbing appendages and changing shape based on the need to perform a particular function.

These bag entities morph into shapes much different than the tube shape we witnessed fleeing the rooks, yet this video feels very similar to what we saw. Although the original video was removed from YouTube, another video of similar entities was filmed on the same hill. It has less convincing elements, but is fascinating nonetheless. The YouTube title is "ALIEN MULTIFORME-CELESTE-GLADYS CORDOVA."

Amsterdam (2011)

Another object fitting the same general description was shown on unexplained-mysteries.com and can be seen on YouTube. It apparently occurred on August 7, 2011 (posted on August 8th). It occurred in Amsterdam and shows a black object floating in the sky. Rather than looking like a plastic bag, it looks more like a black Chinese lantern. The object is high in the sky, just below cloud level, and is clearly self-propelled. At one point it appears to change structure and color.[3]

Chicago, Illinois (2011)

This report is posted on Filer's Files (case #24-2011) and took place at O'Hare International airport at 9:30 p.m. on the evening of August

12, 2011; sunset occurs at about 8 p.m. A man and a woman saw what appeared to be a black bag. They decided it was not a bag as it did not float, dip, or dive, but it moved southeast in a straight line. It was matte black, made no sound, and had no lights. It was smaller than a helicopter, had no blades, and was traveling lower in the sky than a helicopter would. It was traveling faster than a jet. The body was rotating clockwise and seemed to have a rudder that moved in opposite direction to the body. It passed in front of a jet that was taking off. From this description it seems very much like the object seen in Amsterdam.

San Antonio, Texas (2011)

There is very little detail to this sighting, which occurred at 11:40 a.m. on August 23, 2011, but wasn't posted on the National UFO Recording Center Website until October 2011. A person saw a white dot that looked like a plastic bag or jelly fish. It was flying over a neighbor's house, and at first the observer thought it was a bag, but by its behavior realized it was not. The observer states that video was taken, but says the quality is poor, and the object rose and sped off at the time that the camera was produced. The camera is not noted as the cause of the object leaving.[4]

■■■

I do not know what these black-bag entities are. I am reminded of the reports that came out of investigations into strange phenomena at the Sherman Ranch, a 480-acre property located southeast of Ballard, Utah, in the United States. The ranch and the strange events that occurred were investigated by a team of scientists from the National Institute for Discovery Science (NIDS) funded by philanthropist millionaire Robert Bigelow. During the investigation, detailed in the book *Hunt for the Skinwalker*, the intelligence being interacted with on this ranch manifested in varying forms, such as lights, orbs, discs, and creatures that have never been seen before.[5]

Watching the Gladys Cordova video produced the eeriest possibility that hundreds more of these creatures could be hiding among the rocks and were morphed into everyday objects so that they became invisible. At this point we simply don't know what the phenomenon is. It is my hope that the accounts in this book will bring to light additional reports and video so that we can learn more about this odd new arrival.

Bent Beams of Light

Another strange event is described by well-known crop circle researcher turned circle-maker Peter Sorensen. Pete sends this description of his event:[6]

> Unquestionably the strangest thing I have ever seen in my entire life was witnessing what I call "bent searchlights" with the German croppie, Ulrich Kox, late in the summer of 1998. I had seen the famous Amber Gamblers balls of light over Woodborough Hill one night with Colin, Busty, Reg and others, but the spotlights were far stranger.
>
> It occurred in a harvested field in West Stowell after midnight. Ulrich had seen unusual light phenomena that seemed to exhibit intelligent behavior at that location on a couple of occasions before and he brought me there in the hope of seeing more. There was no moon but the stars shone brilliantly, illuminating a very dense carpet of fog just inches thick on the crop stubble.
>
> After nearly two hours we grew weary, but at the very moment that we had agreed to leave, a pair of what looked like World War II spotlights shot up out of the middle of the field for thousands of feet, swinging to and fro as though searching for planes. That was amazing enough, but these beams of light were BENDING as though made of rubber!
>
> They lasted for about seven seconds, long enough that we had no doubt at all what we had witnessed. Then they disappeared without a sound. After a moment of dumbfounded silence Ulrich said, "What was that—some kind of ghost?!"
>
> As soon as I regained my faculties I ran out into the field to the spot where the lights had sprung from, but there was nothing there. We discussed the event for over an hour hoping to see the lights again, but when they didn't return, one of us finally said, "I guess we should go back." And at that very instant the lights reappeared for just a second or two as if to say good night!
>
> The fact that both appearances of the searchlights occurred immediately after we had agreed to depart shows that their source was intelligent and interacting with us.

In conclusion I want to comment on the scientific ramifications. As anyone familiar with physics knows, light travels at 186,000 miles a second and for all practical purposes a beam of light is perfectly straight. So it's impossible for a beam of light to be curved on the size scale that I observed. The only way I can understand what I saw is to hypothesize that it wasn't a *beam* of light but a *plasma* (of glowing gas?). That opens up more questions—like how was it shaped? By a magnetic field? Given that no equipment was visible, what I witnessed would involve a technology more advanced than what humans are capable of at present.

Figure 10:1: Pete Sorensen's artistic rendition of bent beams.

Many witness accounts exists about beams of light arriving in the fields prior to the formation of crop circles, almost as though the fields are being seeded. Some claim to have seen crop circles forming under a beam of light. In no other account than Pete's are the beams of light actually bent. It sounds as though the light could have been refracted through a lens or shield, reminiscent of Matthew William's recounting of the rain stopping over head as he made a crop circle, as if protected with an invisible canopy.

The Norway Spiral and Other Sky Spirals

Hundreds of observers across parts of Norway and Sweden saw an event that became known as the Norway Spiral. It was observed by people heading to work at around 7:50 a.m. local time on December 9, 2009. A similar, though less spectacular, event was also reported in Norway the month before. The December 9th mass sighting of the Spiral was visually recorded by many different cameras. However, most of the renditions seen on the Internet are computer-generated models. Video recordings of the real event as well as the simulated event are posted on YouTube.[7]

There is no question that the Spiral occurred—just curiosity about what caused it. Speculation by skeptics and believers alike results in more questions than answers. This is what was seen: In the light of early dawn, a blue beam shot into the sky leaving a trail of grayish-white, spiraling light. Witnesses say the blue light either came from behind the mountain or out of it. The beam reached a height of about 80,000 feet and stopped midair, and then the spiral expanded before imploding, creating a visual effect that looked to me like a donut ring. The event occurred in the immediate vicinity of Norway on the day that U.S. President Barack Obama arrived in Oslo to accept the Nobel Peace Prize.

Most people were satisfied when the Russians announced that the light show was a failed missile launch of the Bulava ICBM missile. The Russian military claimed what people saw was a rocket motor spinning out of control after the missile was launched from a submarine in the White Sea. The report claimed the missile had previously failed six of its 13 trials, although these failures did not occur as witnessed events.

I was ready to believe this was a failed launch except for the anomalies that kept appearing with continued analysis. I couldn't help but feel the embarrassed Russian official displaying the failed missile launch report was too similar to that of army officer Jessie Marcel holding up pieces of a damaged weather balloon after the suspected UFO crash at Roswell in July 1947. I certainly don't think the Norway Spiral was a UFO crash, but I'm no longer sure it was a missile failure, either.

Dr. Jean-Noel Aubrun, a physicist who has worked in the space industry and for NASA, shared with me his reservations about the Russian failed rocket solution. His primary reasoning was that the spacing of the spiral across its full profile could be qualitatively "explained" by either a perspective effect or a variation in exhaust gas pressure, but it would have taken very unusual conditions to produce the extreme symmetry and regularity of the pattern.[8]

Figure 10.2: Computer rendition of the Norway Spiral by artist Wayne Mason.

Also, as the failed missile trajectory moved through higher levels of thinning atmosphere, the bands within the spiral should have varied significantly in width. Analysis of the visual evidence showed that this did not occur.

Here are some additional problems researchers are having with the Russian missile explanation:

- Sight range: The calculated locations in that region of the world which would have been able to see the missile fired from the White Sea do not tally with the actual sightings in Norway and Sweden.

- Speed of rotation: To match the Russian claims of where the missile was launched and where it was seen, the Spiral would have had to rotate at a speed faster than sound, yet there was no sonic boom.

- The evenly spaced ripples of the Spiral indicate the source was a force with regular impulsion, not that of a failing motor.

- Every rocket launch is carefully recorded. Where is the Russian documentation of this launch?

- Would the Russians really test a rocket over the sky on the day a U.S. president was visiting?

The Norway Spiral is not the only or even the first such sky event. Similar spirals have been seen and filmed over many other cities. The first actually occurred in 1988 in China. More recent events have taken place in Australia on June 7, 2010; Trekhgorny, Russia on December 23, 2011; and Armenia on June 7, 2012: and several more occurred in China. If these are all rocket failures, there is large-scale rocket development underway that is not doing all that well; however, as attention grabbers, the sky spirals are effective counterparts to crop circles in the fields: They certainly can and do focus attention! As time goes on, more evidence will surely present itself to open minds as to what these enigmatic light shows truly are.

Good footage of the varying spirals can be seen on You Tube.[9]

Concluding Thoughts

Research into the black-bag phenomenon needs first to determine if it is an object or creature, then to determine its origin. The problem with the modern-day mentality is that on some level we believe that we know all the mysteries the world has to offer and have seen all the jewels of the Earth. We may not think that we believe this, yet we act as though something undefinable is a miracle. When confronted with the truly unexpected, we scramble to find a place for it.

In 2001 explorers were treated to an unexpected discovery: the largest cave in the world found in Vietnam.[10] Son Doong cave is more than 200 meters (656 feet) wide, 150 meters (492 feet) high, and approximately 9 kilometers (5.6 miles) long. It encompasses caverns big enough to hold a skyscraper. The best part of the underground wonderland is the jungle that exits inside. Past collapses of the roof left holes that allow enough sunlight for an ecosystem to develop and thrive. Exploring the unknown species expected to exist in the pristine environment will fascinate botanists and zoologists for years. Additionally, the life forms inside this jungle have never before seen humans. Is it possible such a place could harbor species we cannot even imagine—species that can morph into black bag shapes and float across our skies?

If the black bag entities are alive, are they terrestrial life forms or alien? We could propose that they have been here all along as they clearly know how to camouflage. The Skinwalker research encountered similarly strange creatures. This research concluded that the life forms were slipping through a dimensional portal. And of course there is still the possibility that the black bags are not alive at all, but represent a new type of material and advanced craft of some kind, or a drone under remote control. It will take considerably more exposure to this phenomenon before we determine what it is.

It is interesting that both the beams of light that were reported by Peter Sorensen as well as Synthia's and my encounter with the black bag felt interactive. Pete describes the beams interacting with the circle-maker's intention to leave, using that decision as a marker of sorts. Synthia and I did not feel the bag interacted with our intentions; rather that it was hanging about to observe us or perhaps be observed by us. The rook attack appeared an unexpected interference. In both phenomena, the desire to make connection was evident. Something may want to be noticed.

Pete's experience with the beams of light and people's experiences with photographic orbs seem to be external expressions of internal spiritual experiences. Many who die and are brought back to life, called a near-death experience (NDE), relate being pulled along tunnels of light and interacting with beings within beams of light. It seems the paradigm shift underway may be a thinning of the veil between the realm of the living and the realm where we go when we leave physical form.

The sky spirals are an enigma. They are interactive only in that they appear in front of large numbers of people and are available to be videotaped. Many of the lights in the sky and UFO-type phenomena have an aversion to being filmed, causing equipment malfunctions as has been described. Not so with the sky spirals. They do not appear to come from another realm or off planet, and I really wasn't sure whether or not to include them at all. However, they do represent new phenomena, whatever their source. I suspect we will find the sky spirals are new technology that will come to light over time.

One of the biggest mysteries of all time is the strange sounds that people are hearing across the world. The sounds are mysterious in many aspects, and no one is able to detect where they come from or what causes them. Some sounds are heard by everyone within a specific hearing distance, which can be several miles; others are heard only by certain individuals within a given area; and some even by people who are totally deaf.

People question whether these sounds come from covert military activity. Some wonder if the Earth is emitting these sounds as tectonic plates shift. Others postulate that how we hear and what we hear is evolving. What we can say for sure is that finding the answers will require ridding our minds of long held assumptions of what is possible and opening to other alternatives. Answers on this topic are unlikely to come from within the box of conventional understanding. This chapter engages three of the biggest sound mysteries of today.

The Hum

A few years ago my mother-in-law, Suzanne Ramsby, began complaining about hearing a low rumble that sounded to her like a diesel truck idling in the distance. Although she searched, she was unable to identify a source or even to fully isolate the direction of the sound. It often disappeared for weeks only to return abruptly as a relentless drone that created a constant, maddening distraction. It caused her to feel irritable and overwhelmed. Suzie's experience is not unique. What she described occurs to hundreds of thousands of people worldwide in a phenomenon that has become known as the Hum.

The Hum was first reported in Bristol, UK, in the 1960s. Although not all people are able to hear it, nonetheless it has become a public health issue. Local Bristol newspaper reports from the 1970s to the present detail the destructive impact the sound has on those who hear it. Headaches and popping eardrums along with a feeling of pressure in the head are a few of the distressing symptoms that accompany the Hum. Several suicides in the Bristol area were directly attributed to the sound's torturous assault, resulting in a government inquiry into the source of the noise.[1]

The Hum is not confined to the UK; it is heard by people all over the world, most notably across Northern Europe, the United States, Canada, Australia, and New Zealand. Within these areas are key sites where the sound activity is more pervasive and received by more people. Locations that are considered hot spots include Bristol, UK (1960s); Taos, New Mexico (1970s); Largs, UK (1980s), Kokomo Indiana (1990s); Auckland, New Zealand; and currently Windsor, Ontario. Many people in the United States know of the phenomenon as the Taos Hum, but in truth we might more accurately call it the Worldwide Hum.

Approximately 5 percent of any people in a high-activity area are subject to hearing the noise. Though this doesn't seem like a large percentage, compare it to other well-known maladies. For example, in the United States the prevalence of glaucoma is approximately 2.1 percent,[2] the prevalence of irritable bowel syndrome is 15 percent,[3] and the prevalence of multiple sclerosis is .09 percent.[4] We would never downplay these serious conditions simply because they don't affect a larger group of people. If you are one of the 5 percent who hear the Hum, it is very significant!

The Hum is said to sound artificial and is more noticeable inside a house or car than outside. It is non-directional, pervasive, and persistent; and described as a hum, rumble, drone, or whirring. It is typically worse around two o'clock in the morning, causing insomnia that results in fatigue. In addition, people suffer other symptoms such as nausea, nosebleeds, difficulty concentrating, headaches, heart palpitations, and severe anxiety, along with a variety of other symptoms.[5] In Taos, complaints to local government were so prevalent that it became a public health concern. Several government-sponsored and independent studies have been conducted in Taos, England, and Australia. The results are astonishing.

Research and Studies

When I first learned of the Hum 20 or so years ago, as an electrical engineer I thought the mystery could be easily solved. I believed very finely tuned, acoustic recording equipment would capture and measure the sound. Trained musicians who hear it relate it to a modulated tone near 41 hz, which wouldn't seem too difficult to capture. This is clearly what government agencies who investigated thought as well. We couldn't have been more wrong!

The most famous and comprehensive government investigation was called the Taos Investigation and was commissioned by the U.S. Congress at the request of New Mexico Congressman Bill Richardson (later to become governor). Under the auspices of the House Permanent Select Committee on Intelligence, on which Bill Richardson served (he is said to have suspected that the sound was related to defense activities), the investigation was carried out by the University of New Mexico over a period of 18 months, and the report was issued in 1995.[6] Like the investigations conducted by the British Government, researchers were baffled. *The conclusion of the report is that the sound is not an acoustic event; no sound waves were detected.* This finding made reasonable the fact that many people who "hear" the Hum are completely deaf.

Acoustic instruments could not detect the sound. It could not be eliminated or affected through acoustic, magnetic, or electrical signals used as barriers. The only tool available to detect it and discern it seemed to be the human body. Details such as frequency, location, direction, intensity, and variations in intensity could only be obtained from Hum sufferers themselves. Two Internet surveys involving a total of 800 Hum sufferers revealed some very interesting results: (Several surveys can be viewed at *www.johndawes.pwp.blueyonder.co.uk* and *www.thehum.info.*)

- The hearing ability of sufferers ranges from excellent to very poor.
- Some sufferers are totally deaf.
- Few people younger than 45 hear it and the largest age group of sufferers is 55.

- Females hear it more often than males.
- Eighty percent of sufferers hear the Hum more often inside a building.
- More sufferers live in the countryside than in city centers.
- A daily cycle in the noise level of the sound exists and reaches a maximum at 2 a.m.
- A relation exists between the Hum and body temperature: Temperatures are above normal when the highest Hum activity is underway.

In 2006, Dr. Tom Moir, a computer engineer at Massey University's Institute of Information and Mathematical Sciences in New Zealand, claims to have recorded the Hum in Auckland. People who have heard the Hum agree that his recording sounds like what they hear. "If this is indeed the Hum, then it's acoustical and not electromagnetic," Dr Moir said.[7] However, there is dispute as to whether this is an actual recording of the mystery sound or of a similar but audible sound. To make matters more confusing, researchers synthetically duplicated the Hum to verify what it sounds like. These synthetic reproductions have ended up on the Internet and are mistaken by many as real.[8]

Hum Vibes

Although the Hum is called a sound and described as a low-frequency drone, research shows it has nothing to do with sound waves. Instead, the inner ear is being stimulated by some type of energy vibration creating the illusion of sound. This is similar in principle to the new generation of hearing aids that use bone conduction to stimulate the perception of sound: "In bone conduction, we kind of bypass the outer ear…we bypass the middle ear, and we stimulate the inner ear directly by vibrating the skull and hearing that vibration through the fluids of the inner ear."[9]

Studies have demonstrated that electromagnetic and radio wave energy sources can produce a vibration that is perceived as sound. In a 1962 study entitled "Human Auditory Systems Response to Modulated Electromagnetic Energy," published in the *Journal of Applied Physiology,* Dr. Allan Frey demonstrated that extremely low frequency electromagnetic energy can induce the perception of sounds in normal and deaf humans.[10] The auditory perception of radio wave frequency was studied in 2003 by Elders and Chou in an article published in *Bioelectromagnetics*. They state:

> Human perception of pulses of RF radiation is a well-established phenomenon that is not an adverse effect. RF-induced sounds are similar to other common sounds such as a click, buzz, hiss, knock or chirp. To hear the sounds, individuals must be capable of hearing high frequency acoustic waves in the kHz range, and the exposure to pulsed RF fields must be in the MHz range. The experimental weight-of-evidence does not support direct stimulation of the central nervous system by RF pulses.[11]

Because electromagnetic frequency can be perceived as sound, tests were carried out inside Faraday Cages (specially constructed, screened chambers built to block electromagnetic waves, including radio waves). Even inside these shielded chambers, Hum hearers could hear the sound. This demonstrated that the sound is not the result of an electromagnetic frequency. Also, the sound phenomena discussed by Elders and Chou resulting from pulsed radio waves were described as a buzz, hiss, knock, click, or chirp, not the dull drones described by Hum hearers. So what vibration is causing the Hum? The Taos Investigation looked at several possibilities. In addition to ruling out an acoustic source, they also ruled out:

- The Schuman resonance, the vibration in the atmosphere created by the discharge of lightning, because there were no changes in magnetometer readings related to the Hum.

- Extremely low frequency (ELF) waves along with radio wave transmission and other frequencies of electromagnetism.

- No correlation could be found to seismic event vibration caused by the movement of the Earth's plates.

People who hear the Hum invariably link it to government or military activity. My mother-in-law was convinced a tunnel was being dug across Long Island Sound. Others suspect the building of underground military bases. In an article titled "The Secret War Against Medford, Oregon," Mark Metcalf suggested the military was beaming Ultra Low Frequency (ULF) waves at Medford, Oregon, during the 1970s. The result was an overnight increase in suicides. His article suggests these might be part of mind-control experiments.[12] The High-Frequency Active Auroral Research Program (H.A.A.R.P.) discussed in Chapter 14 is also frequently cited as the source of the Hum. However, the sound was being reported decades before H.A.A.R.P. was started. Cell towers are also ascribed as a source, although reports of the sound preceded this technology as well.

Although research eliminates ELFs, radio waves, and other forms of electromagnetism, one theory given states that "an interaction is taking place between the electrical power supply and the ionosphere of the Earth creating the vibration that causes the Hum."[13] Hal Rumiani, a former massage therapist in Michigan, felt certain that the Hum he heard was caused by the electric power supply. To test this theory, he arranged to go hundreds of feet underground in an abandoned copper mine. Unfortunately, he found that the Hum was worse there.[14]

It is clear that some type of energy is producing a vibration that simulates the perception of sound in the inner ear. Questions of what it is, where it comes from, and whether or not it has purpose are simply unanswerable at this time. Could it be coming from our planet, could it be the sound from ley lines, or the effect of solar winds interacting with the Earth, or something so new that we don't know what to look for?

One of the problems in ongoing research is that each new project starts from scratch as if no earlier findings exist. Repeating the same tests and finding the same results is a waste of time and resources. The World Hum Database and Mapping Project (*www.thehum.info*) was launched in December 2012 to maintain a detailed mapping of Hum locations, and to provide a Hum-related database for professional and independent researchers. Perhaps more answers will be found through the sharing and coordination of all efforts.

Trumpets From the Sky

A new auditory phenomenon started emanating in 2011—a sound very different from that of the Hum. This is a sound that can be located as coming from the sky, although exactly where in the sky is difficult to pinpoint. It has been described as a low-pitched grumbling that many say sounds like a whale song. In other instances, it has the sound of a group of trumpets blaring. Some people report feeling vibrations along with hearing what they describe as a truly otherworldly sound. Unlike the Hum, everyone present can usually hear this sound and it can be recorded, meaning it is an acoustical vibration. Also, unlike the Hum, in most cases the trumpet sound is audible in short bursts and occurs infrequently.

The eerie noise was first recorded in Florida in March 2011, then in Kiev in the Ukraine on August 11, 2011. It was recorded in Costa Rica on January 9, 2012. Video and audio recordings have been transmitted around the world via the Internet, and new reports continue to arrive. It has now been heard in Conklin, Alberta, Canada, several locations in Russia, Florida, Manitoba in Canada, Nottingham in England, and Asia.[15]

Although firsthand accounts are haunting and some of the recordings are quite convincing, many of the recordings on the Internet are hoaxes. I asked my friend and sound analyst Steve Rapetti to examine these recordings. Steve is a media specialist involved in audio and visual content. His analysis showed that one recording that appeared to be original was re-recorded, altered, and then sent out as a new event.

Steve sent me his report on February 3, 2012. In it he says:

> I believe the video attributed to Czechoslovakia that I did the analysis on was a fake derived from the original from Kiev. I picked the recording from Czech because I could hear the manipulation and decided to try and prove it (fake). Now that I've heard several more, I still sense a lot of copying and creative mischief, but at the heart of it all there is something real to worry about and it's hauntingly Biblical in nature.[16]

Steve's comments are referring to sections of the Book of Revelations that describe angels with blaring trumpets arriving to herald a time of great tribulation on Earth. This connection has concerned many people, especially those who have heard the intensity of the noise and felt the power of it vibrate through their bodies. With no discernible source, it does indeed feel apocalyptic.

As with The Hum, theories as to the source abound. In this case, in addition to Steve's evidence of hoaxing, no substantial research has been conducted. So far theories are:

1. Underground tunneling projects.
2. Vibrations in the Earth's atmosphere due to interactions with increased solar wind.
3. Pressure waves due to the outer and inner envelopes surrounding the solar system compressing as the entire solar system moves into the Galactic Alignment as suggested by some followers of the Maya writings.
4. H.A.A.R.P. technology.
5. Covert global efforts to ward off climate change.
6. Covert weather experiments.
7. The arrival of biblical prophecy. Matthew 24:34 describes angels arriving with the sound of trumpets during a time of great tribulation. The Book of Revelation speaks of the sounding of Seven Trumpets to herald seven apocalyptic events.
8. Sounds from within the Earth. In Steve Rapetti's words, "It (the sound) strongly suggests the possibility of ground induced resonance from the Earth's substrata rubbing together."[17] He cites theories worked on by Einstein related to continental drift. He also considers the extraction of oil and its replacement with salt water to prevent cavitation. Oil functions as a lubricant, facilitating the movement of tectonic plates. Theoretically, the removal of oil increases earthquake and volcanic activity and may also increases the resonant sound as rocks shift, perhaps causing the sounds described.

A firsthand account posted on Disclose.tv is provided by Duncan Taylor of an event that occurred in Scotland in 2012. UFO and strange sounds were seen and heard by police and residents of a town. The event was filmed by Duncan Taylor.

I was awoken by a loud noise at approximately 2:30 am yesterday. I went to the window to see if I could find out where the noise was coming from. It was so loud my windows were vibrating. I spotted a bright light in the sky moving about and pulsating, so I grabbed my camera and managed to get some footage.

Not sure if the light was making the sound, but I've heard of these strange noises from around the world on the Internet and I am shocked it has happened here. I thought they were fake. The noise was heard by my neighbors and local police have had dozens of calls from people who live in the area who heard the noise too, Most are elderly and a lot of them were terrified. Noise disappeared after about 10 minutes.[18]

Government agencies in East Malaysia have taken a strong interest in finding the source of the noise, perhaps because of the possible association with Earthquake activity. A report posted on the Asia One science and tech Website on January 23, 2012 states, "The Science, Technology and Innovation Ministry (in East Malaysia) want to collect audio recordings of the purported strange noises in the sky heard by residents of Kota Samarahan, Sarawak."[19] The report on the Website states that in a SinarHarian report, Deputy Minister Datuk Fadillah Yusuf said the ministry is collecting as much "evidence"[20] as possible on the bizarre happening for a report to be sent to the National Space Agency (Angkasa) for further investigation. The daily also quotes international reports, saying the strange noises heard globally could have originated from H.A.A.R.P. (the High Frequency Active Auroral Research Program), an ionospheric research program based in Gakona, Alaska, in the United States.

Booms Out of Nowhere

Our next odd sound event is affectionately called the Boom. It usually, although not always, arrives at night with enough force to rattle shelves, shake doors, and even crack window panes. The Boom has been heard only a few times and spanning decades, as in Warwick, Rhode Island, with occurrences in 1998 and 2012, or it can occur every night for a period of weeks as in the current episode in Indianapolis, Indiana. Occurrences have dramatically increased since 2007. In the United States, the Boom used to be considered an East Coast event. Now the Boom has been heard in Michigan, Wisconsin, Utah, Texas, Idaho, North Carolina, Louisiana, Ohio, Alabama, Florida, Minnesota, Pennsylvania, New York, and more. Internationally it has been reported in Canada, Tasmania, Swaziland, Australia, and Vietnam, among other places. (The most comprehensive list of reports can be read online at *mysterybooms.blogspot.com.*)

Most describe the Boom as sounding like an explosion. Additional descriptions include sounding like a semi-truck backfiring, a Mack truck hitting a bump, a sonic boom, thunder, or cannon balls. The Boom often occurs with flashes of light, some of which have been identified as possibly space junk hitting the atmosphere. A few accounts include orb or UFO activity. Often the event is heard and felt over very large areas.

Mysterious booms are not unique or new. An NBC News item that aired on September 16, 2011, stated that loud booms have occurred worldwide for a long time.[21] In the Ganges Delta and the Bay of Bengal, they are called Bansal guns; near Seneca Lake in upstate New York they are called Seneca Guns; in coastal areas of Belgium they are called mistpouffers or fog belches; and in Italy they are known as brotondi. The Harami people of Shikoku Japan call them yan. The popular term in the United States is *sky-quake.*

A host of plausible but usually incorrect explanations exist, as described in the September/October 2011 edition of *The Seismological Research Letters.* Seismologist David Hill, scientist emeritus at the U.S. Geological Survey office in Menlo Park, California, made the following suggestions as sources of the sound:[22]

- Rock bursts: sudden release of long-buried rock that result in small, near-surface earthquakes with perceptible jolts and sharp booming sounds.

- Giant waves: booming sounds are heard before tsunamis or extreme waves.

- Methane deposits: the disruption of offshore methane hydrate deposits can lead to explosive venting of high-pressure gas trapped deep within the Earth.

- Meteors: sonic booms can be heard from the shockwave of meteors entering the Earth's atmosphere. The sonic boom may take so much time reaching the Earth's surface from the upper atmosphere that visible signs of the meteor are no longer present.

- Booming sands: can be heard to distances of 6 miles and for as long as 15 minutes. They are attributed to large sand dunes in arid climates with steep faces pointing away from the wind and made of loosely packed, very smooth, almost spherical sand grains. They have been heard in Egypt by

     Bedouins where the sand booms correlated to seismometer activity and suggested small earthquakes.

- Military exercises.

- Quarry blasts.

- Seismic events.

The problem is that most reports of the Boom don't correspond to any of these activities. The few that can be explained through these mechanisms, however, get a lot of attention in the standard news media. MSNBC reports that

> sounds like booming cannons or falling stones accompanied small to moderate earthquakes in England from 1880 to 1916. In 1975, U.S. Geological Survey researchers managed to record both acoustic and seismic signals of an earthquake swarm in California, finding that three earthquakes with magnitudes ranging from 2.0 to 2.8 produced sounds that began within 0.02 seconds of the arrival of seismic waves at the scientists' station. Similar results were seen with quakes in the French Pyrenees in 2004.[23]

However, most reports of the Boom have no such correlation and can't be explained at all. Here are a few of the many Boom reports.

Warwick, Rhode Island

The Boom made local news reports in Warwick, Rhode Island, when it was heard at 11:20 p.m. on December 6, 2012. The Warwick Police Department received nearly 100 phone calls about the noise that was thought to be an explosion. Some residents said that it shook their homes.

Approximately an hour after the initial boom, residents heard a low droning sound variously described as a hum, a distress signal from a boat, and a tug boat. Reports of the Boom also came from witnesses on the other side of Narragansett Bay in Barrington, Rhode Island, who saw a flash of light at the same time that the noise was heard.

Police and fire Departments as well as the Coast Guard searched for the origins of the sounds. They ruled out missing aircraft from the T.F. Green Airport in Warwick and blown electricity transformers. After 50 minutes of trawling the waters of Narragansett Bay, the Coast Guard determined that no ocean vessels were in distress and stopped the search. The Coast Guard determined that the strange flashing light seen in Barrington was that of a lighthouse. The U.S. Geological Survey (USGS) Website did not indicate any seismic activity in New England at the time of the Boom, although there was a small earthquake reported in Maine the next morning. After extensive investigation, officials were not able to locate a source or find the cause.[24]

Clintonville, Wisconsin

In March 2012, residents of Clintonville reported a series of mysteries Booms that occurred for several nights. Residents said they were consistently awakened from sleep. Although the sound was loud and repetitive, officials could not pinpoint the source. The USGS recorded a 1.5 magnitude earthquake and said the noises were consistent with ground trembling. Many residents were unsatisfied with this result, because the seismic activity did not match the timing of when the sounds appeared and for the length that they lasted.

Indianapolis, Indiana

Several residents of Vanderburgh and Warrick Counties in Indiana reported hearing the Boom and feeling vibrations on the nights of January 7 and 8, 2013. Hundreds of people reported hearing several Booms each night, some so loud that houses were said to shake and windows rattle. Public safety agencies conducted an investigation and found no evidence leading to the source of the noises. Those who heard the loud Booms said the sounds came from the sky.

Here are research results:

‣ University of Southern Indiana professor of geology Paul Doss examined seismometer readings and found no disturbances.

‣ The State of Indiana and the Air Guard denied any military activity that would cause a sonic boom.

‣ A meteor was blamed; however Professor Jeff Braun refuted this idea due to lack of visible evidence. The repetition of the sound supports his conclusion.

‣ Tannerite, an exploding target used at outdoor gun ranges in the area, was ruled out as not having enough force.

Local authorities have still not found an explanation. Public speculation includes a blown power transformer, a meth lab explosion, a mine blast at a nearby coal mine, and a sonic boom from some sort of aircraft. No evidence supports any of these theories.[25]

North Carolina

Mysterious booming sounds are occasionally heard on the North Carolina coast, often powerful enough to rattle windows and doors. The latest events occurred in March and September 2011. They cannot be explained by thunderstorms or any man-made sources. Seismographs at the College of Charleston didn't pick up any earthquake activity, and the Charleston Air Force Base didn't report any military aircraft creating sonic booms. In addition, no commercial vessels responded to a U.S. Coast Guard message asking for reports of whether it had been felt offshore. Experts speculate that the Booms are caused by gases released from the sea floor or undersea landslides along the Continental Shelf, the echoed sound of distant thunder, or lightning-like electrical discharges.[26]

Texas (June 2010)

Known as the West Dallas Mystery Booms, West Dallas, Texas, residents regularly hear the Boom. The sound usually occurs late at night, although not always and rattles windows and wakes residents. Most people are unable to determine what direction the Boom comes from or what might cause it. People question: "What kind of power (are) we talking about that rattles windows for up to two miles in all directions... you think it sounds scary inside your house, step outside and listen."[27]

UFO Connection?

Occasionally, the Boom is heard at the same time that unusual lights are seen in the sky. Although it is impossible to say that the lights are in any way connected, two non-ordinary events occurring simultaneously are unlikely to be coincidental. People speculate that the Boom might be the sound of an UFO entering our atmosphere or our dimension, depending on one's perspective. Although there is no evidence of such an occurrence, it makes about as much sense as the scientific suggestions. A YouTube video claiming to have been filmed over Indianapolis just after midnight on January 7, 2013, records a strange sound that is clearly heard against background sirens as several strange lights move in and out of formation on the horizon. Just because we cannot prove these events are connected doesn't mean that they are not.[28]

Concluding Thoughts

Humans hear within a certain range of acoustic frequency. Innumerable activities create waves within this frequency range. Outside of this narrow band are uncountable additional actions creating waves that we might hear if our ears were designed to receive them and our brain to decode them. Perhaps some of these activities are changing and producing sounds within our range of hearing. Noises emitted by the Earth from the movement of tectonic plates with no oil to lubricate the motion fit into this category. Sounds of the solar wind traveling through the Earth's weakening magnetosphere also fit. Perhaps, too, how we receive sound waves—how our brain puts information together—is being altered. It is possible higher intelligence is manipulating the changing parameters to engage us in contact. There are far more possibilities to explore than have been looked at so far.

Few people truly think outside of convention and so assumptions create blindness to other possibilities. NASA engineer Pat Delgado was one who did think outside the box. Following an urge, he began to record radio waves emitted by trees and seemed to capture an unknown conversation. Crazy? Perhaps. But to find the answers to some mysteries, we just might have to get a little bit crazy. Until we can visualize and imagine, we cannot create.

My sense of the direction that we are heading, or have been steered into by another intelligence, is one where all existing boundaries are pushed outward. We are approaching a restart moment where even our five senses may be altered. Entertaining all possibilities is the only way to find answers. When we do, we will undoubtedly laugh at some of the directions we explored; yet without having explored them, we would not have found the path. Embracing possibilities is what is expected of us at this time.

Interaction with unknown intelligence may be inching us another step forward. Though we assume humans have great importance as the kingpin on this beautiful planet, all life is part of the growth underway. To feel secure on this new path we must develop a coherence of love and respect for each others' perspectives. This may not be easy; it is, however, imperative.

The underlying assumptions in all our beliefs are being re-examined. Nowhere is this more evident than in our engagement with death. One of the most difficult aspects of living is losing those we love. Harder than facing our own mortality is the aloneness we are left with when someone close passes. Inevitably we wonder what part of the person carries on afterward and whether it is possible to make contact. Throughout history there have been people who claim special powers that allow them access to the other side. The current shift of reality seems to be lifting the veil for us all. Results from life-after-death research supports our breakthrough and assistance is coming from an unlikely source: spirits of deceased scientists.

While the immediate reaction is to pull back in doubt, it's no longer unusual for people to talk about communication from those who have died. In some regards it is now almost an expectation. Sometimes people hear an actual voice or have a visitation in the form of a vision or dream. More commonly, people receive messages through synchronicity.

Synchronicity seems like coincidence, but as the word implies, there is significant meaning to the coming together of events. The meaning is usually personal and engages the peculiarities and personalities of those involved. For example, after her father's death, Synthia was sitting in her parked car talking to him in her head while she pondered a particular problem. Turning the ignition key, she was startled to hear the opening chords of a song by the Moody Blues, her father's favorite musical group. The lyrics spoke directly to the situation she was thinking about and the synchronicity felt like a communication. Oddly, many people describe synchronistic events with the Moody Blues. This is especially interesting to me because I met Mike Pinder, lead singer and song writer of the band. He shared some of the many unusual situations and synchronicities that inspired the group's music. From the Moody Blues band members to listeners, there are wheels within wheels that create a much bigger story.

Synchronicity for some people involves a symbol that represents a person they loved who has died. A friend of ours tells us that every time he feels deeply connected to his deceased father, he sees not one shooting star, but two—well beyond coincidence. The shooting stars might appear in the sky, in a picture, or in a completely unexpected place such as a commercial van driving past with shooting stars as the logo. Another friend says that a white feather often appears on her husband's favorite chair when she is feeling particularly down and alone. Many people find orbs, beams, and other light phenomena in pictures they take of significant events such as family gatherings.

Another type of interaction is electromagnetic in nature. This includes the inexplicable blinking of lights at significant moments or strange sounds left on an answering machine. My father-in-law died at Christmas in 2000. The family had brought a little Christmas tree to the hospital room along with a radio so he could listen to carols. The lights wouldn't turn on, so the tree was left standing off to the side on a table. At the moment of his death, the Christmas tree lights blinked on and off. Later, as we left the hospital, the radio my brother-in-law carried started to emit static although it wasn't turned on or plugged in.

None of the experiences people have offer proof of the afterlife or the ability to communicate with those who have died. Their significance is in our emotional response and how it changes us. Synchronicity is impactful in the bringing together of two different time lines: the one we are on and the one of the deceased. What is important in the exchange is the sincerity of our desire for contact. Heart-centered action is the attractive force that meshes the two realities.

New Thoughts on Death

The current thinking of many great scientists is that the universe is holographic in nature. Holograms are unique in the way that they record information. All parts of a hologram contain the information that makes the whole, but not in an expected manner. For example, DNA is the blueprint for the whole body and is stored in each cell, yet each cell only represents one aspect of the blueprint. In a hologram, each part is also the entirety. If you tear a holographic picture in half, you will not have two halves of the picture; you will have two smaller duplicate pictures. What will have changed is the picture's clarity. In each splitting, information is lost.

Supposing the universe is a hologram; all parts of it then contain the whole in ever-decreasing degrees of lucidity. Obviously what I am driving at is that, on some level, we have access to those parts that are hidden from view. What we have to do is decide what we include in our definition of the universe. Does the universe only contain what we call life, or does it also contain that which exists before birth and after death? Insights might come from those who have died and returned, something called a near-death experience (NDE).

People who have died and been resuscitated share many similar aspects in their experiences. These reports reveal a distinct continuation of consciousness. Some people, such as Dannion Brinkley, have died multiple times. He and Thomas Benedict Mellon were both dead for well more than an hour before spontaneously reviving. The simple fact of these events challenges religious and scientific beliefs about the afterlife.

Hoping for an NDE is no way to go forward in life-after-death research. We need to be able to reach and break through the veil of separation. If we imagine that the circle of existence is a holographic sphere, with one hemisphere called life and the other death, perhaps we can see both as parts of one whole. With this change in view, communicating with those on the other side of the sphere might seem more tenable and create context for the change. What we may be missing is belief that consciousness continues and that communication is possible.

Certainly many past scientists have believed in the possibility. Thomas Edison, inventor of the phonograph, movie camera, and electric light bulb, modified some of his inventions to create equipment capable of conversing with the other side. This became the foundation of a field of study currently called Instrumental Trans Communication (ITC). Oliver Lodge, inventor of the wireless telegraph, left behind a sealed envelope when he died that contained a mathematical code, which he promised to transmit from the other side. His work fueled experimentation in after-death communication. Professor Gerald Hawkins studied the Oliver Lodge story extensively and believed the code Lodge promised to transmit was coded in the diatomic ratios that appeared in some significant crop circles. Additionally, Guglielmo Marconi, the inventor who bought Oliver Lodge's patents, and scientist-inventor Nicola Tesla also created electronic equipment to engage those in the afterlife.

Life-after-death research has a tremendous pull on people for one very important reason: If our belief in death is replaced with an understanding of the continuation of consciousness, how might we live and behave differently? Many think that changing our relationship with death provides a uniquely powerful inspiration for the quality of living. Changing this one belief would change the world.

Instrumental Trans Communication (ITC) and Electronic Voice Phenomenon (EVP)

Instrumental Trans Communication (ITC) is the field of research that explores the ability of finely tuned instruments to interact and communicate with people who are dead. Electronic Voice Phenomena (EVP) is one area within the larger research of ITC that specializes in engaging and recording spirit voices on electronic media. Technically, EVP represents the origin of the research just as radio and telephone devices predated television and other forms of media that transmit images.[1]

ITC and EVP research hold two assumptions: first, that consciousness exists beyond death, and second, that consciousness can interact with electromagnetic waves. Obviously for ITC and EVP experiments to work, both hypotheses must be correct. Experiments focus on capturing voices on radios, telephones, answering devices, tape recorders, and other types of electronic communication devices as well as capturing the images of people who are dead on video cameras, televisions, and computer monitors.

In EVP, the concept is that unstructured white noise provides a medium that a spirit can manipulate into structured sound. Tape recorders with moving parts make noise that is picked up by the microphones. Sounds are already structured in the background interference due to the consistency of the rotation of the wheels, tape sprockets, and so on. This creates a matrix that the dead can use to create modulated sound that can be fashioned into words. Modern research uses more advanced technology, although this crude method still produces spontaneous recordings.

Recording spirit voices is not restricted to researchers. Many people report unusual voices showing up on their telephone answering machines without being activated by a phone call. Voices also present on tape recorders and cell phones even though there is no intention to connect with a spirit by the person who receives the message. Although the voice is usually somewhat mechanical and the recording full of static, occasionally the message is clear and the voice recognizable as someone the person knew. Every so often the disembodied voice sounds tortured, sad, or lonely, and seems as if it is a lost soul. Some of these "calls" are quite eerie.

Skeptics are quick to point out that the brain is always looking for patterns and will make them out of random events. They say the claims of EVP are no more than apophenia, the experience of seeing meaningful patterns or connections in random or meaningless data. I have heard many different EVP recordings in which I agree that apophenia is obviously happening. And I have heard recordings that were clear, concise, detailed, and informative—not imagined, made up, or frivolous. It's worth noting that the ability to find unseen patterns is also one of the attributes of savants who can perform unusual feats of mathematical calculation. Perhaps many communications whose patterns we simply do not pick up are present in the white noise around us.

In an interview with *The American Magazine* in 1920, Edison said, "I have been at work for some time building an apparatus to see if it is possible for personalities which have left this Earth to communicate with us."[2] Edison was also quoted in the same month and year by *Scientific American,* saying, "I have been thinking for some time of a machine or apparatus which could be operated by personalities which have passed on to another existence or sphere."[3]

Edison's interest in the paranormal was less inspired by an actual belief in life after death than the desire to use science in an arena populated by psychic, mediums, spiritualists, and outright charlatans. Though he made no claims that life exists after death, he did say, "I do claim that it is possible to construct an apparatus which will be so delicate that if there are personalities in another existence or sphere who wish to get in touch with us in this existence or sphere, the apparatus will at least give them a better opportunity to express themselves."[4] He went on to say that this would be better than the tilting tables and raps and Ouija boards and mediums and the other crude methods in use at that time.

Inventor and scientist Nicola Tesla was in fierce competition with Edison to be the first to produce a "spirit telephone." Unfortunately, they both died before producing a reliable device. The machine Edison was working on before his death was called the Ghost Box. His assistant, Dr. Miller Hutchinson, wrote in his diary, "Edison and I are convinced that in the fields of psychic research will yet be discovered facts that will prove of greater significance to the thinking of the human race than all the inventions we have ever made in the field of electricity."[5] After Edison died many looked for the device, but the Ghost Box was never discovered. Synthia's family lived next door to Edison's grandson, Ted Sloan, who told Synthia's mother that he didn't believe the device was ever made. However, in 1991, 70 years after his death, Edison's voice and image appeared on a computer in a Luxembourg ITC experiment with instructions for the present-day research.[6]

Here is quick recap of parts of the modern era of this research:[7]

▸ In 1956, medium Attila von Szalay and researcher Raymond Bayless unintentionally recorded a series of unexplained voices on magnetic tape, the medium of wireless recorders used in WWII and the basis of many recording devices. Bayless reported this in the *Journal of the American Society for Psychical Research*.

▸ In 1959, Swedish film producer Friedrich Juergenson discovered the recognizable voice of his mother in a recording he made of bird songs using a reel-to-reel tape recorder. He later wrote the first book on EVP: *Radio Contact with the Dead*. His book brought several new researchers into the fold and he is considered by most to be the "father of EVP."

▸ In 1967, Dr. Konstantin Raudive from Latvia read a German translation of Juergenson's book. Raudive, a skeptical psychologist, nonetheless conducted hundreds of experiments under laboratory conditions and published his first book, *The Inuudible Become Audible*, in 1968. One experiment was carried out in the recording studio of the Pye Recording Company at their Germany office in 1971. Recording engineers had ensured proper controls in a sound studio built to exclude all external radio and television signals. In 18 minutes they recorded more than 200 different voices. It appeared the spirit world was having a convention with the new technology! His book was re-published in English and renamed *Breakthrough:*

An Amazing Experiment in Electronic Communications with the Dead, coining the phrase Electronic Voice Phenomenon.

▶ In 1967, Edison's spirit allegedly spoke through a West German clairvoyant describing his lifetime efforts to develop equipment for recording voices from the beyond. Edison made suggestions as to how to modify TV sets and tune them to 740 megahertz to get paranormal effects.

▶ In the early 1970s, Raymond Cass from Hull England began EVP research resulting in more than 2,000 examples, establishing him as the pioneer of EVP research in the United Kingdom.

▶ In the 1970s, George Meek, a very successful industrial engineer, retired his job and opened a laboratory in Philadelphia to study energy healing, subtle energy, and EVP. He founded a non-profit research company called the Meta Science Foundation. In 1981, Meek created a device called the Spiricom, which succeeded in communicating with the dead. Conversations were lasting more than one hour in length.

▶ In 1981, electronics engineer Hans-Otto Koenig produced a device called the Generator that used ultrasound as the medium for contacting the spirit world.

▶ In 1986, Swiss electronics engineer Klaus Schreiber obtained pictures of the dead on television by means of an apparatus he called Vidicom. He made audio/video contact with his two deceased wives.

▶ In 1991, on a newly developed version of the Vidicom, Schreiber observed the image and voice of Thomas Edison.

▶ In 1991, Mark Macy began recording spirit faces on Polaroid camera film, which can be seen on his Website (*www.spiritfaces.com*).

▶ In 1999, Steve Cerilli determined that spirit entities can manipulate tube-based shortwave radios, providing a communication link with other planes of existence.

As mentioned at the beginning of this chapter, one of the most remarkable aspects of the ITC research is that it is helped along through information received from the other side. Scientists who are dead have returned to help with the development of the more successful instrumentation. For example, George Meek and his partner, electronic engineer and clairvoyant Bill O'Neil, made contact with a deceased doctor called Doc Nick. Doc Nick suggested that certain audio frequencies be used instead of the traditional white noise, stating that the frequency would "serve as an energy source against which the sounds produced by his vocal cords could be played."[8]

The team was joined by another spirit, Dr. George Jeffries Mueller, who provided specific, detailed, and checkable information. The two spirits helped design Meek's Spiricom, a device that allowed spiritual energy to be transformed into audible voices. Tapes of the Mueller conversations were released to the public, and some can be heard on YouTube (titled "Dialogue between William O'Neill and the Late Dr. George J. Mueller").

The ITC research stalled due to one important limitation: To work, devices needed to be operated by someone possessing psychic skills. Apparently the operators were as important as the device. This theme recurs in all high-strangeness events and may be explained in the Scole Experiment, another research project into life after death.

The Scole Experiment

The Scole Experiment is another example of those on the other side wanting contact with this side. Even more, they wanted scientific recognition as well. The experiment was named after the town of Scole in Norfolk, England, where the project began in 1993. It all started when a spirit message came to two mediums in a small, established, psychic circle led by Robin Foy, an experienced researcher. The message, purportedly from a discarnate spirit, said that "the conditions were right for an important and extended experimental project to occur."[9] The purpose of the experiment was to provide scientific and irrefutable proof of human survival after death.

Experiments consisted of psychic sessions or sittings whose purpose was to demonstrate the presence of discarnate spirits through communications, interactions, and manifestations. The first sittings took place in Norfolk, and then extended to additional controlled experimental sites in the Netherlands, Germany, Switzerland, Spain, and California. What made the sessions different from the average mediumistic séance was that respected scientists and intellectuals were invited as witnesses to validate the results. Two of my friends, Professor Archie Roy and Montague Keen from the British Society for Psychical Research (SPR), were among the invited witnesses.

Apparently, discarnate spirits had been working on the project from the other side for 50 years. These spirits of deceased scientists developed the experiments. At the start of the project, the successes were small but exciting; by the end, incredible feats of manifestation, or materialization, were occurring. Throughout the project the spirits set the agenda, determined the parameters, and established the outcomes for the experiments. The hundreds of meetings that took place were all recorded on audio-tape under Robin Foy's direction.

Two publications on the activities were produced. One, from the British SPR, was a scholarly and objective account of the 37 sittings they witnessed. The second was a book written by two journalists, titled *The Scole Experiment* (Judy Piatkus Publishing, Ltd., 1991), that focused on the story and people involved in the project, and the increasingly impressive paranormal events that occurred. Both publications are very informative in different ways.

The experiments were conducted in the dark with a set number of people present. The mediums conducting the sessions wore luminous bands so that witnesses could see where they were and what they were doing at all times. A table was placed in the middle of the room where the manifestations were focused. The rooms were checked beforehand and verified to have no equipment, hidden compartments, or other deception that might produce the results. During the 37 sittings that were witnessed by members of the SPR, the following extraordinary events occurred:[10]

- Communications and intricate interactions with numerous spirits:
  - Many of whom were deceased scientists.
  - With established personalities and highly distinctive characters, accents, and mannerisms.
  - With whom the dialogue was highly intelligent, witty, informed, and technically precise.
  - Who helped design the research, exercises, and a device to facilitate better results.

▸ In addition to speaking through psychics, voices were sometimes disembodied in specific locations in mid-air, and were captured on tape recorders that had no microphones and on TV sets without aerials. (In other words, no input could be received by ordinary means, only by imprinting the magnetic medium.)

▸ New packages of sealed 35mm Kodak film were left out on the table during proceedings. When the film package was opened and the film developed, pictures of people's faces, animals, and even a circuit showing a refinement in the devices being used were found.

▸ Spirit Lights:

  ◆ Moved around the room in response to investigators' requests.

  ◆ Looked like globes (orbs), pin-pricks, Catherine Wheels, and flashes of light of varying color.

  ◆ Were capable of penetration of solid objects and the observers' bodies.

▸ Items in the room levitated and in some cases disappeared.

▸ Materialization of moving and walking forms, and parts of the body; various objects, such as flowers and jewelry; and taps, raps, and sustained touches from materialized fingers and hands, full handshakes, light kisses, and the feeling of brushing against objects.

▸ Production of sounds such as trumpet sounds from an instrument that had had its mouthpiece removed and to which no group member could physically gain access, and the beating of drums that created a trance like resonance.

If the intent of the spirits was to impress those scientists who watched, they succeeded. British government scientist Piers Eggett attended many sessions and was thoroughly convinced of the honesty of the members and the extraordinary nature of the events.[11] So were my friends Professor Archie Roy and Montague Keen. If the spirits intended to gain widespread scientific investigation, they failed. Allowing scientists to watch proceedings is not the same as allowing scientists to create controlled protocols and procedures with measurable outcomes. In addition, the proofs seemed to be too extravagant, stretching the mind farther than possible. After five years, the experiment had reached the extent of its reach and ended.

The most fascinating aspect of the proceedings was the discussion on where and how the spirits obtained energy to interact with the physical world, enabling them to create audible voices, materialize images, and manifest objects. During a Scole session on December 13, 1993, the spirits were asked what the energy source was. Here is the reply:

> The energy of which we speak is a blend of 'creative energy' from three specific sources. The first we will call "spiritual energy", which we bring with us from our world. The second is human energy, which we take from your bodies during the experiments. And the third is Earth energy which is drawn from "columns" or "reservoirs". These energies were understood and used by the ancients, but this is now forgotten knowledge. We are trying to help humanity to remember.[12]

They described this creative energy as similar to an electromagnetic field. In several sessions, members were given instructions on how to create higher levels of energy needed for manifestations. Electric lighting was not to be used because the current disrupted the special energy being created. Members were advised to meditate before sessions and to maintain positive thoughts, because this increased the rate of vibration in a person's energy field.[13] The use of specific music was encouraged for the same reason. In addition, who was attending the sessions and where they sat mattered. Apparently, different combinations of people in specific alignment creates greater flows of energy. Many of the people present observed that their mental thoughts interacted with the spirits.[14]

As the sessions increased in ability to provide energy for manifestations, the spirits directed the creation of an energetic canopy over the group. This helped raise the energy to create a spiritual doorway. Once the doorway was established and the group energy contained under the canopy, the sophistication and duration of manifestations increased exponentially.[15]

One night, the spirits designed an experiment related to human energy. While a spirit light moved around the room, members were asked to form a circle with their chairs. They were told to sit and lean forward with hands on thighs, pushing against their leg as they did. They were told this created potential energy that the spirit light could use to fuel its luminosity. When the members as a group leaned forward and pressed, the orb was seen to brighten considerably.[16]

Like the ITC recordings, the Scole Experiment does not prove the existence of life after death. It doesn't even provide enough information to slide past the defenses of most people's rational mind. However, if taken at face value, it provides some significant advances into all types of high-strangeness.

Concluding Thoughts

One of the highlights of this information for me is the demonstration of the power of the triangulation among spiritual energy, human energy, and Earth energy. This opens a discussion on the religious significance of the trinity and, for me, brings a new layer of information about the importance of triangles and energy in the strange event that Synthia and I experienced in 1992. I must admit that it had not occurred to either of us that the combination of human, Earth, and spirit generated an entirely new creative energy.

The arena of energy falls more into Synthia's specialized area of work. Subtle energy is the vital life force that flows through all things and creates the template for matter. Many think subtle energy is the substance of the quantum holographic matrix of reality; quite a large concept! The spirits talking through the Scole Experiment seem to indicate that new frequencies are available when the combination of human, Earth, and spirit energies are brought together.

The concentration of Earth energy in certain areas may explain why high-strangeness phenomena tend to focus in specific locations. It is commonly believed that some areas of the planet focus life energy in higher concentrations than in others. Ancient civilizations used this awareness to create megalithic sites such as the pyramids in Egypt and the Yucatan, and the sacred stone circles of North American tribes and European Druids. Harnessing and amplifying this concentration increases the vitality of the planet, nature, and humans—all part of an interconnected whole.

I was stimulated by the idea that a combination of people in specific alignment with each other increases the coherence of energy. We all know the feeling of needing to sit in a certain place at a business meeting or dinner party. One position feels more comfortable than another, thus generating a sense of flow and ease. In the Scole Experiment, the alignment of members allowed an increase in creative energy, which brought ease in manifestation. Synthia agrees that in her work, alignment and coherence among herself, her client, and a higher energy produces a flow that supports the person's healing process.

Combinations of people may also be the attractive force for other high-strangeness events such UFO and orbs. Certain individuals seem sought out as key players, perhaps because they carry more vital force and are in some type of alignment with the intent of the higher intelligence/spirit/ET/ghost. These people may not even realize that they fulfill this role, yet provide the link that can be used for a manifestation. Could the combination of people and their alignment with each other be involved in differences in perception of high-strangeness events, such as happened with Dr. Steven Greer's sky watch at Woodborough Hill?

Of course I immediately think of the crop circles. There may be more reasons than we presently realize for the crop formations to be placed in precise positions with specific alignments and for crop artists to feel compelled to put them in particular fields. I suspect the ability of the mind to interact with phenomena is increased with the triangulation of human, Earth, and spirit energy, providing the flow that allows a person making a crop circle to connect with a person wanting a crop circle and then to produce that wished-for design in a particular field. I am reminded of the importance crop circle researchers and artists place on following their feelings and of being compelled to create. In Chapter 6, I remarked that the answers and growth in relation to crop circles would be found in the interactions between researchers and crop artists. It is a conclusion circle-maker Julian Richardson had come to as well. Now is the time for us to deepen this understanding.

I am left with many questions related to crop circles. It seems many of the mysterious happenings might be created through the combination of spiritual, human, and Earth energy aligned together. Could this explain Peter Sorensen's bent beams of light in Chapter 10? Could they have been a manifestation derived from this combination? The spirits said that electric current disrupts creative energy. Could high concentrations of creative energy disrupt electrical instruments, as described in Chapter 5? Might the degree of interference of the equipment relate to the amount of creative energy generated? Do researchers and enthusiasts visiting the circles have as much generative capacity as the circle-makers? Is it the generation of creative energy that causes spontaneous healing? I think of the energy canopy over the Scole members and wonder if an energy canopy protected Matthew Williams and the team of circle-makers from the rain in Chapter 6. What a colossal experiment indeed!

The point of this chapter is really to ask whether consciousness survives death and whether we have the ability to connect with the deceased. I believe the answer to both is yes. Happily, these experiments give us an easy tool for experimentation. Consider a person with whom you connect who has passed, include people to assist you, use a tape recorder, and go to a place in nature where the energy feels strong to you. Arrange yourself and the others until you feel comfortable with the placement of each person. Turn on the tape machine. Connect with each other, connect with the Earth, and connect with your deceased loved one. Ask questions out loud, waiting in between until it feels right to ask another. When you are done, go home and play back the tape. Play it at faster and slower speeds. You may be surprised by what you hear, although you may not be successful immediately. You may need to find ways to elevate the energy of the group or make better connection with the deceased. The key is to not give up. The research reveals that both sides require practice!

PART IV

Hidden Technology

Cocooned in Hidden Technology *by Wayne Mason.*

Paradigm shifts occur amid chaos and confusion; the old breaks down as the new emerges. The pandemonium of our times informs us that we are right on target for change. Pressure mounts in our personal lives and we see its reflection in social, economic, environmental, and global tension.

The leaders of the current era naturally resist the shift underway. They fear losing control and advantage, and are driven to preserve what is crumbling. Out of this mindset arise technology, practices, and legislation that, although hidden from public view, monumentally impact our lives. If we wonder whether change is truly here, we can confirm it by how aggressively it is opposed.

Hidden technology is moving forward with disregard for the public's right to be an informed part of the decision-making. We have a choice as to how we respond. We can grumble and moan, or we can step up and meet the challenge. Clues as to how might come from non-ordinary reality.

A few years back colleagues started sending me information on a new phenomenon called chemtrails, vapor trails in the sky formed from the emissions of jet engines. I wasn't sure why people were so concerned, as all aircraft leave trails in the sky; they are called contrails, meaning trails made from condensation. According to the Aviation Explorer Website, contrails are "aviation smog" made up of ice, CO_2, soot particles, aerosols and chemical substances.[1] Essentially, the exhausts of aircraft engines or wingtip vortices make artificial cirrus clouds. Because contrails are a naturel result of air flight, I really couldn't see what the fuss was all about. The e-mails kept coming, however, and people kept insisting that the emissions called chemtrails were different.

For one thing, chemtrails don't look like regular contrails. They are thick and tube-shaped. In addition, they do not disperse quickly, as do ordinary contrails, but maintain a presence in the sky for much longer periods of time. Whereas contrails disperse and disappear, chemtrails spread outward, but do not disappear. The oddest thing about them, however, is the patterns they make. The planes leaving these mystery trails don't simply fly from point A to B, leaving a trail behind them; they crisscross back and forth over areas of the sky, leaving grid-like patterns that remain for hours. When the patterns are first laid down, they look like a netting of vapor. Within a few hours, although the crisscrossing can still be seen, each line spreads out until the edges seem to meet, forming a sheet. The effect dims the brightness of the sky. These sightings began sometime in the 1990s and were brought to worldwide attention in 1997 through an article by journalist William Thomas in a winter edition for the *Environmental News Service,* an excellent online journal for global environmental news.[2]

I heard what people were saying, but it wasn't until 2007 that I saw an event that convinced me my friends and colleagues are right:

Something odd is going on. Synthia and I live on a small farm in Connecticut located on a flight path for aircraft into and out of the busy New York airports. As a result of all the e-mails, I began to pay more attention to the regular flights. Sitting outside the barn and watching the sky, I realized how seldom people today actually look into the sky. What used to be the most natural thing in the world is now a rarity. On most days, what I saw being emitted from the craft overhead were normal contrails. Then, on January 23, 2007, at around 5 p.m., I got an excited call from a friend suggesting I go out and look into the sky.

In fact, I had already seen what my friend was alerting me to and had run inside to get my camera when his call came. In the sky were four aircraft flying at different altitudes, two traveling south–north and two traveling west–east. As they moved, the south–north crossed the line of the west–east vapor trails, although still at different altitudes. They created what looked like a net overhead. Of course, I had been told that this was what happened, but frankly I didn't understand how odd it really was or how planned and precisely executed it appeared. At first I wondered if this was some type of military exercise and if the trails were simply a marking device to measure precision. However, that didn't explain why they were reported as occurring across the planet in nearly every country. Once produced, the trails spread out exceptionally quickly, although the vapor still remains quite thick. It creates a covering across the sky and diminishes sunlight. I was intrigued and began to look into this subject in earnest.

What I found was a lot of denial on the part of the government and military on one side, and a lot of theories with very little evidence on the other. The distrust and lack of concrete evidence is a common occurrence when the agencies involved refuse to acknowledge that a phenomenon exists or provide any information about it. Meanwhile, skeptics have a great time debunking everything.

I am certain that a phenomenon does exist; however, I find the answers provided by both skeptics and theorists to be insufficient. What is needed is a focused investigation enlisting scientists, engineers, and government representatives. Some will say this has already been done and point to the interesting array of qualified speakers at well-known chemtrail conventions. What is often presented are many credible and possible theories, but still with little concrete evidence beyond deduction.

There are excellent Websites that track information and need our support. One of the most important is the Chemtrail Tracking USA message board, which keeps real-time information on chemtrail sightings with concurrent radar and aircraft activity. You can log on at *groups.yahoo.com/group/chemtrailtrackingusa.* The more information we amass, the better able we will be to see the big picture.

Differences Between Contrails and Chemtrails

The first argument put forward by skeptics is that contrails can and do share some of the characteristics of chemtrails under certain conditions. For example, one of the characteristics of a chemtrail is that it lasts for several hours, and contrails can also last for several hours if the atmospheric temperature and humidity are conducive. Low temperatures with high humidity and stable temperature stratification will keep the vapors from mixing with ambient air, allowing contrails to hang in the sky for several hours. However, chemtrails appear under unstable atmospheric conditions at higher temperatures and lower humidity; in other words, long-lasting chemtrails occur in conditions unsupportive of long-lasting contrails.

It doesn't take looking at too many chemtrails or even pictures of them to see that there is a different quality to the vapor emitted compared to regular engine exhaust. Whereas the latter is generally white or possibly gray, chemtrails are highly reflective and often appear with a red or pinkish tint. Colors in vapor indicate chemicals and clearly there is a different composition between the contrail emissions and those we are calling chemtrails.

However, the greatest evidence that chemtrails are not contrails is that many planes have been witnessed and photographed dispersing substances at high altitudes through a multiple array of nozzles attached to the wing assembly of the craft. It is very similar to the traditional forms of crop dusting. Aircraft leave contrails behind engines, not through a series of nozzles on the wings. Some pictures reveal eight trails coming from one wing, as can be seen on the excellent website of the Carnicom Institute, a research organization for the betterment of humanity.[3] These trails are clearly not engine exhaust.

The biggest difference between the trails I witnessed in 2007 and aircraft exhaust was the behavior of the planes. Aircraft fly from one destination to another, presumably carrying passengers or cargo. Yet the planes I saw over the farm in 2007 flew in formation, crisscrossing the sky to create a grid. Others observe circular flight paths or zig-zag patterns. The patterned trails they leave cannot be passed off as a convergence of airline contrails; something much more organized and precise is underway.

Simple observation quickly discerns the difference between chem-trails and contrails, yet governments are fast to deny. They are also emphatic that this is a myth, nothing more than conspiracy theories. Interestingly, the FAA has been known to deny aircraft are in an area even as observers are watching them fly overhead.

I had a similar experience on Thursday, January 10, 2013, between 2:10 and 2:20 p.m. I observed three planes flying in parallel formation, leaving thick, dense, white trails that I considered to be chemtrails spreading behind them. The aircraft were traveling approximately west to east. Within the spreading trail I could see numerous veins or root-like tentacles dispersing outward from the core of the trails. As I was observing and photographing, two commercial aircraft approached diagonally from approximately north to south and crossed through the chemtrails at almost right angles. Prior to crossing the chemtrails, the two aircraft were producing normal vapor trails that were dissipating a short distance behind them at a rate consistent with the forward motion of the craft. Then something interesting happened: The moment these aircraft passed through the mysterious trails, their own trails changed, remaining suspended in the air like those they passed through. It was clear they had dragged the materials of the chemtrail along with them as they passed through.

After capturing this on camera, I went indoors to see if I could trace the aircraft on radar tracker software available on the Internet (at: *www.flightradar24.com/*). I was looking for five aircraft, but oddly only the two southbound commercial airliners were shown on radar. As I surmised, they were headed toward the New York airports from Europe. However, the three other craft, which had produced the mysterious trails, were not shown. This was very interesting, because the FAA has the option to use a five-minute delay on live radar. Apparently, they decided to remove these three crafts within that five-minute window.

The list of reasons why chemtrails are not contrails goes on. For example, contrails cannot be turned on and off at will, yet many wit-nesses report that occurring. One article on the Website World Affairs

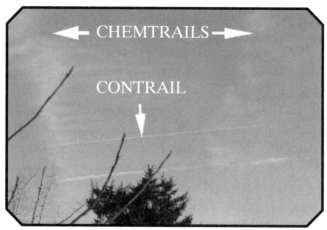

*Figure 13.1: Commercial airlines dragging chemtrail materials
after crossing their trails.*

Brief states that numerous witnesses claim to have seen aircraft abruptly turning its exhaust off and then back on. When one such incident was reported through a local TV station, the response was that these were government Lear jets conducting experiments into the formation of ice crystals. The only problem was that the aircraft were not small jets but large military craft.[4] What is important about this exchange is that the government did not deny that this was something different than ordinary craft and ordinary vapors.

Finally, contrails do not show up on radar, and chemtrails do. Ingredients in the spray seem to interfere with weather radar, and weathermen were put on the spot to explain it. In a broadcast in 2010 on News Channel 10 (Key West, Florida), areas of radar interference over the area were shown. The weatherman explained that it was part of a military exercise: Military airplanes were dropping aluminum-coated strips called chaff as part of anti-radar or radar scrambling drills. One weatherman explained that these strips could take a day to drop out of the sky, adding, "When you see a pattern like this [he then showed several pictures of typical chemtrails], you can rest assured that something is going on."

How refreshing to have a little bit of truth! The chemtrails were not contrails after all, but military anti-radar exercises. Although this didn't explain why it was necessary to perform these exercises again and again all across the globe, it was nice to know that we could rest assured that something was going on!

Chemtrail Analysis

If we accept, as I do, that there is something to the chemtrails, then what is being sprayed and why? Those who are doing the spraying know the answer and, as with most such phenomena, it is the secrecy that spawns suspicion and thoughts of harmful conspiracy.

Several types of analysis have been conducted on the fallout from these trails. Ideally, what we need is real-time analysis of the chemtrail in the air. This has yet to be accomplished for the obvious logistical and financial obstacles, but it is the smoking gun that is needed. Other analysis falls short of the mark. Here are a few of the main ones:

▸ After chemtrail activity, people often see fibers that look like cobwebs across the landscape. One such event occurred in eastern Oregon on November 2 and November 4, 1999. Some of the white cobwebs were collected by Q-tip and placed in plastic bags. Analysis of filaments extracted from a sample indicates some type of a polymer that is both extremely elastic as well as adhesive.[5] Ill health effects have been reported in association with the fibers, making one think of Morgellons disease (discussed in Chapter 2).

▸ In an article written by William Thomas and Erminia Cassani, two samples of a brown, gelatinous goo collected in 1998 and suspected to be residue from chemtrails were analyzed in EPA-approved labs. Although there were variations to the composition, lab results found protozoans that are temperature resistant, bacteria Pseudomonas flourescens (a TNT and fuel-eating bacteria patented by the Pentagon for bioremediation), infectious Streptomyces, and a fluorescent bacteria often used as a biomarker in lab tests. Also present was a restriction enzyme used for gene splicing. Pseudomonas fluorescens is well known for causing upper respiratory infections, and many of those who handled the substance became ill. The overwhelming picture was of germ warfare. The labs involved have stopped answering inquires and skeptics are highly critical of the findings.[6]

▸ 2001 rainfall samples collected in Santa Fe, New Mexico, revealed higher than normal levels of elemental magnesium, barium, aluminum, and strontium. Samples were taken directly after aerosol spraying (chemtrails).[7]

▸ Photographs taken by pilots of chemtrails reveal that they are ejecting particulate matter in the air that scatters light. In view of the increase in asthma and upper respiratory conditions in children today, the Carnicom Institute is calling for air quality control organizations to study this subject further.[8] According to government insiders, the EPA was told to stand down on the issue.[9]

▶ As stated earlier, the biggest problem with the analysis is that actual samples of chemtrails have not been obtained in the air. All other samples are indicative, but not conclusive. The Attorney General's Office (AGO) in New Mexico sent pictures and analysis presented from the public to a physicist at an organization called New Mexicans for Science and Reason (NMSR). The NMSR Website published a report with their conclusions. The AGO reviewed letters sent to their office expressing concerns that certain aircraft were spraying biological or chemical materials into the atmosphere for unspecified purposes. They published a report concluding that there was no evidence that the vapor trails were anything other than normal contrails discharged from jet aircraft. Then the report took an odd turn by stating, "That is not to say that there could not be an occasional, purposeful experimental release."[10]

Suspicions: Theories to Conspiracies

If we accept that there is something to the chemtrail controversy, even if we can't say what it is all about, the next natural question is why. What is the purpose of the aerosol spraying? There are many theories from creating an environment conducive to alien inhabitants to biological warfare to saving the planet from global warming. None of the theories have reliable evidence. I know different people will argue with both sides of this statement, yet for me, this is truly an observable and mysterious phenomenon with no provable answer.

Weather modification is probably the number-one theory of the purpose of chemtrails. The 2005 Weather Modification Research and Technology Act enacted in the first sitting of the 109th congress, act S 517, fueled speculation that weather modification was at the root of the chemtrails. Changing the chemical composition of the atmosphere might allow the alleviation of drought, lessen the intensity of superstorms, and reverse global warming. A 2008 article in Chemical and Engineering News revealed that Nobel Prize winner in Chemistry Paul Crutzen along with many other scientists is speculating on the possible injection of sulfur into the atmosphere.[11] It's worth noting that the Earth's natural cooling ability includes volcanic eruptions that disperse sulfur and particulate matter into the atmosphere that reflect sunlight.

Biological warfare is a worry for many based on the analysis of the brown goo reported on by William Thomas and the reports of illness and/or mental confusion following exposure to chemtrails. Thomas's report of a combination of Pseudomonas flourescens, whose patent is owned by the Pentagon, along with infectious agents and gene-splicing enzymes, was a powerful indicator in this direction. Add that a similar combination is part of the constituents in a Maryland company said to supply agents of germ warfare, and full grown paranoia sets in.[12] However, there is not sufficient evidence that these biological agents truly are present. The labs involved backtracked on statements, fueling speculation that they were leaned on or found the alternative news attention too intense. More samples, more labs, and more research must be done before any definitive answer can come from this arena.

Another theory relates to military use. According to the Rense.com there are several military projects using aerosol spraying as part of communication enhancement. In one such project, the barium salts in the aerosol spray set up an electrical and chemical environment that supports radio frequency ducting for a specific warfare system called the Variable Terrain Radio Parabolic Equation (VTRPE). Ducting refers to the salts forming a path from one point to another that can conduct radio frequency over the horizon. This is part of a Radio Frequency Mission Planner system that produces 3-D terrain on a television-type screen, used especially in Afghanistan and Iraq.[13] The best evidence for this information comes from the government insider who is called AC Griffith. His story follows.

Answers From the Inside

Two government insiders broke ranks and talked publicly about chemtrails as a government project called Clover Leaf. Ted Gunderson is a former FBI Agent, once head of the Los Angeles Division. He claims the chemtrails are part of a government program under the auspices of the United Nations and is of top-secret importance. He names bases where unmarked military planes fly from and emphases that commercial airplanes have been outfitted with nozzles for the aerosol spraying program. He links the ingredients being sprayed from the planes to the massive fish and bird deaths occurring around the globe and clearly feels great concern for human health.[14]

Many people have difficulty with his testimony because in some of his disclosures he links the CIA with Satanic cults. If we take belief in Satan away from the proceedings and consider the cult a front for a CIA operation, it becomes more believable. Mr. Gunderson's testimony ranges over many past conspiracies, such as the shootings of JFK and Bobby Kennedy, Ruby Ridge, 9/11, and more. It is easy to consider him a conspiracy theorist and dismiss him, yet at one time he held enormous responsibility for the well-being of this country. I can understand that this might cause great confusion, but it doesn't take much listening to realize that, though the topics Mr. Gunderson covers feel crazy, he is not. He is clear, concise, cognizant, and informed. He is also emotional, so that it would be easy to dismiss him yet I fear that would be a mistake.

The next government insider to come forward is a man called A.C. Griffith. His testimony can be heard on a YouTube video titled "Ex-Government Employee Talks About CHEMTRAILS on The PowerHour Program." Griffith, now deceased, was formerly with the National Security Agency (NSA) with top-secret cryptographic clearance. More recently he worked in affiliation with the CIA. He claimed to be one of the few who personally got inside the aerosol spraying program at Wright-Patterson Air Force Base, where the program is being administered.

Griffith confirms that commercial airlines have been outfitted with aerosol nozzles on the wings and confirms earlier speculation that this is part of VTRPE. He says the people involved in setting up different parts never see the entire picture and do not know what the end game is. He claims that people who learn too much and confront the project are killed. The picture he portrays is alarming.[15]

For me, the most moving insider story comes from an airplane mechanic who accidentally stumbled on the project. His statement can be seen on YouTube (labeled "Chemtrail Aircraft Mechanic Speaks"). It can also be found at the Carnicom Institute Website. Remaining anonymous, he describes being asked to work on an aircraft, and finding a system of piping and valves that had no relation to the waste disposal system where they were installed. His curiosity was rewarded by immediate suspension. When he began to research Internet sites, he received an anonymous communication stating that "Curiosity killed the Cat." Hoax? Read for yourself and decide. For me it had the chilling voice of authenticity, most notable in the knowledgeable detail of the job of being an airplane mechanic.[16]

The American Association for the Advancement of Science Symposium

Policymakers, scientists, engineers, and journalists gathered at a meeting of the American Association for the Advancement of Science (AAAS) in San Diego, California, from February 18 to 22, 2010. The meeting was focused on the plausibility of a worldwide geo-engineering campaign to artificially engineer the Earth's climate and combat global warming. The ideas presented included spraying aerosol aluminum and other particles into the sky to block the sun.[17] While protestors gathered outside the building demanding answers to chemtrails, these scientists insisted that no such aerosol spraying program was underway.

However, the program they are proposing seeks to spray an aluminum compound that has four times the reflective surface of other contenders like sulfur. The idea is to dump 10 to 20 mega-tons of this substance per year into the stratosphere to reflect sunlight back into space. David Keith, a leading scientist and expert in the field of geo-engineering, discussed potential future risks as well as benefits. Benefits included a cooler atmosphere and less melting of ice caps, and therefore one would assume fewer of the superstorms associated with climate change. Apparently there are no real risks to an action of this nature or none that have been studied.[18]

When audience member Dane Wigington, a solar expert, asked about the toxic effect of highly reactive materials like small particles of aluminum on soil, water, and human health, Keith replied, "Our collaborators working on the aerosol scheme have investigated this. It was one of the first things we looked at and the effects don't even come anywhere near being a health hazard. We have not published results; however, it was one of the first things we looked into. If you are looking at the sheer number of particles released, it's not even close to becoming an issue."

Wigington fired back: "So let me clarify: ten megatons of aluminum dumped into the atmosphere would have no human health impacts?"

Keith took a deep breath and replied: "So, so, let me be more careful here. Let us separate out the toxicological question. We have only just begun to research the aluminum and have published nothing."

The possible diminishment of the ozone layer or damage to the ionosphere had not been addressed. Oddly, Keith concluded by saying, "We haven't done anything serious on aluminum and there could be something terrible that we find tomorrow that we haven't looked at." Meanwhile soil samples from all over the world are reportedly showing increasing amounts of aluminum, barium, and other materials. You can see reports on this conference on YouTube (entitled "What in the World Are They Spraying? (Chemtrails)").[19]

The AAAS may not have conducted full research on the harmful health effects of spraying aluminum in the atmosphere, but there are several areas we suggest they investigate. Current general cancer risk statistics are staggering. Now, the risk of getting cancer in the United States is one of every three women and one of every two men. The risk of dying from cancer is one of every five women and one in every four men.[20] You can increase your risk of getting cancer by making poor lifestyle choices such as smoking and drinking; you cannot guarantee that you won't get cancer by living clean. That is because the major cause of cancer is genetic mutation caused by an oncogene, or cancer-producing substances, from environmental pollution, including heavy metals, pesticides, and solvents. Aluminum is the most abundant metal to be found in the Earth's crust (8 percent), but is not found free in nature. Though it is not considered highly toxic in small doses, it is implicated as a factor in breast cancer and Alzheimer's disease. Another risk to investigate is the growing problem with Vitamin D deficiency. Vitamin D is produced in the body in response to the sun; spraying reflective material into the atmosphere can only worsen Vitamin D deficiency, further impacting cancer rates, autoimmune disorders, and bone disorders.

Before experiments reach the stage of funding this one reported at the San Diego conference has, it should certainly have conducted the necessary health studies. Interestingly, Monsanto, the producer of genetically modified food, has taken out a new patent titled "Stress tolerant plants and methods thereof." It addresses all forms of abiotic stress including cold, drought, flood, heat, UV stress, ozone increases, acid rain, pollution, salt stress, heavy metals, mineralized soils, and other stressors. Under heavy metals is the intent to increase aluminum resistance of the plants. Coincidence? Maybe—or maybe not.

Michael J. Murphy is a journalist and political activist from the Los Angeles area. He was at the conference and made the previous material available to the public. From his remarks in an article posted on *countercurrents.org*, David Keith doesn't seem to be a bad guy; he did go outside the symposium to talk with protesters about chemtrails and address their concerns. He didn't seem to realize, however, that a program was already underway, probably not for the reasons of global warming but for military purposes.

Concluding Thoughts

The popular Website of the Carnicom Institute keeps a visitors record for the chemtrail part of the site. The record shows that weather modification companies and government agencies are the primary repeat visitors to this site.[21] Project Censored publishes an annual collection of the top 25 censored news stories and has done so for 35 years. In the 2012 September release, Rady Ananda's article, "Atmospheric Geoengineering: Weather Manipulation, Contrails and Chemtrails," ranked as the ninth-most-censored story in the United States.[22] If there are no chemtrails, why on Earth can't we discuss it?

This subject of chemtrails takes so many twists and turns it's like a rollercoaster ride. The best I can say is my money is with a combined military project and global warming reversal project piggybacked on each other—one the public will accept, the other hidden within it. When all is said and done, global warming is a national security issue for all countries and a moral issue related to our grandchildren and the Earth. We do have to address the many ways we wage war with the planet and challenge its ability to support us. However, before we jump on board a high-sci project with the ability to damage the planet even further, we must look at all the ramifications, and, like Native people, think of the consequences seven generations into the future.

I believe as we continue to flirt with technology that has the ability to destroy the planet, we can anticipate a multitude of new phenomena. If we are correct that other dimensions, off-planet intelligence, or even the dead are impacted by what we do here and now, some of the phenomena we have been discussing throughout this book may be aimed at providing tools we need in order to address these concerns.

205

Chapter 14: The
Ionosphere: The
New Frontier
of Hidden
Technology

The ionosphere is a layer of the Earth's upper atmosphere located about 60–90 kilometers (37.3–55.9 miles) above the Earth's surface. The structure and nature of the ionosphere produces natural phenomena such as lightning and the aurora borealis. As the name suggests, the ionosphere is comprised of ions (charged particles) along with highly charged electrons. The ions and charged electrons are formed when molecules and atoms are ruptured by the sun's rays and broken into unstable elements. By this action the ionosphere protects the Earth from the harmful effects of solar radiation with help from the ozone layer and magnetosphere.

The extreme importance of the ionosphere in protecting life should make experimenting with it sacrosanct. Unfortunately, that is not the case. Some of the most far-reaching covert projects to emerge over the last 40 years involve pulsed electromagnetic waves in ionospheric heating technology. The scientific projects have been cloaked in secrecy, intrigue, and suspicion, causing grave misgivings by scientists and public alike.

The ionosphere is central to all of our telecommunication systems. It reflects short-wave (high-frequency [HF]) radio waves, making it possible to transmit an HF signal from one area to a receiver beyond the curve of the Earth. The HF transmission hits the higher layer of the ionosphere, which reflects the signal back to Earth at a point far from where it left. This allows the transmission of a signal to travel beyond the curvature of the Earth, something Ultra High Frequency (UHF) radio transmissions cannot do.

Cell phones and other wireless devices use UHF in surface, or ground, transmissions, which are limited to relatively short distances, because electromagnetic waves are unable to bend. They must be beamed through towers or satellites to achieve distances greater than the horizon. It is the reflective properties of the ionosphere that make it the new frontier of hidden technology.

Using the ionosphere presents unique challenges. It is an interactive system that absorbs and transmits solar radiation, so its ability to reflect HF radio waves is changeable. It is impacted by increases in solar activity such as solar flares and sun spots. In addition, the ionosphere has daily variances as ions and highly charged electrons that are formed during the day under the influence of the sun recombine at night. It also has seasonal and geographical variations most notable in the higher layers of the atmosphere. Any technology that relies on the ionosphere must take these deviations into account, one of the reasons research into this layer is drawing such attention.[1]

Ionospheric covert programs have been represented to the public as over-the-horizon radar. The first such project started in the 1970s with a disruption called the Woodpecker.

The Russian Woodpecker

When I worked for regional government in Great Britain, I was a communications officer, overseeing the communication aspects of major civil emergency planning and preparedness. I was involved in creating and maintaining systems to provide undisturbed government communications during extreme events such as nuclear war. When I took my post in the 1970s, preparations to counter a nuclear confrontation with Russia was top priority.

My job was to ensure functional communication in underground control facilities where military, police, and government leaders would establish command during an attack. In such an event, radio transmissions in the frequency bands established for Citizen Bands, Amateur Radio (HAM) networks, as well as frequencies permanently allocated for government and military use would be commandeered. I regularly visited three underground control facilities for systems maintenance.

You can imagine my concern when one day in the mid-1970s I turned on a HAM radio receiver in one of the facilities and heard something unfamiliar and disturbing: loud, rapid bursts of a popping noise that sounded like a submachine gun was being pulsed in streams that stopped for short periods, then returned. The sound was disrupting frequency bands allocated by international agreements for government and commercial use, and the interference was so strong that speakers sounded as though they were about to dismantle.

The sound created continual interference that moved across different shortwave radio bands and was reported worldwide. It wasn't long before the public began to lodge complaints to the highest levels of international government. Due to its cadence, the sound was called the Woodpecker. Attempts to locate the source eventually resulted in triangulating the signal to a location in the Soviet Union. The power was estimated to be around 10 megawatts, in those days one of the largest radio transmissions on Earth.

The interference was disabling parts of the communications system established for emergency operations and commercial air travel. This was a serious breach in national security and public safety, and nobody knew what to do about it. The mysterious signal was unacknowledged by the Soviets, who were the source. Without admitting culpability, they eventually shifted the frequencies being transmitted, largely due to the interference they were causing long-range air-to-ground communications used by commercial airliners. Some believed Woodpecker was a Soviet mind-control or weather-control experiment. These were not idle speculations.

Investigation eventually revealed that the signal was coming from an arrangement of Tesla-type transmitters traced to an installation in the cities of Riga and Gomel, near Chernobyl. UK experts concluded that the Woodpecker was an over-the-horizon radar (OTH) system, publicly confirmed after the fall of the Soviet Union when the Soviets acknowledged that the Woodpecker was the Duga-3, an early-warning radar system. The device was aimed northward and covered the continental United States. The sound began in July 1976, became less frequent in the late1980s, and disappeared altogether in December 1989 with the dissolution of the Soviet Union.[2]

Over-the-horizon radar bounces signals off the ionosphere to travel beyond the curvature of the Earth. Interestingly, it was reported that in 1977 the U.S. government sold the Soviets a supermagnet that was used in the Woodpecker device. According to an article in *Paranoia Magazine* in 2008, the magnet weighed 40 tons and was capable of generating a magnetic field 250,000 times more powerful than that of the Earth's magnetic field.[3] (Additional information from that article is reported on Philip Coppens's Website (*hwww.philipcoppens.com/woodpecker. html*).)

The speculation that the Woodpecker was involved in mind control experiments was supported on many fronts. The measured signal was in the frequency range that impacted the human brain in the arena of psychological activity.

- Dr. Andrew Michrowski, technologies specialist with the Canadian Department of State, and president of the Planetary Association for Clean Energy (PACE), wrote that the "U.S.S.R. signals have been assessed by the Environmental Protection Agency [...] to be psychoactive."[4]

- In 1984, a research specialist in California, Dr. Ross Adey, obtained a Soviet mini-Woodpecker transmitter called the LIDA. It was described as a "distant treatment apparatus"[5] said to treat psychological problems, including sleeplessness, hypertension, and neurotic disturbances. Apparently the device was used experimentally as a replacement for tranquilizers and other drugs to avoid unwanted side effects. Operating at 40 MHz, the LIDA pulsed low-frequency radio waves with the intention of stimulating electromagnetic current in the brain to produce a trance-like state.

- Lt. Colonel Thomas Bearden, USAF (Ret.), claimed that the signal was responsible for weather modification responsible for a drought in the western United States, according to an article on the *Paranoia* magazine Website.[6] The draught severely affected farming and economics in 1976.

Specifics about the Woodpecker project, called Steel Yard in government circles, are still classified. It seems suspect that this project should still be so classified 30 years later. Could it be that there were more ramifications than were admitted? Considering that this massive energy beam was located very close to Chernobyl and the energy that powered it came from the Chernobyl Nuclear Power Station, was it a coincidence that Reactor 4 had a disastrous meltdown in 1986?

With regard to ancient prophecy, Chernobyl means wormwood, and Wormwood is the name of a star in Revelation 8:10–11: "The third angel sounded his trumpet and a great star, blazing like a torch, fell from the sky on a third of the rivers and on the springs of water—the name of the star is Wormwood. A third of the waters turned bitter, and many people died from the waters that had become bitter." As far as we know the Woodpecker project has ended, but a stronger, more alarming project has emerged to take its place, this time operated by the U.S government: H.A.A.R.P.

The Untuned H.A.A.R.P.

H.A.A.R.P. is a research and development program for exploring, understanding, and using the ionosphere. It stands for High Frequency Active Auroral Research Program, and it is run by the U.S. military at a facility located in Gakona, Alaska. According to the official government Website, "H.A.A.R.P. is a scientific endeavor aimed at studying the properties and behavior of the ionosphere with particular emphasis on being able to understand and use it to enhance communications and surveillance systems for both civilian and defense purposes."[7] The program is funded by several branches of the U.S. military and several universities, and is supplied by commercial companies.

Today's sophisticated wireless society depends on consistency in electronic performance and communications for virtually all aspects of life. Far beyond being able to access Facebook and Twitter on our handheld cell phones, telecommunications systems are essential for national security (guiding missiles, communicating with submarines, and so forth). Understanding the ionosphere seems to be a socially responsible endeavor; however, H.A.A.R.P. goes much further. It seeks not only to understand, but also to manipulate and control this region of the atmosphere. Using high-power transmitters operating in the high-frequency (HF) range called Ionospheric Research Instruments (IRI), areas of the ionosphere are "temporarily excited" for scientific study."[8] The implications of this could be quite grave.

The program is said to allow governments to detect underground mineral reserves and communicate with underground miners, communicate with submarines deep in the ocean, and enhance other aspects of telecommunications. Although defense purposes are not clearly stated, as the government Website explains, the project does have military applications. That is an astounding understatement. The ability to predict and manipulate conditions in the ionosphere would allow a government to "see" over the horizon, shield military activity from radar observation, disrupt military communications of enemies, create natural weather disasters, and create geological disruption such as earthquakes.[9] Essentially, it would allow governments to use weather and geology as global weaponry. If this seems like the Star Wars weapon plan that was supposedly tabled in the 1980s, it just might be.

Bernard Eastlund (1938–2007) discovered the technique of ionospheric heating. Eastlund authored three patents. (U.S. Patents #4,686,605, #4,712,155, and #5,038,664 related to this technique.)[10] The H.A.A.R.P. facility is an advancement on his original ideas. It sends high-powered beams of electromagnetic waves directly at a single point in the ionosphere. The government Website reports that at the Alaskan site there are 180 transmitting towers, each with two pairs of dipole antennas transmitting at more than 10 billion watts.[11] The complete array of antennas, steered by computers, sends a narrow beam of high-powered pulsed radio signals upward toward one spot of the ionosphere.

The radio waves heat the ionosphere causing it to absorb and store more energy. The small area that receives the HF radio waves expands and is pushed into higher altitudes, forming a bubble in the ionosphere. Inside this expanded area, energy is accumulated and amplified. The bubble is highly reflective so that HF signals can be bounced off to points well beyond the horizon. ELF (extremely low frequency) and microwave signals can also be reflected in what is called the "lens effect."

Commercial applications of Eastlund's original patents provided a theoretical mechanism for transporting energy around the globe without the need for pipelines. Eastlund's first two patents were allegedly bought by the Atlantic Richfield Company (ARCO) with this in mind. The idea is that this technology will allow access and use of natural gas reserves that are too remote to pipe. Imagine converting the gas at a remote location into electrical energy on site, then bouncing it off the heated atmospheric lens to customers around the globe.

Fears about the government's use of this technology, however, take a much different turn. It is believed their interest quickly shifted from over-the-horizon radar and spy potential to weaponry. As U.S. military documents put it, H.A.A.R.P. aims to learn how to "exploit the ionosphere for Department of Defense purposes."[12] Researchers say that the heated bubble in the ionosphere accumulates and amplifies the energy being beamed into it with the potential to be discharged in a nuclear-sized explosion. Bouncing it off the lens allows the "bomb" to be detonated at distances far from the computer-generated source, and, because it is not a nuclear bomb, there would be no radiation after the detonation—just a devastating blast stronger than a nuclear bomb killing those in the area. This argument is countered with claims that the amount of energy being beamed could not possibly fuel such a device and that HF beams dissipate en route to the ionosphere.

The concerns of using H.A.A.R.P. to initiate nuclear-type detonations parallel concerns that the same technology is being used in weather-control experiments not to improve farming and food growing conditions or alleviate drought in South Africa, but rather as a form of weaponry. The reasoning is that changes in the ionosphere are reflected in dynamics in the gulfstream. Supper heating one area might result in shifts in the gulfstream, which would affect weather patterns.

Controlling weather seems like science fiction, especially using it in warfare. However, consider the response of U.S. Secretary of Defense William S. Cohen on April 28, 1997, in a keynote address at the Conference on Terrorism, Weapons of Mass Destruction, and U.S. Strategy at the University of Georgia in Athens. When asked a question about terrorism, part of Cohen's response was: "Others are engaging even in an eco-type terrorism whereby they can alter the climate, set off earthquakes and volcanoes remotely through the use of electromagnetic waves."[13] Clearly, even two decades ago the technology was in development. Weather-related phenomena will be further discussed in Chapter 15.

Skepticism, and not just from conspiracy theorists, over the intent of H.A.A.R.P. is such that it is even suspected of involvement in the huge earthquake and tsunami in Japan on March 11, 2011. *MIT Technology Review* reported on a presentation by Dimitar Ouzounov at the NASA Goddard Space Flight Centre in Maryland, noting that "before the M9 earthquake, the total electron content of the ionosphere increased dramatically over the epicentre, reaching a maximum three days before the quake struck. At the same time, satellite observations showed a big increase in infrared emissions from above the epicentre, which peaked in the hours before the quake. In other words, the atmosphere was heating up."[14] The MIT article went on to speculate whether H.A.A.R.P. could be responsible.

Press releases and other information from the military on H.A.A.R.P. continually downplay what the program is capable of doing. Publicity documents insist that the H.A.A.R.P. project is no different than other ionospheric heaters operating safely throughout the world in places such as Arecibo, Puerto Rico, Tromso, Norway, and locations in Russia. Many people wonder if the Norway Spiral and other sky spirals are the result of electromagnetic pulsing from such facilities. No evidence exists, but that does not mean it isn't there.

Concluding Thoughts

It is difficult to know whether manipulating our ionosphere is safe or not. It is impossible to know the true intent of the government and corporate interests in H.A.A.R.P., or how realistic the fears about it are. I am sure I am not the only one wondering whether the extreme warming of the atmosphere in the current climate change is related to our heating segments of the ionosphere. The truth is that we do not have to prove that this technology is unsafe; the government has to prove to us that it *is* safe. This planet is not owned by corporations or ruled by governments; the people might be, but the planet is not.

Those who say the government would not proceed with technology that was dangerous or use the public as guinea pigs have been asleep. The government has a very poor record of not putting public safety ahead of corporate profit. Consider how the FDA has allowed corporations to introduce genetically modified foods into the public food banks with no long-term studies, or even requirement of labeling so that people can choose if they want this type of food. The folly of this was made clear in recent European studies that reveal these foods are cancer promoting.[15] We are all an experiment under Montesano's endeavor to enlarge the company purse under the auspices of the government.

The government has an even worse record for truthfully disclosing public harm in areas involving national security. It is difficult to trust the intentions or responsible management in something as vital to our well-being as the ionosphere. Should we destroy the ionosphere with our experiments, the intent for doing so will be a moot point. Before his death, Bernard Eastlund said, "The public must be involved in the development of the concept from the start...the public itself must want to accept the risks involved."[16] The problem has always been the exclusion of any dissenting opinion, outside scientific debate, or public deliberation before the spending of massive sums of money to experiment with our future.

This planet is a self-regulating system that supplies life. It has been here long before our civilizations and, if all goes well, will continue long after we are gone. We assume it is our right to interfere with the homeostatic mechanisms—that we should be allowed to unravel anything that we want to exploit. That is the hubris of our current mentality. It is the mentality we are leaving behind in the shift underway.

The question for those who care to resist is: how? How can you protect yourself from the harmful effects of technology or confront it politically? The movie *Avatar* touched those who saw it with the beauty of the vision of oneness and connection. It fell short in believing that the power in that connection is greater than the power of war and destruction. But what if it is?

When we engage in political action, we are investing our belief in the idea that the principles our system is based on will work if we apply the proper pressure in the proper channels. It's important to take this kind of action and ask our representatives to bring the concerns of H.A.A.R.P. into a congressional committee. Bill Richardson did so for the Hum, and we can and should pursue this avenue, if for no other reason than to have tried. We can all initiate internet petitions and use the Internet to keep the questions on the table.

Spiritual action is a more difficult concept to grapple with. Many will shake their heads and say that spiritual action works in spiritual domains and this is purely a physical issue. In Part II, the crop circles demonstrated that synchronicity exits between one person's thoughts and another's. We saw that the thoughts of one person compel action in another and that there is a force that I call higher mind orchestrating events. The Scole Experiment identified the elements involved: alignment among human energy, Earth energy, and spiritual energy. The question we have to answer is whether we can invest our belief in the idea that these principles can work in great and meaningful ways. We will never know if we do not try. Examples of how are found in the Conclusion.

Somehow, weather seems to be at the center of many hidden technologies. Whether this is due to a desire to find solutions to climate change or whether climate change is an excuse for experimenting with weather patterns may be irrelevant. Either way, boundaries are being crossed.

I have studied meteorology and kept weather records since 1961. As a kid, all I ever wanted for Christmas and birthdays were books on the sciences, with weather at the top of the list. I spent more of my time looking into the sky than most people, developing an awareness of clouds and a good knowledge of the synoptic charts issued by meteorological organizations around the world.

Consequently, I take an interest in all things skyward and tend to notice subtle changes that many people don't regard as unusual. Sometimes it pays off. The many references throughout this chapter to radar images and cloud pictures can be seen on my Website (*www.colinandrews.net*.)

Radar Images

Radar tracks weather by detecting water droplets in the atmosphere related to cloud density. On occasion it perceives large-scale forest fires because of the particulate matter in the sky. As we saw in Chapter 13, it also picks up the reflective material in chemtrails. Most weather tracking systems use satellite imaging of cloud cover in concert with radar imaging to visualize changing conditions and make forecasts. It's possible to differentiate and observe different elements in the atmosphere by separating satellite images from radar images. Most weather stations make their forecasting systems available to the public. (My Website offers links into most global geological and weather monitoring systems.[1])

Through my Website I am in communication with several thousands of international visitors daily. On January 15, 2010, a man who lives in the southern part of West Australia e-mailed to say that he was seeing something very odd on the Australian Bureau of Meteorology (BOM) weather radar and suggested that I take a look. His e-mail began a three-year investigation that is still ongoing.

The man was alerting me to an unusual radar pattern that formed a perfect donut-shape on the weather screen. It faded within a few hours of its arrival. By the time I saw the e-mail and checked the BOM national radar imaging, the mysterious large ring had mostly dissipated; I was able to see it on a time loop. The satellite and radar composite showed an unusual white ring that spread across a small region of southern West Australia. Several hours later in the same area, a large counterclockwise rotation appeared in the atmosphere, indicating a high pressure system. Radar showed a condensation trail off the coastline and also a series of three small spiraling arms of condensation in the area coinciding with the location of the center of this unusual ring.

In the Southern Hemisphere, counterclockwise rotations are high pressure systems; clockwise rotations indicate low pressure. Typically, high pressure systems are present on clear days with no clouds and no precipitation, and therefore do not create images on radar. On this particular day there was no reflective precipitation that would have created the radar image seen. The composite satellite imagery revealed no cloud related weather over the entire south West Australia. So what activated the weather radar and created a perfectly symmetrical geometry?

I suggested to my Australian informant that he write directly to BOM or the regional office and ask for an explanation. The following e-mail was sent from the Kalgoorlie-Boulder meteorological station to him on January 18, 2010, and he forwarded it to me:

> Early Saturday there were sort of concentric circles of echoes between 200 Kms and 400 Kms from Kalgoorlie-Boulder. However there was no weather around this area from which radar signals might have been reflected. It would therefore seem to be due to what is referred to as "anomalous propagation" (false echoes) or even possibly dust in the atmosphere. Regards, Kalgoorlie-Boulder Met. Office.[2]

It was very interesting that the Met Office acknowledged not knowing the cause of the strange radar reading. Offering two possibilities was honest and straightforward, but geometry of this kind must have some kind of explanation. It was clear that the radar image did not reflect an actual substance in the atmosphere, as that would be seen on satellite. Therefore, the only conclusion is that the geometry was an electromagnetic interference pattern. But what caused the strange interference? This was the beginning of a mystery hunt.

The Expanding Picture

I immediately posted the geometric radar image. Within a few days, people from across Australia were alerting me to additional odd patterns on radar imaging. Everyone who contacted me agreed that these artifacts had not been seen before. The images covered a wide range of designs. All were circular in nature with different features radiating from the center. They included donut shapes, rings, straight spokes as in bicycle wheels, multiple curved radial arms, and concentric rings. Some of the geometries emanated very unusual colors. In standard weather radar, colors indicate the degree of precipitation; in these interference patterns, new colors were appearing that defied standard interpretation, and their meanings are still unknown. Following is a list of the radar images received in the first couple months of 2010 with date (mm/dd/yy), description and location. (This is also available on my Website.)

01/15/10   White donut ring Southern West Australia (W.A.). **Start of the phenomenon.**

01/22/10   Donut with white and black radiating spokes around red center, North coast W.A.

01/22/10   White concentric rings, Victoria (Vic.)

01/27/10   Counter-clockwise, curved arms radiating from bright orange center, Vic.

01/28/10   Black, radiating spokes around solid black center, north coast of W.A.

01/28/10   Radiating "feathers" emitting rainbow colors north coast of W.A.

02/02/10   Dense white donut in the middle of Queensland (QLD)

02/03/10	Radiating white spokes northeast coast QLD
02/03/10	White concentric rings, north coast QLD
02/04/10	Red circle around bright red center, center of QLD
02/08/10	Concentric rings west coast of W.A.
02/10/10	Black radiating arms from solid black center, north coast of WA
02/10/10	Curved arms radiating from red ring, Vic.
02/11/10	Concentric rings north coast of W.A.
02/11/10	White concentric rings, NSW
02/15/10	Radiating rainbow spokes, west coast of W.A.
02/19/10	Radiating curved counterclockwise arms around red center Vic.

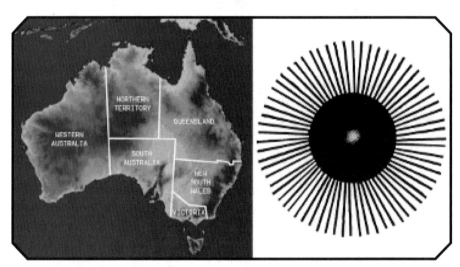

Figure 15.1: (left) A map of Australia. (right) Sample radar image.

As the months progressed, I continued to post dates, freeze-frame pictures, and satellite loops of the BOM radar anomalies as people across Australia alerted me to odd occurrences. Gradually a pattern began to emerge. Each radar interference image was centered over a radar station and was therefore the result of information, or misinformation, from that station. A BOM employee shared that they thought the corrupt information was the result of interference from an unknown source. He wrote:

I am a Bureau of Meteorology tech who works on the radars. Just had a look at the images from the [W.A.] area. The level 1 rain threshold is either set too low, hence picking up noise, or there is someone working nearby on a transmitting device which falls within the bandwidth of our radio, hence the radio "speckle" interference. Noticed the "swept gain" attenuates the signal out, out to so many km's. The idea of AP "Anomalous Propagation" is often when there is a temperature inversion, and the radar picks up "false echoes" off the atmosphere. Regards[3]

After thanking him for getting in touch and sending me his technical explanation, I asked how powerful and at what frequency a nearby transmitting device would need to be to interfere with equipment. I added: "Is it conceivable that the same effect could be the result of transmissions beamed from above instead of from the ground? I believe that the US/Australian/UK/Canadian H.A.A.R.P. experimental installations are thought to be responsible for some new, previously unseen atmospheric phenomenon. Thinking outside the box, is it an outside possibility that the effects seen on Australian Met radar were created by frequency interference from the H.A.A.R.P. network similar to what you have suggested caused by ground based interference, but from satellites above?"

BOM agent James Butler was very good to reply, saying: "Re: The round radar problem in WA; it is a BOM Radar unit which has its lower rain level threshold setup too low, ie too sensitive, which gives the noisy radar reading like that. Nothing to do with HAARP, which, as you know, is in Alaska. I see images like this a lot as I work for the Bureau of Meteorology in QLD. Regards."[4]

It is a fact that many of the rings seen on radar systems are the result of incomplete radar returns, inversions, and out-of-trim settings on the ground equipment. However, there is no evidence that this is the case for all of them. If the event of January 2010 was caused by the rain level being set too low, then how likely is it that the escalating numbers of events were all radar stations with rain settings set too low? If the radar rings are caused by a ground-based rogue transmission, why, after all these years of using radar, should this become such a sudden and widespread issue? Is it not possible that the rogue transmission could be a high-power emission from H.A.A.R.P.?

The official explanations simply do not add up. Instead, they lead back to the original question and add a few more: What type of interference created patterns like this, where did it originate, and why and how have so many stations across Australia become involved?

On February 4, 2010, BOM placed a caption above their radar on the TV screen: *"Please note that we are experiencing technical issues with the radar images resulting in circular discs appearing unexpectedly at times. We will endeavor to look at this problem as quickly as possible."*

That statement changed over the months, but it still confirms that the Bureau does not know the source of the interference. As of this writing, it reads: *"If you notice any circular patterns or straight lines originating from the centre of the radar location, this is due to occasional interference to the radar data. The Bureau is currently investigating ways to reduce these interferences."*

At the time of this writing, BOM is still trying to resolve the problem. Meanwhile, the media began to pay attention, and on April 2, 2010, national and local newspapers picked up on the mystery. The *Telegraph* headline read "Bizarre Theories Circling Weather Bureau." In the article, the radar patterns were labeled as "the digital-age equivalent of crop circles—mysterious patterns appearing on the Bureau of Meteorology's national radar system without any explanation."[5] Information from this story was repeated in other newspapers across Australia.[6]

Weather Connections

When the radar anomalies were first reported in 2010, Australia was in the midst of the worst drought in a thousand years, a 10-year-long event affecting large areas across the vast country. Climate experts believe it is the beginning of an increasing trend related to global warming. The official end of the arid period was announced on May 11, 2012, which meant the government could stop paying subsidies to affected farmers for the reason of exceptional circumstances. In fact, the drought had been alleviated in 2010 with tropical storm Olga followed by the worst storm in Australia's history on March 6, 2012.[7]

On January 16, 2010, the day the large white donut ring arrived on the radar in southern West Australia, people were experiencing a variety of weather extremes. A farmer who owned land where the radar interference pattern was cited reported that the days around the event were exceptionally hot. A couple in Sydney (eastern Australia) said they witnessed a very strange reddish haze around the sun two days after the radar ring had appeared in the western part of the country. Within 17 days, tropical storm Olga appeared and distinguished herself with her atypical behavior. The storm maneuvered across the country, making landfall three different times.

After all was said and done, instead of the widespread damage expected across vast areas of Australia from Olga, a good soaking was given to seriously parched areas suffering water shortages. The interesting thing about Olga was the way in which the storm seemed to be maneuvered around the country, with depressions and upper troughs forming in time to steer her in different directions. Many weather stations and even NASA commented on the unusual pattern.

In the week it took for Olga to make her journey across the country down under, five atypical radar interference patterns occurred in West Australia and Victoria. Though this does not in any way prove a link, it is an interesting coincidence. The observations on my Website drew the attention of BOM and elicited e-mails from professional meteorologists both in and outside of BOM who told me that I was not the only person wondering what was going on. Many of these radar patterns and weather had never been seen by professionals before. This is not just a casual curiosity; this is a scientific mystery.

Even more interesting are the two occasions when new weather systems developed from dramatic interference patterns. The first occurred on February 19, 2010, in Australia (February 18th in the United States). An amazing symbol appeared on the national radar emanating from a facility in Melbourne: a black and red counter-clockwise spiral surrounding a red-flared spiral center. I had witnessed a radiating ring similar to this on January 27, 2010, and noticed then that the lower levels of the atmosphere began to rotate in the same counter-clockwise direction as the radar pattern. Now I watched a second time as a pressure system formed under the radar symbol in an unprecedented physical reflection of the radar image. Normally the weather occurs first and then is reflected by the radar. I assumed the first event was an odd coincidence in which frequency interference created a technical artifact that coincided with a new pressure system. Watching it occur for a second time, I had the eerie feeling of weather modification. Could the radar interference be a reflection of an electromagnetic pulse that was interacting with the atmosphere to modify weather?

On March 6, 2012, the Big Dry ended with the worst storm in 156 years. Golf ball–sized hail pelted Melbourne and super-cell thunderstorms rocked across Australia, unleashing tornados and causing massive flooding. The storm was the final stage in a sudden, extreme shift in weather from super drought to superstorms.

Today, the radar interference is unabated, and weather extremes are cascading. During 2012 strange, unexplained radar patterns appeared across the country on January 8th and 17th, February 4th and 17th, April 17th, May 4th, 15th, and 29th, June 18th, July 20th and 26th, September 1st, November 20th and 29th, and December 2nd. On February 16, 2013, in W.A., a ruby-red Catherine wheel burst across the radar to set the scene for the post-2012 era.

The summer of 2012 saw the second hottest temperatures ever recorded in Australia, as extreme heat, flooding, and cyclones ravaged the continent. For example, Perth recorded its second hottest summer on record and the hottest summer in more than 30 years. Victoria recorded its hottest November day, with temperatures reaching close to 46 degrees Celsius (114.8 degrees Fahrenheit).

According to the official statement from the Bureau of Meteorology the summer of 2012-2013 was the warmest since records began in 1910 and included the hottest day on record, across all of Australia and the Southern Hemisphere.[8] If indeed the radar interference is a by-product of the Australian government's weather modification project, it doesn't seem to be helping.

Unusual Flying Objects and Strange Weather?

On February 25, 2010, what must have been a very large object was seen on radar just off the coast of Sydney, moving southeast across the Tasman Sea. The object had the shape of a bird with wings fully extended or an aircraft. In some ways it looked like a satellite with two solar panels, although it was far too large and low-flying to be a satellite. Its approximate position was 35 degrees 10 minutes south, 152 degrees 5 minutes east.

Radar loops are available to the public in sequences of four frames that are played back in short animation. The first frame in a sequence is dropped off as a new fourth frame is captured, so that each sequence only goes back four frames from the present time. The strange object was seen in the first and last frames of a sequence.

In the first frame, the object was very close to Sydney. It disappeared in the next frame and was replaced with a first-of-its-kind interference pattern that appeared as a narrow, bright orange ring centered over the city. In the third frame, the ring had disappeared as well as the object. In the final frame, the winged object was hundreds of miles over the Tasman Sea, heading in a southeasterly direction toward New Zealand.

When radar imaging was separated from satellite imaging, the orange ring was seen only on radar, as would be expected, and the winged object was viewed only on radar as well. The satellite image did not show either, but did show an enormous cloud canopy rapidly moving from the north toward the northeast coast of Australia, deepening as it approached. The huge storm followed the path of the flying object, and half an hour after the object had moved off the coast and disappeared from radar, a second radar interference pattern appeared off the northern coast of W.A., many hundreds of miles to the west.

On the following day, February 26th, three parallel white lines formed on the weather radar screens across parts of Australia: one on the northwest coast, another on the southwest, and a third in the southeast over Melbourne. They were all aligned west to east and looked like an underlying grid system. For several weeks prior to these lines appearing, a single white line had appeared numerous times over Melbourne. I had queried BOM as to what might cause the single line, and they suggested it could be an effect of a large building obscuring the radar return. Now, in light of the arrival of two more lines on opposite coasts hundreds of miles away, sharing the same alignment and forming what looked like a national grid, this seemed doubtful.

On February 27th, the colossal storm seen on radar on the 25th covered more than half of the landmass of Australia. It stretched into the heart of the continent while half of the storm was still out to sea off the north coast. At that moment, a quarter of the nation's radar installations were taken out of service. BOM issued a notice saying *"Radar*

Service is currently unavailable due to: Sorry outage information is currently unavailable." The stations affected were Mt Gambier, Esperence, Albany, Geraldton, Hobart, Giles, Alice Springs, Moree, Willis Island, Broome, and Canarvon.

Figure 15.2: White, single lines that appeared February 26, 2010.

Since the original e-mail exchange with BOM, several more communications had taken place in which employees revealed that they did not know the source or cause of the mystery. I am of the opinion that the object flying over Sydney was part of a designed manipulation or adjustment of the large weather system that was approaching. The radar interference was a by-product of weather modification work. The burst of radar to the west of the storm may have been an electromagnetic effect of technology that was steering the monster weather system.

At the time that the numerous stations went off air, I wondered if BOM might be installing new technology, trying to filter out the effects of weather modification on the standard network and reduce the visibility of unusual objects in the sky. All the signs suggested that what was taking place across Australia on February 25th–27th was a national event and not related to the coincidental malfunctioning of individual radar stations.

Links to ChemTrails?

Anyone who has watched the development of chemtrails since the 1990s will know of the associated radar anomalies such as those on the Carnicom Institute's Website. It wasn't long before visitors to my site posted questions wondering whether chemtrails were causing the Australian radar irregularities. From the evidence and witness reports I have gathered, it doesn't seem that there is a correlation between chemtrail activity in Australia and this radar artifact.

Although considerable reports of chemtrails arose in Australia during this time period, there didn't seem to be any correlation to the radar images. However, there are several other considerations. For one, chemtrails last in the sky for many hours. If they were creating a reflective surface showing up on radar, the images would last for the same amount of time as the chemtrail. Instead, the radar images are gone within minutes. In addition, chemtrail radar images seen on weather channels reflect the same line or diffusion pattern as the dispersing aerosol spray. All things taken into consideration, I believe this is a new and different phenomenon.

H.A.A.R.P. Connections

It is true that many of the radar rings are the result of incomplete radar returns, inversions, and out-of-trim settings on the ground equipment, but there is no identifying the source. The artifacts are not random or isolated. Some scientists have expressed the opinion that H.A.A.R.P., jointly operated among the United States, United Kingdom, Canada, and Australian governments, is causing the interference. The H.A.A.R.P. program certainly has the capability and mission statement to modify weather, but would the sister installation in Exmouth in Western Australia leave radar imprints?

On January 22, 2010, two unique interference patterns were seen by millions of viewers. A new design appeared over the city of Melbourne consisting of 14 white, broken concentric rings centered on and straddled over a large area of cloud as seen on the satellite. Thirty seconds later, another radar pattern appeared over the northwest coast consisting of 70 thin black spokes radiating out of a solid black circle; in the center was a small bright orange or red dot. Published data from the H.A.A.R.P. installation in Alaska stated that the power to the antenna array had been increased that same day.

Full study of the radar anomalies involves several disciplines that are highly technical and specialized. It is not easy when classified projects further obscure the picture. The following statement was sent to me from an engineer working for BOM who asked not to be named for fear he would lose his job:

> As I understand it, the Alaskan Tesla transmitting system which we all know as HAARP, transmits at ultralow frequency, which I will not go into in this email, but they would never show up as effects on weather radar. It is designed for sub level use, i.e. under water and through the crust of the earth. Sometimes it is used for ionization too, (upper atmosphere) not sure how and at what frequency. Documentation on this would be hard to get, as it has certain classifications.[9]

This letter points out how much in-depth and serious research needs to be done. Recording the phenomenon sets the stage for continued study as governments and organizations are urged to be transparent in the research they do that affects us all. It is difficult for me to think governments of any kind would purposefully manufacture a tsunami; I have trouble believing this is the new warfare. We all breathe the same air. I am perfectly able to accept that weather modification exists, but I tend to see it in a more fundamental desire to create better farming conditions or combat global warming, however misguided. There are many who will say how wrong I am. I have to say that the truth is I really don't know the motive or the extent of the program.

Experts Explain

Throughout my investigation I have been in touch with the BOM and also have sent information to various scientists. The replies are interesting. Dr. Bruce Maccabee, an American optical physicist formerly employed by the U.S. Navy (*www.brumac.8k.com*), wrote a letter that is posted on my Website.

After sending him radar pictures, he wrote:

I presume these are typical rotating radars that scan around 360 degrees every ten - fifteen seconds or so, recording the distances to reflective targets at each angle. I presume that electronic interference "properly applied" could make strange patterns on radar (creating spurious targets). However, electronic interference, if from an external source, would come from one direction unless the interfering source were able to travel around the radar antenna so that it was always within the radar beam. Hard to imagine an interfering source that could stay within the beam. 'Internally generated interference might do it.

I think I know what could cause a spoke. A radar "spoke" would be created if along some direction angle theta with a direction width of "delta theta" there was something that gave the equivalent of essentially continuous reflection at all distances (some amount of reflection at all distances within range) and at angle theta plus delta theta, extending for another delta theta, there is no reflection or minimal reflection and then at theta plus 2 x delta theta there is another spoke of width delta theta with continuous reflection at all distances, and so on around a circle.

A spiral would require, at a particular angle theta, a series of strong reflections at varying distances, and this series of distances would change with angle theta such that a series of curved lines of reflection would be created, making a collection of spiral patterns all ending at the same center. One main thing that strikes me as "impossible" is the fact that strange targets are seen all the way around (360 deg).

Obviously this requires either a signal input that is independent of direction of the radar antenna, such as an internal (noise or jamming) source, or something in the atmosphere that surrounds each radar station, or something that actually travels around each radar station in order to remain within the radar beam. Each of these "explanations" is as bizarre as the phenomenon itself.

Maybe these are "radar agriglyphs" (crop circles). LOL[10]

I also received the following from Malcolm Kitchen, of the British Meteorological Office on March 14, 2010:

Colin, your email has been passed onto me for reply. I have looked at the sample image and my guess would be that this and similar patterns do not have a meteorological origin. There can be several causes of geometric ring or spoke patterns:

a) If there is an unexpected increase in the amount of electrical noise in the radar system. This noise tends to "break through" at a particular range because the effective gain is higher at long range to compensate for the inverse square fall off in the signal. Having said that, the smaller "holes" in your sample image at extreme range don't fit this.

b) when the engineers are checking or calibrating the radar, they may inject artificial signals into the system but forget to turn off the data supply to the outside world. This can result in ring patterns.

c) Interference from other radars or noise sources can produce spoke patterns, particularly when two radars which are close together in frequency are pointing at each other.

The UK weather radar network also suffers from similar artifacts to some extent (maybe one or two incidents per month on average).[11]

Two other employees from the Australian Bureau of Meteorology suggested that the radar ring was possibly caused by a rogue frequency transmitted close to the government installation. A reader reports his equipment that measures ULF pulses from the Sun found that 12-hour recordings for January were normal except for the one recorded on January 15, 2010 in which levels more than doubled.[12]

Weather Modification Projects

Though we cannot say with certainty that the radar interference is from weather modification experiments and/or the electromagnetic effect of H.A.A.R.P., we can say with surety that both programs are underway in Australia and around the world. Demonstrating a connection between the H.A.A.R.P. activities and radar anomalies is something different. As was seen in Chapter 14, there is no attempt to hide the H.A.A.R.P. program, only its true activity. In Australia, the U.S. Navy runs a H.A.A.R.P. facility in Exmouth, which is easily seen on Google Earth. It is comprised of a pentagon-shaped array of transmitters and buildings.

The 2010 Association for the Advancement of Science Symposium, reported on in Chapter 13, appeared to believe significant geo-engineering isn't yet underway. However, Weather Modification Incorporated is a company that does just that. Its Website lists all the projects it is contracted for around the world. It is staggering. Thirty-six weather modification projects are underway by this company in the United States; 30 projects are listed in all other countries combined. And these projects represent only one company.[13]

The number-one weather modification project in Australia is in Queensland. In 2008, during the midst of what would amount to a 10-year drought, rain fell in Queensland and created massive flooding. It rained after two days of cloud seeding conducted by a company named Australian Rain Technologies that offers "rainfall enhancement" services. Theoretically, rainfall is produced by introducing electrically charged droplets into a naturally occurring cloud via an ATLANT ion-emitting device. Each ATLANT device incorporates "a high voltage generator connected to a large network of thin wires of a metal composition supported on a framework with a series of pyramids on top."[14] If anyone doubts the serious nature of this company please look at *www.australianrain.com.au.*

In January 2008, the *Courier Mail* reported on this weather seeding project. The article quotes Queensland Sustainability Minister Andrew McNamara as planning to spend $7.6 million over four years to test cloud-seeding. New South Wales (NSW) already spent four years conducting a cloud seeding test that increased the rainfall by 14 percent.[15] Australia's weather modifying programs are in direct conflict with Australia's agreement as a signatory nation to the 1978 United Nation's Treaty that bans environmental modification systems: the United Nations Convention on the Prohibition of Military or Any Other Hostile Use of Environmental Modification Techniques.[16]

One unexpected outcome is the response of the insurance companies and their concern about providing compensation for damage
resulting from manipulated events. Basically, the insurance industry
wants to redefine the term "natural event" to mean only natural events
and leave out any weather manipulation/modification or earth-shaking
events from the policies. Insurance companies don't want to be liable for
providing compensation for what the government, military, and intelligence agencies are creating with weather manipulation technologies.[17]

When companies argue over who foots the bill, you know the technology is real and in use.

Concluding Thoughts

At this time it is impossible to say what technology is involved with
the radar anomolies in Australila. I believe there is a weather connection, but real answers must come from scientists with more knowledge.
What we can say is that people have been involved with influencing
weather for millenia and success did not relate to technology, but to
mind and heart connection.

Native people have a long tradition surrounding the spiritual qual-
ities of nature including weather, clouds, and rain. This tradtion continues today. Says one North American Tribe, "The rain dance is still
an important part of Native American consciousness, just as we are
concerned with the amount of rainfall even in the modern world."[18]

Indian Country Website states:

Recently, during the ski season, the managers of a ski resort in
Park City, Utah, invited a group of Uintah Dancers to perform
a dance that would hopefully bring much needed snow to their
bare resort. They danced, and the next day it snowed, and it kept
snowing for three days. Who is to judge the power of prayer or
belief? As the Native people of this land, we are accustomed to
prayer and certain beliefs and traditions, and dancing for rain
has been and remains to this day, one of our traditions. We
daily give thanks to our Creator and our Ancestors, for having
gifted us with those beautiful beliefs and traditions. Aho.[19]

Many societies around the world have sacred dance or ritual to produce rain. Apart from the Native Americans and Aboriginal people in

Australia, Romanian ceremonies known as paparuda and caloian are still in use. Some United States farmers attempt to bring rain during droughts through prayer. These rituals differ greatly in their specifics, but share a common action through ritual and/or spiritual means.

Going back to Part II of this book, we demonstrated that sincere intent connected with a higher intelligence that produced interaction with lights in the sky, orbs, and the orchestration of the art of circle-makers with the request of circle enthusiasts. British crop circle-maker Matthew Williams claims that he asked for the rain to stop during the construction of a crop circle design and a donut-shape appeared below the clouds over their heads, stopping the rain inside the crop circle. He said it was raining outside the circle, but not inside where they worked. We saw in the Scole Experiment the importance of Earth energy. Can we stretch ourselves a little further to embrace the intellegence within nature and interact with it?

I know for many that the idea that we can influence the physical world in this way will seem absurd. I hope after reading the Conclusion to this book they might change their mind.

Throughout this book we have been exploring the interaction of mind and matter. We have discovered a telepathic link between crop circle-makers and crop circle enthusiasts and suggested that an underlying connection exits among people. We are proposing that we are each tuned to an orchestrating force that choreographs the synchronicities that guide us. It may seem to you that the links we are suggesting are wildly speculative and outside the realm of reality. However, the military does not; it recognizes the mind as one of the most important military weapons. Methods to use it include mind control and mental weaponry. In fact, the only part of our speculation not explored by the military is that of an orchestrating intelligence. The consequences are extreme.

Mind control covers a broad spectrum of activity. The first and most obvious is manipulating the public mind through propaganda. Every nation engages in propaganda, targeting both citizen and enemy. If the belief is that a government is stronger than it actually is, control is easier to maintain. In today's society the government has massive tools at hand for manipulating opinion. Mass and social media provide access to nearly everyone on the planet. Facebook, Twitter, personal e-mail—all are culled to determine the psychology of the nation. The U.S. Department of Defense (DOD) readily admits to developing computer algorithms to mine data from social media in order to understand "group dynamics and forecast trends."[1] Additionally, whistleblower Edward Snowden has informed the world that the National Security Agency (NSA) is mining e-mails and telephone calls of the entire United States, a practice previously denied before this revelation.

Psychology introduces the use of emotion to manipulate the mind, because strong emotions produce a portal of entry into the psyche. Any message a government wishes to impart with the intention that it become part of the national gestalt can be introduced on waves of emotional energy. It is a tried and true technique: Use an event that generates strong feelings, then introduce a rallying call to action. Finally, success in manipulation is guaranteed when a nation's citizenry is united through group exaltation. Whether the underdog or victor; they must believe in the superiority of their culture and beliefs. Consequently, propaganda begins early and is part of national identity.

These are minor and obvious uses of the mind in war, and this does not represent the limits of the ways in which it is influenced. Lt. Col. John Alexander published an article as far back as the 1980s advocating the introduction of extra-sensory perception (ESP), telepathy, and the use of mind over matter, or psychokinesis, for military use. In reality, his article was an acknowledgment of what was already underway within a division of Special Operations called Psychological Operations, or PsyOps. At the time of the article, PsyOps programs were using a psychic technique for spying called remote viewing (a topic covered further in Chapter 18). Also by this time, telepathy had joined the arsenal of tools that included subliminal messaging and control over mass media to manipulate public opinion.

It is outside of the scope and mission of this book to fully cover this topic. Our intent is only to introduce some key advances that we need to be aware of as we enter a new time in history. At this point, we are still at the crossroads of change, and the information here sends us down a path that is frightening to consider. It is said that if a mind can be controlled via mind control techniques, it would pose a threat greater than a nuclear bomb. Regrettably, I have to tell those of you who might have missed the headlines: We have reached that place.

An article on the Website Democratic Underground discusses a 1980s document titled "From PSYOP to MindWar: The Psychology of Victory," coauthored by then-Colonel Paul E. Vallely, the Commander of the 7th Psychological Operations Group, United States Army Reserve, Presidio of San Francisco, California. The article is a military discussion paper that is a chilling directive for the future. It states that Mind War should employ subliminal brainwashing technology as well as weapons that directly attack the targeted population's central nervous system and brain functioning: "There are some purely natural conditions under which minds may become more or less receptive to ideas, and Mind War should take full advantage of such phenomena *as atmospheric electromagnetic activity, air ionization, and extremely low frequency waves."*[2] (author's emphasis)

The italics are mine and meant to underscore the reality. In 1980 this was written for the future; that future is now. Secret projects such as H.A.A.R.P. and drones that spy on citizens and can kill from a command at a remote location are the reality of these decisions. The persistent belief that H.A.A.R.P. and chemtrails are involved in mind control may be true. The groundwork has been laid at the highest levels for such programs to be used against citizenry and enemy alike. Indeed, it seems the government may have difficulty telling the two apart.

Vallely ends his discussion paper by pointing out that the media is key in reaching virtually all people on Earth to ensure that the "correct" message is reinforced. Accepting that news media is now entertainment, infiltration of propaganda is assured.

The Neuroscience of War

In the early 1990s I met Masahiro Kahata at a crop circle workshop in New York City. Masahiro is a scientist and computer programmer working in the realm of brainwave technology. He worked with Synthia and me in brainwave monitoring experiments inside and near crop circles in England. He holds many patents and is the first person I know to demonstrate equipment that can translate thought into computer action.

The last time we saw Masahiro was in 2009 at the Washington, DC, ExoPolitico Conference. Masahiro brought his newest brainwave equipment and asked us to meet him to try it out. Synthia and I took turns being connected to the computer through a headset. The picture on the screen showed mountains and valleys; the task was to move the cursor through the terrain using mental commands. It was an amazing experience. The type of thought that we typically engage in could not move the cursor. Intention had to be finely focused. This involved bringing both hemispheres of the brain into coherence. When coherence was achieved, the cursor moved through the scenery on command. The feeling that came with the ability was astounding. It felt as though the location of perception actually moved from one side of the head into the center. It was similar to being able to find hidden images from the Magic Eye pictures.

It seemed miraculous that Masahiro had figured a way to take brain signals and turn them into computer commands. His device was designed to help people develop the abilities of their mind by teaching them how to shift into coherence. Once the experience was achieved on the machine, the feeling was imprinted in the body and could be reproduced for other activities such as visualization and remote viewing. Masahiro was giving people relatively inexpensive tools to use for techniques that harness the power of our minds

The military has taken this type of technology five steps beyond. On February 6, 2012, an article in the UK national newspaper, *The Guardian,* described some of the new technology. The headline read "Neuroscience Could Mean Soldiers Controlling Weapons with Minds." The article revealed breakthroughs in neuroscience such as Masahiro's self-development machine applied to war, not as a training tool but as a weapon. The article states, "Soldiers could have their minds plugged directly into weapons systems, undergo brain scans during recruitment and take courses of neural stimulation to boost their learning if the armed forces embrace the latest developments in neuroscience to hone the performance of their troops."[3] The technology is called brain-machine interface (BMI) and is being considered in the use of instructing drones and other military weaponry.

Is this sounding like *Star Trek*'s Borg civilization where humans and machines are melded? Sadly, the neuroscientists whose work is being transformed into military application developed it to benefit humanity through improved treatments for brain disease and mental illness.[4] The security applications were never envisaged. The science they are developing is revolutionary and has the power to change how we relate our minds to matter. Yet in our sad state of affairs, the major funding of this work is for war.

Commanding weapons is only one part of the many ways neuroscience breakthroughs are being converted to military use. On April 8, 2012, the *New York Post* reported that the Pentagon is creating "telepathic troops."[5] This refers to troops wearing special helmets that are fitted with electrodes that allow soldiers to communicate telepathically on the battlefield. Brain signals will be read and used to send warnings without speaking.

The technology works by computers picking up brain signals of soldiers' thoughts and communicating them to control centers. The soldiers are taught to think specific codes to represent specific conditions. For example, they learn codes for "it is safe to proceed," "don't proceed," "target ahead," "fire when ready," and so on. The commands can be transferred to other troops without a word spoken or radio device used. Commands such as "call in helicopter" or "enemy ahead" are presently working; other code structures are about 45 percent accurate according to a report in the *Daily Mail* (UK).[6] Naturally there are intentions for this statistic to improve. The 4-million-dollar synthetic telepathy research project is being conducted at facilities across the country and funded by the Pentagon. Military scientists believe by 2017 that silently communicating soldiers will be in action.[7]

The problem is obvious: We are not always in control of our thoughts. Our minds become unbalanced by fear or anger, and we imagine dangers where none exist. We have all heard a noise in the basement and prepared for an intruder when only a mouse was present! What happens on the battlefield when fatigue, PTSD, or injury creates a distorted picture? The only way to fully control the mind is to eliminate emotion—give the human mind over to the control of the machine for the machine to use as a tool of perception. Then we really will be the Borg.

The mind-machine interface is not the extent of military neuroscience projects. Scientists seeking to alleviate the symptoms of dementia and age related memory loss determined that passing a weak electrical signal through the skull, called transcranial direct current stimulation (tDCS), can improve people's performance in some tasks. The military has begun its own research using tDCS to improve a soldier's ability to spot roadside bombs, snipers, and other hidden threats in a virtual reality training program used by U.S. troops bound for the Middle East.[8] One more technological tool is brain-scanning binoculars. The binoculars pick up on a soldier's unconscious recognition of a potential threat and bring it to his conscious attention. Because the human brain can process images such as targets much faster than we are consciously aware, the binoculars are expected to provide significant advantages in terms of speed and accuracy of information-gathering.[9]

The problem with all this new technology is that we don't know what it will do to people's mental balance. There is a reason we don't consciously process information as quickly as a machine; it overwhelms our mind and emotions. Our soldiers are once again being used as guinea pigs as the military by-passes the quality of being human.

Synthia and I are not the only people concerned about the use of such dehumanizing technology. Scientists, civil rights groups, peace advocates, and allegedly even congressional members such as former representative Dennis Kucinich (Democrat from Ohio), have raised concerns. Maybe that's why redistricting was conducted that stole the congressional seat held by Kucinich. The problem is that the public is not hearing concerns or listening when they do. Media controlled brains are operating as the government planned. Behavioral economist Dan Ariely, author of *Predictably Irrational,* states in a 2008 Ted Partner Series Forum, "If the decision is too difficult for us, we will choose what is chosen for us."[10] What is being chosen for us may not lead where we want to go.

Mind Games out of Control

Interfering with people's minds is an experiment with a high level of uncertainty. What happens when the interference creates an inner tension that breaks? People are bowing now under the current level of daily stress; how much worse will it get if they are bombarded by thoughts and directions that are not in alignment with their own inner integrity? Consider this: Over a six-week period in early 2009, four wives of soldiers at Fort Bragg were murdered by their husbands newly home from Afghanistan. Three of the four domestic murder cases involved Special Operations soldiers.[11] In fact, Fort Bragg is the Army headquarters for Special Forces and Special Operations soldiers. Hundreds have been deployed from this station in the fight against terrorism. Special Operations is the division where mind control experiments are being conducted. Coincidence? Four murders in six weeks perpetrated by people from the same Special Ops facility seems alarming to say the least.

Another curiosity: Pilot Clayton Osbon was flying an A320 commercial aircraft from New York to Las Vegas on March 27, 2012, when he began to act erratically. He scolded air traffic controllers and repeated phrases such as "We're not going to Vegas" and "We're all going down." When he left the cockpit, the copilot took control and directed passengers to tackle Osborn and restrain him, which they did. Osborn was arrested on landing in Amarillo, Texas, with no explanation for what happened.[12] Just a few days earlier, a flight attendant on an American Airlines flight grabbed the public address microphone and ranted for 15 minutes on the plane's public-address system. She said, "I'm not responsible for this plane crashing," and continued in such a vein, making comments that the plane would crash if they didn't go back to the gate.[13]

These two episodes were blamed on exhaustion. The sad truth is that pilots often fly in a state of exhaustion and flight attendants are also sleep deprived with the flight schedules they maintain. That is not unusual. What is unusual is two trained airline personnel melting down within days of each other and saying virtually the same thing. Many people, such as author James Bearden, wonder if they were affected by mind control experiments.

Curious and Curiouser

Another inexplicable event occurred on May 17, 2008, involving twin sisters on the M6 motorway in England, who were observed by police on motorway monitoring cameras. The two women were running in the fast lane. A police car was dispatched and, because the day happened to be one in which the BBC was filming for the reality show *Traffic Cops,* the BBC television crew was dispatched as well. (The account can be viewed on Youtube, accessible through my Website.[14])

The police saw that the women were not behaving normally: They were standing perfectly still in the roadway although several reports had come in to the police control room verifying that two women were running into the fast lanes of the busy motorways. Then, as the police approached, both women ran out into the traffic and were hit by oncoming vehicles. One twin was hit and thrown over a vehicle, and was then driven over by a large truck. They both lay unconscious. Emergency vehicles were called, as they clearly had sustained serious injuries. Suddenly, the second twin moved from a state of unconsciousness to complete recovery, and resumed her irrational behavior by fighting with police. She repeatedly screamed to nearby people, "Call the police."

Then, amazingly, the twin who had been run over got up as well! The twins continued to fight the police and run down the highway. They didn't seem aware of their surroundings, didn't appear to feel pain, exhibited super-human strength, and seemed telepathically connected. They screamed statements such as "They're trying to take our organs" and both repeatedly called for the police. In the end they were subdued, yet it took seven men to contain one of the women and transfer her to an ambulance.

The police on the scene suspected that the women were under the influence of drugs and perhaps had a suicide pact. Medical examinations revealed no drugs or alcohol in either woman's system. A police officer on site speaking to the television film crew said, "I don't think she comprehended in any way how seriously injured she actually was. Very strange, very, very, strange indeed: you start to wonder what is going on here. There is something seriously wrong in this incident," and Detective Superintendent Dave Garrett said, "The reasons for the two events may never be truly known or understood. "[15] When I posted this video on my Website, it received thousands of visitors. Watching it is viscerally upsetting, as it demonstrates something outside of known reality.

A similar encounter occurred near Waterbury in Connecticut. A retired policeman working as a long-run truck driver was traveling on Interstate 84. At about 5 a.m. one day in December 2003, he was driving behind a car whose passenger door opened. To his horror, he watched first as a foot, then a leg, and finally the body of a large man fell out of the car. The man lay crumpled as if severely injured. The truck driver pulled to the side and called 911. The body had bumped, rolled, and skidded about 75 yards. Before he could reach the man, the car he fell out of backed up and one of the other passengers leaned over him. The man then got up as if completely healed, and walked over to the astonished trucker and gave him a few words of marital advice. He then said, "You can't die if you don't really want to." At that, he joined the others in the car and they drove off. The former police officer said, "After having spent 20 years as a police officer on patrol, I can recognize a seriously injured person. And he was a seriously injured person."[16]

Concluding Thoughts

People have a built-in sense of self and a need for internal consistency and integrity. Integrity means wholeness; when we are pushed too far, we fragment. Mind control experiments are just that: experiments. Although they might bring great returns on the battlefield, we have no idea what the cost will be to the individual who becomes part of the machine mind. In this dilemma we are faced with the ultimate opportunity to understand the power of being human. What is it that makes us different from a machine?

If it is true that the military is using telepathy enhanced with technology such as ionized particles and ULF waves, then we are faced with a difficult dilemma: Can we be sure the voice we hear that compels us in a particular direction is our own? Is some of the synchronicity that binds events together orchestrated by a military agenda? This is difficult territory and one with which I have familiarity.

One night in August 2000, as I was falling asleep, I heard a distinct voice in my head say, "It's time to go public with this now." There was a strong emphasis on the word "now." I knew exactly what this meant: It was time for me to announce findings from a two-year study that 80 percent of crop circles in England during that time could be explained as man-made events. Making such an announcement was emotionally devastating. It was an admission that I had inadvertently led people down a path that wasn't completely true. The immensity of what that meant on a spiritual level was crushing, and the decision to reveal my findings was one I had been avoiding. And then I heard the voice.

The next morning I awoke up to the telephone ringing. Picking up the receiver, I was greeted by a television producer at the BBC. "Hi Colin," she said. "I woke up this morning and had the feeling you might have something for us on the crop circles. Do you?" At one time, when crop circle mania was at its height, I received regular calls from this BBC contact. She hadn't called me in years. Later that day, a BBC crew met me at a crop circle at Alton Barnes, where I made the statement that ostracized me from the crop circle community.

Some of the people who have heard this story are convinced that the BBC woman and I were interfered with and thoughts were put in our heads by the military. As my work fell apart, I, too, wondered if this was true. How can we tell the difference between mind control and interacting with the higher mind?

Synthia was quite clear in her conviction that the voice was not mind control. She reasoned that if the voice was in alignment with my inner truth, congruent with my inner sense of self, and heightened my sense of coherence, then my mind was not being overridden with a command; it was interfacing with higher consciousness. I had to agree. Revealing my research results was incredibly difficult, yet it was the truth and speaking it enhanced my inner congruence. This has become the measure I use to test feelings of being compelled: Does acting increase or decrease my sense congruence?

The unethical use of machines such as drones to spy on and kill while controlled by individuals in an underground bunker thousands of miles away and the use of technology to override another's mind—these things are criminal offenses. We must stand for full government transparency and be prepared for a future based on the decisions we are making today.

As so often happens, science fiction seems a prelude to science. It sometimes appears as though a new idea has to reach our imagination before it can reach our intellect. If we look back to *Star Trek* and consider Jean Luc Picard as he faced this dilemma as a Borg, he provides the answer. What we are as humans—a mind with will, intent, and heartfelt emotion—is far more powerful than what we can currently imagine.

Bridging the Edge

Future Visioning *by Wayne Mason.*

A paradigm changes when people stop believing in the old one. Then we are available to see something new. We may have been previously exposed to these new ideas and perhaps scoffed at their impossibility. The vanguards of the new are often ridiculed because the view they present is incomprehensible, whereas the old still holds sway. The stairway to change is climbed in stages. Consider the metaphor in the blockbuster movie *Avatar*. The audience is wooed by the worldview of Pandora and is introduced to a way of relating through senses, feelings, and intuition. Greed and exploitation are outmoded. Sadly the movie did not develop this theme to resolution and demonstrate the power of collective consciousness. It ended in the typical fashion of solving problems through war and destruction, but what if there were another way?

Chapter 17:
Other Minds,
Other
Intelligences

Throughout this book we have been discussing interaction with another form of consciousness. We call it a higher mind, higher consciousness, or orchestrating principle. We also describe it as related to UFO and mysterious phenomena. At this point, we need to try to define what it is and look at its actions to determine its motivation. A tall order indeed!

My conclusion is that we are interacting with many different minds and multiple intelligences that fall into two groups. There is the mind/intelligence of interaction with UFOs, orbs, and those who have died. Then there is the orchestrating force that brings the right people to the right place for interactions to occur. It creates synchronicity and guides our contact with each other as our intentions are coordinated. To say that we are intermingling with just one intelligence is akin to proposing that humans are the only life form on Earth.

Each type of engagement may represent a specific life form—a different "species" in a multi-dimensional universe. Like ourselves, each is a spiritual force embodied in form, although we cannot say for sure what the force or the form is. The beings might be called extraterrestrials, angels, light beings, demons, ghosts, astral bodies, wayebs, guides, totems, ascended masters, or any number of names. They may come from other planets or be associated with different dimensions of this planet. They may be souls who have died or are yet to be born. They may come from our future. They may be our higher selves. They may be all of these things. They are other voices, other nations, traveling with us in the matrix.

What is the intelligence behind the orchestrations? It is easier to look at what it does rather than what it is. It interacts with the deepest part of who we are and seems to drive the direction of our evolution. It coheres, whispers in our mind, creates dreams and influences future direction. It is primarily invisible and perhaps has even cloaked itself within us. It functions in our subconscious, is invasive, and, though respectful of our self-will, manages to get its own way. It is both us and something else. It permeates the whole structure of humanity, possibly through the function of our mirror neurons and a thousand other neural networks we have yet to discover. This intelligence infuses, binds together, and evolves all life forms of all species of all dimensions in reality.

If reality and consciousness are holographic, then the higher mind we speak of is that of the unified whole. From this perspective, the evolution of the whole is the motivation behind the orchestration. Current statistics from climatologists say the mean extinction for three-fourths of the Earth's surface at the current rate of environmental decline is calculated to occur in the year 2039.[1] What harm humans are perpetrating might represent a breach in the fabric of reality so significant that many intelligences are involved in supporting our choice toward a shift in paradigm.

We cannot be forced along this path; we can only be influenced. The voice within that resonates with the holographic matrix can be touched, and when it is, we can be compelled to follow. However, we do so with free will. Currently, humanity operates from personal advantage and greed, believing that we are in competition with other aspects of the whole. War is the solution we use to solve our problems. Hawkins said that we can never fully see the new mindstep we are going through; it is too foreign from our current view. Terms like galactic citizen sounds like a bad comic strip story, yet that is where we are headed. We truly are at the edge of reality.

Entangled

The other voices with whom we are in dialogue exist in a range of frequency. Some are closer to us in form and consciousness, and are consequently more easily contacted. Others are vibrations of light, sound, and thought that impress our senses and stimulate our feelings. Still others take forms we can identify with or manifest their energy for short periods on electronic media so that we can converse. Suggestions are made through these links: Scientists are impressed with radical new ideas, engineers are inspired to see new forms of technology, and everyone who interacts is brought closer to the inner-self, which resonates with the larger whole. The answers we need are all inside at deep and primal levels. The interactions underway are helping us access these answers.

Whatever the beings are that we call ET (extraterrestrial), I do not feel we need to prove they are here or real. For me, they are fact because I have experienced them. Others will have to find their own proof. They are closest to us in form and are the ones who appear and communicate. They are involved with us, are interested in our dilemmas, and influence our affairs.

It is impossible to truly know their motives. Some people are convinced that there are good ET's and bad ones. For me, they are engaged with us in the overlap of dimensions and caught in the travail of the crossroads we are in. Ascertaining their intent can only come through communication.

The following stories are examples of what is occurring across the world.

Our Field

On November 17, 1976, crop circles were not yet known in England and extraterrestrials were only talked about in fringe magazines. Steven Spielberg's classic movie *Close Encounters of the Third Kind* would not be out for another year. Polite people didn't discuss UFOs; that was for the crazies. So when two friends, Joyce Bowles and Ted Pratt, had a close encounter—one that predicted the coming of crop circles—there was no incentive for them to come forward and tell their story. Nonetheless, they did. The very next day they brought the ridicule of the nation upon themselves when they told what had happened to them.

The incident occurred when the couple was driving along the A272 toward Winchester. They were about to turn left onto a narrow country lane at Chilcomb to pick up Joyce's children from a friend's home. As Joyce steered the little Morris Mini left, an orange light suddenly dropped out of the sky and stopped at ground level behind a high hedge. Suddenly, the car engine stalled, the lights tripled in brilliance, and the car came to a stop on a grassy verge.

Several tall beings emerged from the direction of the light. One proceeded to the driver's side window and peered into the vehicle.

Joyce and Ted both described the being as tall, white, and having bright red eyes. The next thing either remembered was that the beings and the light were gone, and the car engine suddenly started. Several hours had passed. They drove in a greatly confused state to the nearby farmhouse where Joyce's children waited.

Several days later they were involved in a second event that occurred in the same area. This time the couple experienced two hours of missing time and then found themselves several miles away near Southampton. During the period of missing time, they remembered being taken toward the light and into a craft. They were shown what looked like some kind of star chart with many different symbols consisting of circles, circles inside concentric rings, and dumbbells (two circles connected with a straight line). They received an odd telepathic transmission from the beings. They heard, "This is our field." They had no idea what was meant by those words.

The following year (1977) in that field, the first circle of the modern era of crop circles appeared. Over the next few years, the designs would evolve to include all the symbols on the chart that Joyce and Ted had seen, all within easy sight of "Our Field." One thing on which the couple refused to elaborate was what they called a serious and dire message given to them by the beings about the future health of the environment. Years later, I personally investigated this case, talking to Ted Pratt's wife and Joyce Bowles's close friends, Peggy and Don Tuersley. Though I learned much more than is public knowledge, the message was never disclosed. My gut tells me that it was the same message heard during an unknown transmission that interrupted a news program in 1977 (as we will see).

Interestingly, the location of the field where the Bowles/Pratt encounter occurred was close to my home and those of Pat Delgado, Busty Taylor, and Terence Meaden, the first coordinated research team. It was within 500 yards of the public house that was frequented by Doug Bower and Dave Chorley, the men who claimed to have made all the early crop circles. The stage was set, the actors ready, and, out of the mix, the crop circle mystery was born.

A strange collaboration of the Pratt/Bowles event came about 34 years later. Synthia and I met with a team of researchers in Wales in August 2010 to talk with "Ken," a retired policeman. Ken told us that on the same night that Joyce Bowles and Ted Pratt saw the tall beings, he also saw such a being on the outskirts of Bristol, about 40 miles east of the field where Joyce and Ted had their encounter. Ken was returning home after his shift when he saw what he called a very tall "spaceman"[2] standing outside the main gates of the military complex in Bristol. It would appear more was going on than apparent.

Radio Introductions

Until my regression with Professor Jim Harder in 1997, I had no memory of my childhood experience with ET. I heard the TV announcement of Ted and Joyce after their experience and found it curious, especially because it occurred so close to my home. My first involvement with extraterrestrial and the idea that they were concerned with life on this planet occurred on November 26, 1977, when I heard the unknown transmission.

I have always had a fascination with radios and communication systems. On that night in 1977, I was unpacking my first tape recorder, purchased to record material broadcasting on an intricate communications system that I had constructed. The tape recorder was a brand new, 5 ¼ inch, reel-to-reel machine measuring 2 feet square and 6 inches deep. To activate the machine to record, I had to select two levers and then adjust sound filters to remove background interference. I was figuring out the machine and, as a test run, selected "record" as I slid the microphone across the carpeted floor toward the TV set. It was 5:10 p.m. and I had the Independent Television News program running in the background, only partly listening as I worked.

Almost immediately, the picture on the screen began to break up into small speckles or dots, and the news presenter's voice broke and faded into the background. The news program covered central-southern England and was broadcast from one of two large transmitters at Hannington. Within moments the picture was completely gone and the newscaster's report was replaced by a strange, modulated mechanical voice. For the next six minutes, this voice gave a strong message to nearly a million people. (A recording of the actual message in full can be heard on my DVD *Conscious Circles.*[3])

This is a portion of the transcript that southern England heard on *ITN News,* (Independent Television Network, transmitted on Channel 3) on November 26, 1977, and that I recorded:

This is the voice of Vrillon, a representative of the Ashtar Galactic Command speaking to you. For many years you have seen us as lights in the skies. We speak to you now in peace and wisdom as we have done to your brothers and sisters all over this, your planet Earth.

We come to warn you of the destiny of your race and your world so that you may communicate to your fellow beings the course you must take to avoid the disaster which threatens your world and the beings on our worlds around you. This is in order that you may share in the great awakening, as the planet passes into a New Age....

The New Age can be a time of great peace and evolution for your race, but only if your rulers are made aware of the evil forces that can overshadow their judgments.

Be still now and listen, for your chance may not come again.

All your weapons of evil must be removed. The time for conflict is now past and the race of which you are a part may proceed to the higher stages of its evolution if you show yourselves worthy to do this. You have but a short time to learn to live together in peace and goodwill.

Be aware also that there are many false prophets and guides operating in your world. They will suck your energy from you—the energy you call money—and will put it to evil ends and give you worthless dross in return.

Your inner divine self will protect you from this. You must learn to be sensitive to the voice within that can tell you what is truth and what is confusion, chaos and untruth. Learn to listen to the voice of truth which is within you and you will lead yourselves onto the path of evolution.

This is our message to our dear friends. We have watched you growing for many years as you too have watched our lights in your skies. You know now that we are here and that there are more beings on and around your Earth than your scientists admit.

The transmission ended with these words: *"We are now leaving the plane of your existence."*

The interrupted television news broadcast caused hundreds of calls to the police and television studio. Four in-depth investigations by the Independent Broadcasting Authority (IBA) and the British government could not account for the event. I won't try to prove that this was a real transmission from an extraterrestrial source. I will say that at the time this occurred, there was no known technology that could override and replace a national broadcast for six minutes. No one since has claimed to have hoaxed it.

I have often wondered whether this first recording on my new machine was more than a coincidence and was actually an orchestrated event. Since I began talking about this incident, a number of people have e-mailed to say that they also heard the transmission that day. Many reported feeling compelled to turn on the TV or were otherwise unexpectedly hearing the transmission. The message was ahead of its time, geared more for today than 40 years ago. Yet even for those who dismissed it as a hoax, a seed was planted. Forty years ago the decisions were being made that make today what is; apparently, the need was seen for intervention.

Another interesting correlation occurred with a crop circle that arrived on August 15, 2005, forming at the base of the second television transmitter that covered southern England. It was a spectacular crop circle consisting of a large-headed being with almond-shaped eyes holding what looked like a CD-type disc covered in patterns. The disc was constructed of bits representing an ASCI computer code with a high degree of mathematical sophistication. When it first appeared, no one knew what the patterns meant. My friend and fellow researcher Paul Vigay, sadly no longer with us, deciphered the binary sequences on the disc and translated them into decimal equivalents. He then looked them up in the ASCII character set to reveal the message. Remarkably, it was virtually the same as that heard on the television news broadcast, and I suspect also the same as conveyed to Joyce Bowles and Ted Pratt. It read: "Beware the bearers of FALSE gifts & their BROKEN PROMISES. Much PAIN but still time (unknown damaged word here). There is GOOD out there. We Oppose DECEPTION . Conduit CLOSING (BELL SOUND)."

I think we can say the message was sent.

Edward Belbruno's Route to the Moon

One interaction with a higher mind that inspired a scientific innovation happened to mathematician Edward Belbruno, a friend who is affiliated with Princeton University. His research focuses on celestial mechanics, dynamical systems, astrodynamics, astrophysics, and cosmology. From 1985 to 1990 he was an orbital analyst at the Jet Propulsion Laboratory (JPL), a NASA center in Pasadena, California, where he developed the first systemic application of the Chaos Theory to space travel. His theory, called the Fuzzy Boundary Theory, provided a means to construct very low-energy paths for spacecraft to obtain lunar orbit.

His theory was initially developed in 1986 to provide a way to get a hypothetical spacecraft to the Moon. He was given only a few months to come up with a trajectory to the Moon that would go into orbit with no fuel, known as ballistic capture. Such trajectories did not exist at that time; his colleagues concluded that they did not exist. Because he was an artist, Edward explored finding a desired route to the Moon by doing a painting of the Earth-Moon system using bold brushstrokes in Van Gogh style, working very fast so he wouldn't be thinking and being guided instead by his unconscious. Examining his finished work, the pattern of brushstrokes revealed the desired trajectory, which was then found using a computer simulation with realistic modeling and the final conclusion gave rise to a new way to get to the Moon with much less fuel. This route and accompanying methodology was a new approach to space travel; it promised to save substantial money to place a spacecraft in orbit around the Moon because no fuel was required.

Originally, Edward's application of the Chaos Theory was not accepted. He says, "These ideas were not well received since they were so new and not the way they (astrodynamicists) did trajectory design at the time. In January 1990 my boss told me that I was to be let go from my regular mission design job—mainly because the work I was doing in my spare time of ballistic capture transfers was not appreciated." Edward explained that his low-energy trajectory made the current three day trip to the moon a two year venture. He added that his discovery would require "smaller spacecraft that would be less expensive and require fewer people to be employed by the Center which, I was told, was not desirable."[4]

Edward's theory was put to the test when Japanese lunar orbiter probe, Hagoromo, lost its transmitter and was unable to communicate with its command probe, *Hiten*, which was orbiting Earth. Using conventional trajectory transfers, the command probe was unable to enter lunar orbit to re-establish contact due to low levels of fuel. Edward devised a ballistic capture trajectory that required little fuel and saved the Japanese mission. The incident was published in an article entitled "Through the Fuzzy Boundary: A New Route to the Moon" in Carl Sagan's *Planetary Report* (May/June 1992). What few realize, however, is that Edward believes his ideas may have come from another mind. He has agreed here to share some of his inspiring story.

"The fact that I was being let go from my job was a terrible experience. I was shattered. I felt like my life was over. Later that day I asked the Universe to help me. I was helped way beyond my comprehension."

Two months later, in April 1990, Edward says an engineer named James Miller arrived at his door. Miller was asking for help with the compromised probe mission that Japan was desperate to salvage. Edward says:

The moment he asked me, the solution suddenly jumped into my mind, like a light going off. It was a solution I had not considered in the previous five years. It was weird, using the Sun's gravity, requiring Muses A (*Hiten*) to go one million miles *beyond* the Moon, then falling back to the Moon and into lunar orbit using my theory of ballistic capture, requiring no fuel. I had never thought of this before. But yet, I felt confident it would work. I had an inner knowing.

The engineer did not believe the agency would go for it, but they did. The new method would take the probe five months to achieve orbit, substantially less than the two years of Edward Belbruno's original theory. In April 1992, the *Hiten* probe was taken out of Earth's orbit to begin the five-month journey into Lunar orbit using little to no fuel.

In the meantime, Edward decided to move from Pasadena to St. Paul, Minnesota, with his girlfriend, Elena. He says, "While *Hiten* was on its way to the Moon, we were driving to St. Paul, Minnesota in my Jeep Wrangler."

The couple stopped for a dinner break just north of Caspar, Wyoming, and the trip took a new direction. They argued over the route because, for some unknown reason, Elena was determined to take an easterly direction for about 70 miles on a small, one-lane road that ultimately led to Thunder Basin National Grasslands. Eventually Edward agreed, and around 7 p.m. they started on the new route.

Edward reports that once on the road,

it was very unusual. It was slightly foggy and we saw a number of animals near the road, so I had to drive with some caution. The road was only one lane in each direction. After driving for a couple of hours, I noticed not a single car passed us in either direction. This was unusual. I was concerned that we could run out of gas. Then suddenly, I was relieved to see a sign saying we were entering Thunder Basin National Grasslands. I knew that the tiny town of Wright was not far away.

The road headed down a decline as we drove into the basin. Off in the distance, at the bottom of the basin, perhaps about two miles away, I saw a very bright red light. I couldn't imagine what it was and said to Elena that it must be a construction site, not thinking how ridiculous that sounded since it was in a park about 11 p.m. at night. As we got to the bottom of the basin and the road leveled off, I kept my eyes on the red light. As we got closer, maybe a half mile away, I saw that the light was straight ahead. However, I noticed that it was not on the side of the road, but in the center of the road. This concerned me.

As I got closer, about one quarter mile away, I noticed something else that alarmed me. The light was not a point source, but the boundary of a square. This was very strange. I said to Elena that it must be an advertising sign on a tractor trailer that had jack-knifed across the road. My mind was racing to make sense of it. As I got closer, about 50 feet away, I abruptly stopped. The red square was huge and not on the road, but about 20 feet above the road. Its base was about 40 feet, the width of the entire road, and the height was also about 40 feet. I saw it was on the back of a much larger black square object that was on the road and extended well over the road on both sides and with a vertical height of about 60 feet. The red square was right in the center of it.

The road was totally blocked by this object. I could not get around it. It seemed clear that whatever it was, it intended to block the road. It wasn't doing anything except sitting there, silently. Elena and I just stared at it. The light was bright, but you could look at it. Elena was scared and I was totally stunned. I had seen nothing remotely like this before. Being a scientist, I was completely at a loss for words.

It just sat there—then suddenly it lifted off of the road. It was silent. It was amazing to see. It stopped rising and the base of the black square hovered at about 50 feet off of the ground for about 20 minutes. I was totally in awe. Then suddenly, the black square with the red square boundary in the center of it, started to rotate. As it rotated, it became clear that we were looking at the back of a large rectangular craft about 100 feet long. It stopped rotating and the long rectangle, mainly black with a slight bluish glow, hovered off the road. It just stayed still. Elena said that I should walk under it. I said, "No way, it could be dangerous" and then said, "Why don't you walk under it?" So, there we sat in the car watching this thing hover above the road. It was completely silent. There was nothing threatening about it. It was almost as if it was doing this as a demonstration.

Suddenly it did a little oscillating motion, then slowly moved away silently, going north. It was very pleasant and beautiful. My mind was racing to try and make sense of this. When it was a couple of miles north with the red square barely visible in the back, I got out of my Jeep and stood in the road, watching the rectangle fly away. Then I got back into my car and just drove away on the road. I was in a daze.

As I drove away in shock, not noticing where I was going, I felt Elena shaking me strongly, saying, 'They're waiting for us!' She was very frightened. I looked ahead and saw an intense white light oscillating in a rapid fashion, like a strobe light, on the left side of the road. I wanted to stop. However, it was frightening. When I slowed down, I saw a number of things and a lot of activity. This situation was very scary, with the bright strobe like light going on and off rapidly. When I went to stop, Elena started screaming very loudly and she started to panic, threatening to jump out of the car. I decided not to stop. We made it to a hotel about an hour later. It should have been 12 midnight or so, but it was 3 a.m.

In St. Paul, a month later, I happily found out that *Hiten* successfully arrived at the Moon on the new transfer. Carl Sagan asked me to write an article about the rescue of *Hiten* for his journal, *The Planetary Report*. As I was proof reading it, I ended by saying that *Hiten* arrived at the Moon on October 2, 1991.

I scratched my head then had the startling realization that when my car was blocked by the huge rectangular craft in Wyoming, that was precisely when *Hiten* arrived at the Moon!

After this realization, it was like I was hit by a lightning bolt. Was this a coincidence? If not, what did it mean? Was I being informed that *Hiten* had arrived? Why was this being done? Was my work on the transfer influenced? If so, by what?

Since then, my view of the world has changed. I had always thought that the human race was in control of its own destiny. My experience indicated that this was not the case. Our reality is far more complex than I ever imagined, and is not what it seems at all."

The story of the rescue of *Hiten* and Edward's theory is written up in the book *Fly Me to the Moon* (Princeton University Press, 2007). (His Websites are *www.edbelbruno.com* and *www.belbrunoart.com.*)

Concluding Thoughts

Through the years of my research I wasn't sure of the motives of the ET. Hearing the stories of abductees, I wondered if parts of the extraterrestrial presence were malevolent. Some abduction researchers speculated that a genetic program is underway to in some way preserve one of the ET species from extinction.

My concerns undoubtedly rose from the mindset of distrust that is currently prevalent. The prevailing belief is that human action is naturally geared to personal advantage and therefore no one can be fully trusted because self-gratification is the highest goal. In this mindset, the unaccountable and frightening actions of another species can only be seen as dangerous.

Interactions with the phenomena have changed me. What I have come to believe is that the motive of the ET presence is prompted from the need to stabilize our actions. They are giving us a small breathing space in which to evolve toward needed emotional coherence to reverse the damage we have done to this planet. It is probably not the survival of the planet that is at stake, but human survival, along with a few thousand plant and animal species living on it.

Each of us—human, ET, angel, ghost—is responsible to hear and follow the voice within that is connected to the larger whole. It is the single directive for finding a life of joy. Edward Belbruno works with orbit trajectories. He maps gravitational forces and the interactions of bodies to find pathways that will transfer an object from one part of space to another. Similar to salmon riding the backwash of currents to swim up a waterfall, Edward's work finds ways to ride the forces inherent in nature. He says, "Each of us has a pathway that is prepared for us. It may not be where we think we want to go, but when we are in synch with it, life flows. When we are not, we have unnecessary struggle."

Finding the path that has been designed for our passage requires listening to the cues around us that interact with our inner sense of self to create the voice that compels and inspires us forward. The evolution of consciousness requires us to pay attention at a level few have been tuned into. This is where we are today: learning how to listen.

Chapter 18: Homo Noeticus: The Conscious Human
By Synthia Andrews

The mindstep we are taking involves more than modifying how we think; it involves using new tools of perception. If evolution of our consciousness is the motivation behind the intelligent force that is compelling us, then our abilities and capabilities must advance in order to make connection. In doing this we are becoming the New Human.

New levels of reality represent new frequencies; different dimensions vibrate at different rates. As we engage high-strangeness events, change is initiated as pathways of perception in our body-mind are nudged open. These avenues and the abilities they enable are already present and functioning. We are wired to participate in greater levels of reality; the wiring has only been waiting for our awakening.

Words carry preconceived ideas, and the topics in this book can stimulate our biases. We need to move beyond semantics to the underlying experiences that words represent. For some, discussion of spirituality sounds too New Age or even religious. Those of that sensitivity are often interested in phenomenology and not in discussions of indwelling consciousness. Others feel phenomena take our attention away from spirit. Perhaps we can look at the two as different sides of the same coin. Spirituality means infused with spirit. Everything is infused with spirit; the universe is a spiritual experiment. Phenomena occur as the result of spirit moving in form. The two are reflections of the other.

In the early chapters of this book, Colin revealed that the orchestration of events between crop circle-makers, researchers, and enthusiasts occurred because people listened to an inner voice and followed feelings of being compelled. We read of Edward Belbruno's drive down silent roads in the middle of the night to fulfill a call to a meeting he had no idea he was to attend. To engage non-ordinary reality, we are asked to step outside the boundaries of rational behavior and be willing to trust a communication that is happening on a deep, inner level. We don't necessarily know what we are communicating with or why; we can only follow our feelings. Many people are willing, but they are not sure how.

Developing Perception

Developing perception requires paying attention to the body and the mind while understanding and using the emotions. Non-ordinary reality engages us differently than day-to-day life. During high-strangeness events, we are communicating and receiving information that is carried on waves of subtle energy. To perceive this information, we use processing functions that are normally subconscious. The exchange occurs through complex interactions among our body, mind, and emotions. To fully engage the non-ordinary, we need to pay attention to our inner voice and observe our emotions, felt sensations, and intuition as we communicate with another mind. The following are some characteristics of the experience:

- People feel prompted to act by a sense of urgency or need to move. They may have no idea of where they want to go or why; they just need to move. When they do, it "feels right." It is often described as a magnetic attraction; when moving toward the pull, the body relaxes and a sense of flow can be felt. Resisting it provokes agitation. Following the sensation of opening leads the circle-maker to the exact field to place the crop circle, takes the researcher to the spot where the UFO appears, prepares us to dialogue.

- Communications are often imprinted directly into a person's mind, sometimes as an image or as words, but more often as an inner knowing. For example, someone will know they need to drive down a certain road, meditate on a specific design, or explore a certain mathematical equation. They have an image that an inner confidence and/or excitement carries into action.

- Emotion is the key to communication and motivation. Emotions communicate intent and create connection. The purely biological fear people can experience when faced with the unexplained is sometimes alleviated through the communication of waves of calming, peaceful emotions that convey safety. This type of transference seems to accompany many encounters.

- Following a compulsion or inner knowing produces elevated brainwave states in the super-beta or even gamma range. These are states of singular focus and high creativity. Other sights and sounds disappear. This is often accompanied by transcendent emotions of gratitude, awe, wonder, and compassion.

- During high-strangeness events, ordinary markers of reality, such as time, take on new attributes. The ambiance suddenly changes and it can feel like being in a bubble. Time can be extended so that a lot can happen in a short period, or nothing happens yet hours have gone by.

- When communication is received, the idea or thought arrives with a sense of satisfaction and relief. Often a rush of energy will move through the body accompanied by tingling, goose bumps, or vibration.

- Connection with another mind is a whole body event. The body opens and the mind becomes receptive. Transcendent emotions, goose bumps, and other physical confirmations are felt.

- Fear is the natural response to the unknown. Overwhelming fear can close perceptions, shut down the mind, and freeze the body. Because the function of fear is to provide safety, maximizing a sense of safety can help manage fear. It may seem obvious, but a meditation practice, prayer, belief, or fallback position that provides a sense of safety is a good thing to have and to practice on a daily basis. For safety to be present when needed, working through our fear needs to be second nature.

- Danger is conveyed with feelings of dread, reluctance, and withdrawal. Continuing to go forward produces extreme discomfort, even causing shivers and weakness. Sometimes these are signs of overwhelm and the danger is an internal break with the continuity of reality. Whether the risk is physical danger or psychological overwhelm, the signals need to be considered.

Contact with non-ordinary reality is likely to increase as we move forward. Being able to discern messages and respond provides us with inspiration for technological ideas, scientific advances, and new awareness. Receiving and responding depend on the development of our perception; the more connected we are to our body, the better able we are to read energy and understand our emotions, allowing better navigation through the changing terrain. (For those who wish to explore this further, my books *The Path of Energy* (Career Press/New Page Books, 2011) and *The Path of Emotion* (Career Press/New Page Books, 2013) provide easy-to-use guidelines.)

Is the Body Changing?

Developing the skills necessary to travel in different realms requires mental, psychological, and energetic adjustment. New neural networks are created, but is it possible that our physical body is changing, too?

In recent years there has been an explosion of reports of exceptional new abilities, especially in children. There have always been cases of child savants, but the incidence seems to be rising. Usually such children are wired just a bit differently; they may be autistic or have an attention deficit disorder that gives rise to gifts of understanding, musical ability, scientific aptitudes, or psychic perceptions. These progeny are often called Indigo Children. Dr. Andrija Puharich, a respected parapsychologist, studied the abilities of these children as far back as the 1960s, calling them Star Kids.

The aptitudes of these young people demonstrate the plasticity of the brain. Imagine a young boy in China who can see in the dark reading a book in pitch blackness. Daniel Tammet sees numbers in his head as pictures, shapes, and patterns. He sees textures and flashes of light, ripples across surfaces that translate somehow to the answers to mathematical problems. Daniel is able to perform advanced mathematical calculations instantly in his head, correct to decimal points into the 100s. The powers these kids have demonstrate that we are capable of much higher functioning than is expressed under normal circumstances. Accessing these greater abilities is the evolution underway.

Many people remark that today's children seem to access more of their inner abilities. They intuitively know things beyond their training and are psychically open, demonstrating telepathic and even psychokinetic abilities. This means they can communicate by transferring thought and can mentally affect matter. If this represents the New Human, then we are developing the psychic side of our nature. The term coined by noted author John White, parapsychology and consciousness researcher, is "Homo noeticus."

Many of the researchers who study Indigo Children believe they are part of a hybrid human/extraterrestrial race. I don't claim to know the answer to this question, but I wonder if it isn't more about the entire species awakening. As humans we have extraordinary spiritual capabilities that have been submerged, especially since the industrial revolution. When children are born, they are still connected to the realm they just left with memories and abilities adults have long forgotten. In the hands of parents who cannot recognize, hear, or see the dimension they come from, the pathways are soon closed down.

Right now, people across all spectra are awakening. They are better able to recognize the innate wisdom and connection to pre-life dimension that exist in their children. Children don't have to close down in order to fit in and can express more of their potential. This may even be allowing high-level souls to come through. In actuality, we don't really know what extraterrestrial beings or high level souls really are. They may well be the same thing. We can say that today's children represent our evolution of consciousness.

Mystics from all religions describe humans as light beings; the greater our spiritual awareness, the greater the radiance of our light. Quantum physics also declares that light is the building block of matter. Current studies in cell biology agree. Our DNA seems to express light, and light is the carrier of information that organizes our body. The pineal gland is especially calibrated to receive and respond to light. If evolution begins with the expansion of inner light, might we begin to see changes in these physical structures?

DNA Transformation

Much attention is paid to the idea that DNA was originally 12-stranded and that awakening our consciousness means restoring these disabled strands. Physically, DNA is a double-stranded helix. The idea that it was once 12-stranded was developed in a channeling session by Barbara Marciniak. After speaking with Barbara two years ago when she wrote the foreword to my book *The Path of Energy,* I came to a different understanding: that the channeling suggested that the two strands of physical DNA have counterparts of additional strands of light. In the Super String Theory of physics, the Universe is made of vibrating strings of light. The deepest, most indivisible level of matter is made of patterns of vibration that provide form. DNA is a superconductor, storing light and information to organize the body. Why would it not reduce to vibrations of light?

Though this may seem farfetched, an article published in a peer-reviewed journal called *Cell Biophysics* revealed the importance of light and DNA as far back as 1984. The article declared that the biological light produced during metabolism, called biophotons, is largely released from the DNA within each cell. More importantly, the light is highly coherent.[1] This means that all the photons in the light produced by DNA are aligned in the same direction. Coherence is the quality in lasers that allows them to be used for creating holograms. Does the light produced by DNA create three-dimensional perception? Does it interact with how we perceive and experience reality?

Recent research discovered the existence of four-stranded DNA.[2] Immediately people wondered if this means we are evolving and heading toward our original 12-stranded condition. However, the four-stranded DNA are only found in the phase of cell division where DNA is replicating, the S-phase, and the quadruple-helix appears at the moment to be an error in replication. This may explain how cell mutations result in cancer. This is very exciting news for healing and perhaps even preventing cancer, but four-stranded DNA doesn't necessarily indicate evolution. On the other hand, the research is still developing and is one to watch in the future.

Despite the number of strands that are actually present, the evolution of consciousness may best be represented by the amount of internal light that DNA transmits. Biophotons emitted by DNA were first discovered by Professor Fritz-Albert Popp at the International Institute of Biophysics in Germany. His research shows that biophoton emissions radiate through our cellular network conveying information.[3] Interactions with new frequency and higher mind seem to impact the vibration of our DNA and its capacity to store, conduct, and emit light. This could mean the mystics were correct and transformation is the result of increasing our inner light.

One way to amplify light within is to increase the coherence of our energy field. This happens when our body, mind, and emotions are working in concert with our spirit. Masahiro Kahata's machine trains people to create inner coherence. The effect was powerful and produced immediate ability to focus and use mental energy. The same effect can be achieved through a meditation practice.

Experiments with water crystals conducted by Dr. Masaru Emoto reveal that the energy of thoughts and emotion impact form. His unorthodox experiments show that different thoughts and emotions effect the formation of water crystals and produce different patterns. Emoto demonstrated this by having people project specific emotions and thoughts toward water as it froze, then examined the crystals that formed under a microscope. Water subjected to thoughts of love while freezing produced crystalline structures that were more elaborate and symmetrical than those that formed when focused on by people holding negative thoughts.[4]

Pineal Gland

The pineal gland is the size of a grain of sand and sits in the back of the brain at the level of the nose. It receives and responds to light and electromagnetic energy. Spiritually, the pineal gland corresponds to the Third Eye chakra, related to psychic ability, intuition, wisdom, and insight. It is called the doorway to inter-dimensional experiences and a portal to self-awareness, higher consciousness, and states of bliss. In addition to melatonin, the pineal produces a molecule associated with altered states of consciousness, Dimethytyptamine (DMT). DMT is a neuropeptide that acts as a natural hallucinogen. It was first discovered in the human body in the 1950s and is involved with lucid dreaming, near-death experiences, and out-of-body astral travel.[5] It is called the Spirit Molecule and is clearly important to experiencing non-ordinary reality.

Within the past 30 years a new crystal formation made of calcite has been found in the tissue of the pineal gland. Hydroxyapatite crystals are often found in the pineal gland; however, calcite is not. The new crystal formations are small (usually under 20 microns) and have sharp edges with a rough surface. First reported in the late 1970s and early 1980s, early studies thought they were the result of the inability of aging cells to break down calcium.[6] The standard treatment for the prevention of osteoporosis during this time period was the use of excessive amounts of calcium. At the same time, a near epidemic of Vitamin D deficiency, a nutrient needed to metabolize calcium and incorporate it into bone tissue, made this a reasonable theory. However, further study shows these crystals are functional; they are not an accident of metabolism.

A 2002 Israeli study revealed that the calcite crystals interact with external electromagnetic fields. The same study theorized that the crystals interacted with the more usual hydroxyapatite crystals that are piezoelectric, meaning they release electricity when placed under mechanical pressure.[7] Crystals act as transmitters, receivers, and amplifiers of frequency, making them useful in watches and computer technology. It is possible the interaction between two pineal crystals are adjusting levels of light in the body or helping to receive new frequencies. The interaction may result in the release of DMT such that we can shift perception during high-strangeness events. The study of this is only beginning and opens many possibilities.

Remote Viewing: Part of the New Frontier

We are being prompted to use our minds in new ways. We are in constant receipt of psychic information that filters into our awareness as gut instinct and intuition. Making the process conscious is the challenge of shifting into a new paradigm. Dean Radin from the Noetic Sciences defines telepathy as feeling at a distance, and telepathy may be the foundation of ESP abilities. One of the easiest and safest advanced mind techniques to use is remote viewing.

Remote viewing (RV) is the ability to see the details of something from a distance. It is a natural ability that we use on a regular basis. Every time we talk to someone on the phone and create a picture in our mind about where the other person is, we are accessing this ability—however, not necessarily as we might imagine. The vivid pictures of where the other person is standing and what he or she is doing are likely to be manufactured by the imagination. Underneath the details that have been in-filled are other pieces of information. They are below the radar of awareness, yet they convey accurate information. Impressions, shapes, textures, smells, and other non-distinct details reveal true information about the place, event, or person viewed. These fragments of information form the basis for remote viewing.

RV was one of the psychic techniques used by military intelligence talked about in Chapter 16. Impressive results from research conducted between 1972 and 1975 by Ingo Swann, Russell Targ, and Harold Puthoff in a project called Stargate resulted in a recruiting and training program by the military to use RV for the collection of intelligence information.[8] The project was renamed and moved several times, ending within the Defense Intelligence Agency (DIA), where it was supposedly terminated in November 1995. Many of the highly successful viewers from the program now run business consulting agencies based on these techniques.

The ability to see events, scenes and objects is said to be 15 percent accurate with untrained people with no special propensity.[9] However, Colin has met and worked with several of the best RV people in the business. According to remote viewers including Sergeant Edward Dames, Dr. Simeon Hein, and Dr. Courtney Brown, people with natural ability who receive further training can expect to be 60–65 percent accurate. Dr. Joe McMoneagle, one of the military's psychic spies, confirms this in his book *The Ultimate Time Machine*.[10]

According to McMoneagle, key traits required for successful viewing are:[11]

- Self-selection. A person must want to do it.
- Openness to the probability of paranormal information transfer.
- Artistic talent and the capability to express perceptions.
- The capability for imaginative (out-of-the-box) solutions to problems.
- A strong motivation to achieve an outcome.

Colin is himself a very accomplished remote viewer. He reports:

There is something quite shocking about the ability to see distant scenes without any form of physical contact. No wires, no TV, radio or even discussion with others at that distant location—just you, your mind, and clear intent to know something about it. Remote viewing is for me one of the most exciting and mind blowing human abilities.

*My first attempt to remotely view was with my daughter Mandy
when she was about 10 or 11. We carried out an experiment with
me acting as the viewer and Mandy providing targets. The results
were incredible. Mandy sketched a bicycle in a simple side view
with two wheels and a handle bar. She placed her sketch into a
sealed envelope. I was in an adjacent room. Focusing on the envelope, I found myself in a white/gray misty place where I saw two
wheels and a steering wheel. I sketched it as the side view of a
motor car. When we compared the content of Mandy's sketch in
the envelope and my remotely viewed image, it was astounding.
Placing her sketch over mine, the two wheels of her bicycle aligned
with the two wheels of my car. Holding them up to the bright light,
one could see that her handle bars exactly positioned to my car
steering wheel. Everything was drawn to the size and proportion.*

Colin and Mandy's experiment reveals the accuracy of the technique and the problem with interpreting the images received in the
RV. It is a problem that is difficult to overcome. If Colin simply drew
what he saw, the wheels and arc of the steering wheel, it would have
been more accurate than letting his mind interpret what he saw as a
car and infilling details. This is an issue with high-strangeness events as
well. We are conditioned to infill what we perceive with comparisons
to what we know. It is the natural outcome of how the brain searches
for known patterns, responsible for the apophenia discussed in Chapter 12 in relation to electronic voice messages from the dead. It may
explain why witnesses of high-strangeness events often have much
different memories of what happened: Each person's brain supplies
details taken from previous experiences.

As much as we need to clear the mind from past comparisons, we
also need to have faith that what we see has elements of truth. An
experience Colin and I had 15 years later shows the development of the
skill. He reports this event during a trip we took to Orlando, Florida:

*Synthia and I went to separate rooms where Synthia was to focus
on an object in or outside the room and draw a picture of it, not one
of her better skills, placing it in an envelope. From the other room I
used RV techniques to view the target. When something formed on
the milky, dull screen in my mind's eye, I first saw one image, then*

another. The first was an upside-down curved dish with a wing nut in its center. I tried not to interpret and simply sketched it. Then I saw something very different: four definite blades at 90-degree angles, like helicopter blades but stationary and wider in proportion. I drew them as I saw them.

I joined Synthia sure that the experiment had not worked. I showed her my drawings and said, "I've gotten two objects, each very different." Synthia pulled her poorly drawn sketch out of the hotel envelope, saying, "It was supposed to be the ceiling fan in the room."

It was immediately obvious that both of my remote viewing images were correct. My helicopter blades were the four blades of the ceiling fan, and the upside down dish was the fan's lower assembly. Placing my two images together, the complete ceiling fan was captured. There was more to it than that: The position of the stationary blades I had sketched were exactly where the blades had come to rest on the actual fan in the room. The proportions of fan blades and its underbelly design were remarkably accurate. I was truly shocked.

I must say it is aggravating that while I am always blown away by the results, Synthia never is. She seems to find it all totally natural, while for me, it is miraculous.

Learning RV techniques helps the mind receive impressions from other realms. It trains us to let go of preconceived ideas and be open to exactly what is. It is also a technique that can be used to investigate high-strangeness events. This final story of Colin's reveals how helpful it can be.

On January 17, 2012, Colin received a telephone call from friend Annie Haslam, the English rock singer and songwriter for the group Renaissance. Annie now lives in Pennsylvania and had taken a photograph of her backyard during the heavy snowstorm of October 31, 2011, that immobilized New England. Afterward, she put her camera away and forgot about the pictures until she was looking through her computer files on January 16, 2012. Then she found a strange object on the digital photograph. Here is Colin's account:

Of the seven pictures Annie took of her backyard in the storm of October 31st, one had two very clear golden discs on them. The discs appeared almost identical with a symbol engraved on the side of each. They looked to be hovering at very low level over the left-hand boundary of her property. I must admit when Annie sent me a high-resolution copy of the photo, the second taken that day, I had not seen anything quite like it. (It can be viewed on my Website at www.colinandrews.net/UFO-7-Colin_Andrews.html.*)*

I ran through a series of questions with Annie to eliminate obvious possibilities like the reflection from a lamp. From the questions, I learned that she did not remember seeing the discs with her naked eye. We went step-by-step through the room and could not identify a possible light source. I asked her to take pictures of her room so I could see for myself. For obvious security reasons she was hesitant. I soon became convinced that her picture was worth investigating and committed to pursuing a detailed study.

I contacted several experts including UFO researchers, photographic analysts, ancient script and glyph analysts, and my trusted friend and retired British journalist David Haith, for his critical eye and vast experience as a journalist. I spent many weeks investigating this single photograph, along with several world experts who were as intrigued as I. The photographic analysis indicated the object was not a reflection and was definitely outside the room. If this were true, this was one of the best photographs of a UFO ever taken.

After a few days, I asked remote viewer Dr. Simeon Hein, founder of the Institute for Resonance, an RV training center, if he would be prepared to remote view a target I was researching. He agreed. He knew nothing about the photo or what was on it. I approached Simeon via e-mail on January 25, 2012. We agreed that I would place the target in an envelope, seal it, and put a number and date on it. Later the next day Simeon carried out his remote viewing on the contents of the envelope. On January 27th he sent me this: "Hi Colin: Here are the results— Target: Colin's Envelope Picture.[12]

"When I first started viewing this target, it's white and shaped liked a Hershey's Kiss or something like that. Round, hollow,

smooth. Polished. Exotic. But then I keep getting the feeling that it's not real, it only looks that way on the outside, like very good reproduction. And that it could be damaging to you in some way. A trick. You have a choice about this, but proceed carefully. Ask for more information. 'Look before you leap.'"

To say I was surprised is putting it lightly. I was shocked and sure he was wrong. I asked several questions for clarification and he added: "Yes, Colin, I detected a very fine grooved pattern etched on the surface. I can also tell you that I was thinking about the Kecksburg 1965 crashed object a number of times during the session, but kept pushing it out of my mind."

Simeon sent me the notes and sketches produced during the session. In his notes were these comments: Hard, Flat, manmade. Hershey's Kiss, Break Recon. Heavy, round, manmade. Groove pattern, thin slotted, open. A UFO A False. Smoke and Mirrors. Hollow and smooth.

What Simeon said went against the opinion of the experts and everyone who had seen the photographs. According to the viewing by Simeon, this was an exotic-looking object, round and smooth, hollow and looked like UFO or Hershey's Kiss, and was manmade. He also thought this was smoke and mirrors and for some reason kept seeing the famous crashed UFO incident alleged to have taken place near Kecksburg, Pennsylvania, in 1965. What was I to make of this?

My answer arrived in a tearful phone call from Annie on February 20th. She was very upset, saying she had found the answer to the discs and was deeply sorry for the weeks of work involved. She told me that she happened to be sitting in a different room while talking on the phone to her attorney. She looked out the window and noticed the objects were back! This time, however, she could see them as a reflection on the window caused by a halogen lamp. The disc she saw was identical to one of the discs in the picture. The second disc was a distortion on the window, which doubled the effect, showing two reflections. It was as simple as that. She had not realized before because she rarely used the room and thought she had taken the picture from her kitchen window. The views were nearly identical.

The description matched in every detail Simeon's remote view. The halogen lamp was round, hard, and smooth with a groove pattern on its surface. It was hollow and looked very much indeed like the famous ad popular American chocolate known as a Hershey's Kiss. The lamp did resemble what some claimed was a UFO retrieved near Kecksburg, Pennsylvania. The only thing that Simeon was wrong about was that there was no purposeful trick. It was a simple mistake carried too far by enthusiasm.

Russel Targ, one of the original RV specialists, says that one of the most valuable uses for remote viewing is as a tool for self-discovery: "As you get familiar with remote viewing, you realize your awareness fills all of space-time...so it's clear that you couldn't possibly be just made of meat and potatoes."[13] This is the essence of developing our perceptive capacity—to understand that we are much more than we envisage and the universe is more magical than we allow.

Concluding Thoughts

Training ourselves to use techniques such as RV can help us look for answers in new arenas. If this is a holographic universe, within each of us are pathways to the answers we need. We are used to thinking of animals as being less smart than us and inanimate objects contributing nothing to the process of intelligence. Yet intelligence exists in everything around us. Everything is vibration, and all that we know scientifically has come from experimenting with matter. How else did David Bohm discover the cloud of an atom's electron orbits, or Heidelberg discover the uncertainly principle? As we learn to communicate with the intelligence in nature, all manner of possibilities arise.

Instead of seeding clouds with ionized particles to produce rain, can we interact with the intelligence within weather? Not a strange thought to Native people, but to the Western mind, it is impossible. The only way to find out the limits of possibility is to develop our telepathic communication and RV skills and use them.

We often forget that we are surrounded on this planet by intelligent species, neglecting to recognize any intelligence that isn't like ours. I recently went into our rabbit hutch to open the doors to the outside runs. A squirrel had managed to get inside and when I came in, he freaked out. He was hurling himself from wall to wall in frenzy.

I started talking to him and reached out with my mind and emotion to send him a wave of calm safety. He immediately stopped jumping around and looked at me. I created an image in my mind of the hole he used to come into the shed. As I talked, quietly and calmly, he walked by me and went out the hole.

We are in communication with everything around us through our transmission of thought and emotion; half of what we see is a reaction to what we transmit. If we create internal coherence while holding the awareness that communication is occurring, we might begin to change the world and take up the mantle of the New Human.

Conclusion

The first time I saw a crop circle, my mind and emotions were over-whelmed. The sense of awe has never left. In one word, my gut reaction to the reason for the circle phenomenon to arrive is response. They arrived in response to our call for something better, for a way to return to balance. They demonstrate what is possible. The universe supports our call for a different road. The crop circle phenomenon represents a non-human intelligence actively at work through us. We have been responded to and engaged on a united journey with other beings. The route that the phenomenon took was not immediately obvious.

The crossroads we are at is real. The combination of what we value and what we fear has given rise to a way of life that is not sustainable. The secret technologies in this book are only the tip of what governments and corporations employ to try to mitigate the consequences of our actions and control the populace as systems become strained. Robots are made to look like insects to fly inside houses to spy; remote-controlled aircraft are aimed to seek and kill from afar; street lighting poles are cameras and sensors follow our every move. Citizens in England are captured on surveillance film an average of 300 times in the course of one day. What is presented as real food is a mixture of genes joined together from many species with pesticides spliced in as well. We have no idea what the consequences of these choices will be, yet they are undertaken without consent from the public. Right now, we are physically and spiritually in trouble, not from an external intrusion, but from our own imbalance.

On the other hand, every day we discover that there is more to the universe than we can possibly imagine. Wherever we look we find magnificence. CERN takes us into the smallest spaces of subatomic reality to demonstrate that the principles that govern the world are entangled and interactive. Astronomers have found a structure in space estimated to be four billion light years across and held together in one system by unknown and unseen force fields. The smallest and largest objects say the same thing: Everything is connected and everything is interrelated.[1]

Given the extent of what we do not know and what we are discovering, high-strangeness events should not tax our belief; we should be aghast at the prevailing attitude that nothing new is possible. The first human attribute being challenged in the change underway is hubris. We are not the pinnacle of what the universe has to offer, and our technology cannot replace the principles on which life is based. Like our body, the balance of Earth is maintained through principles more intricate and interwoven than our medicine or geoscience comprehends.

The interactions we have with non-human intelligence occur within. The exchange is subtle, sometimes so delicate that it arrives in our brains as our own thoughts or inspirations. Closer reflection, however, reveals a connection to the part of us that is resonating with the larger whole. Dr Rupert Sheldrake postulates the existence of a morphic field that contains the combined developmental information collected by the experiences of a given species. Members of a species have access to this information through resonance of their individual field with that of the group mind, or morphic field.[2] I would take this one step further, suggesting a quantum field of consciousness that contains all reality and to which we have access. Through resonance, higher influences speak, and if we are aligned we receive the message. Once we are open, an enormous range of new potential gathers and forms; new phenomena are signs that the Akashic Field, or morphic field, is responding to our awakening.

Part of this awakening is reflected in changes in our principles; the other part is the development of hidden abilities. The principles and abilities are not new; rather they are forgotten. The principles can be found in indigenous wisdom that honors the Earth and the place of Earth spirits of which humans are only one within the cosmos. The abilities are asleep within us.

Greed and dishonesty in all their forms can no longer be tolerated or sustained. Rather than being a trial and tribulation, what we have before us is an incredible adventure. With our hearts and minds open to what is presenting itself, we can be what nature intended for us: fully functioning spiritual and dimensional beings.

The Next Step

The crop circle interaction, UFO contacts, and other high-strangeness events are a training ground. We are being trained in how to move inside to feel energy, engage other intelligence, exchange information, and find solutions. Unusual phenomena don't just happen; we are an equal part of the equation that creates them. We are the spirit that lives on this plane and interacts with matter in this frequency. Other minds can contact and connect with us, but we are the ones who must act here. Now the question is: What will we do with what we have learned?

The new direction requires sincerity on a level that we rarely feel or from which we seldom act. The mindset that separates us from each other must actively be shifted. When the overriding belief is that we are each ultimately alone, then we will always seek our own advantage and be suspicious of the motives of others. We are not alone; we are part of something much bigger and more incredible than we realize.

Right now we divide ourselves into polarities. We group ourselves into nations, races, political parties, genders, economic classes, and so on. We look for our differences instead of our similarities even though we are much more alike than we are different. Let us return to where this book began: with Native prophecy.

John Kimmey is the current representative for the Hopi Elders. At the 2009 Tipping Point Conference he made a moving speech to the congregation in which he identified the times we are in as the later days of the Hopi Time of Purification. In the address, Kimmey declared that our difficulties are the result of man-made polarities created through the misunderstanding of the laws of nature, which he called universal principles. The imbalances in society, he suggested, can be traced to imbalances within individuals; whatever we carry internally is reflected externally. The disruption of natural cycles, polarized politics, economic extremes, and other social issues are the result of these internal imbalances.

To survive the days of purification, the Hopi instruction is for each of us to examine the imbalances in our personal lives and address the common problems of our times through cooperation "as family rather than neighbors."[3] The tool we have to use is our intention. He says, "This crisis is demanding that we employ a previously overlooked faculty of human nature, namely our Divinity. This faculty has always been active, but almost completely ignored in this last century. It is through the filter of our hearts and emotions that we can reawaken this reliable source of Truth."[4] (John Kimmey's full speech can be read at *www.greatmystery.org/nl/cancun2012hopi.*)

The first reaction I usually encounter when talking to people about global family and consciousness is: "Yeah, but don't forget, we've got terrorism out there and crazy people are killing each other every day." It's true; those things exist. The desire for self-protection is natural. The question is whether our protective actions are working—or is there a better way? Terrorism reflects the degree to which the planet is out of balance. What is it that is out of balance and how can it be adjusted? The only way to find those answers is through communication.

From the perspective of off-planet intelligence, the effects of the actions of Earthlings to the continuity of the fabric of consciousness might look like galactic terrorism. The decision could be made to eliminate us, and no doubt we would consider that an act of evil. Instead, we are experiencing an attempt at engagement and contact seems to have only one aim: communication. Can we extend that same hand to other people, political parties, nations, and even nature?

As Bill Clinton once said, we cannot kill our way out of our troubles. There will always be another enemy and another threat. If we continue down this path, the only answer is to further isolate ourselves—lock our families in the house, never take our eyes off our kids, and experience life through virtual reality. On the other hand, every person has a family; every enemy loves someone. The seeds of what connect us are present and if we can extend our identity from that of self to that of global family, miracles can happen.

Taking Action

The action steps for us to take must come from within. No one from the outside can tell us what we should do or what road is ours. The biggest challenge of this time is learning to listen and trust the senses we left behind. We can take political action, social action, love more, recycle, reuse, and repair. We can live simply and exploit less. Whatever we decide to do has to come from an inner impulse and reflect an inner truth. What is needed now more than ever are practices of reflection to balance the internal polarities each of us carry.

Many people think the current system is broken and we must wait until it collapses before we can create something better. However, as former Republican governor of Louisiana "Buddy" Roemer said, "Washington is not broken, it's bought."[5] We are all complicit. We have given our power to leaders who don't lead. We venerate celebrities who live excessive lives and buy stock in companies that put profits before people and planet. Our choices reveal that we value money, power, and comfort.

The shift underway is about what we value and where we choose to put our attention. We need to support those things that sustain life and reflect on what our actions give birth to. We need to take back our power and realize that we provide the fuel that drives the system. Although inner truth must motivate our actions, here are some suggestions for sparking inspiration:

- Buy products from companies that: treat employees well, give back to the community, and produce products we need with as little impact as possible to the Earth.

- Use the stock market as a tool for doing good things in the world. Invest in companies that produce innovative products and move the world in the direction of the future. Change the criterion from that of making the most return to that of doing the most good with each investment dollar.

- Spend time each day connecting with nature: plant a garden and grow some of your own food, take a walk in the woods, look at the sky at night.

- Leaders must lead where we want to go or they lose power. Provide direction to the leaders we have chosen.

- Create heart-centered action.

- Strengthen connections with family and friends.

- Choose to see people in terms of their wholeness, not in terms of where they have disappointed. This does not mean letting people get away with murder. Everyone must face the consequences of their actions; however, we can still see their humanity and divinity.

- Practice being mindful and responsible. Everything one says, everything one does, everything one thinks has an impact on every other being in the world.
- As much as possible, buy, act, and be cruelty free.
- Create an intention-based community such as the groups in the next section.
- Act with respect for self, family, community, Earth, ancestors, elders, other entities, and all life.
- Act as if you believe that we are not alone.

As we move through this shifting time, some things will fall away, and others will rise and replace them. This is the natural cycle. The power of spirit moving in systems can be seen all around us. Each of us needs to find something that inspires us and then become involved. We are part of the consciousness that is moving spirit in matter.

We have talked of consciousness with no attempt to define what it is. There is no adequate definition. Consciousness is the act of aware-ness, the substance of form, and the force through which we experience life. It is personal and collective. It directs. It is carried on energy, yet is not energy; it is something beyond. When we extend our awareness and intent to use the force of our consciousness, we can change the world.

The Global Consciousness Project (GCP) is a parapsychology experiment begun in 1998, and funded by the Institute of Noetic Sci-ences. The project was developed after 20 years of experiments at the Princeton Engineering Anomalies Research Lab, known as PEAR. Run by Roger D. Nelson, the experiments appeared to show that electronic noise-based, random number generators are influenced by human con-sciousness. When the minds of many people come together in one aim, they form a coherent force and the random generators show a less-ran-dom, more organized sequence of data.

There are 70 random generators around the planet monitoring out-put signals. The findings suggest that world focusing events such as the death of Princess Diana, the falling of the Berlin Wall, and the 9/11 attack on the World Trade Center show distinct statistical changes in the degree of randomness of the generators. The degree to which the generators become more organized is not related to whether the event is positive or negative; it is related to how much emotion the event engenders. These results seem to imply that we are all linked together in a field of energy.

What I find most fascinating is that a preliminary spike in organization occurs several hours or even days before an event, foreshadowing its arrival. Research conducted by Dean Radin, as discussed in Chapter 3, suggests that the random generators are not the only precognitive receivers of events; our subconscious culls the same information from the ambiance around us and we feel events that are about to occur in our body.[6] The more we pay attention to our body, the more we feel our connection to the field and the more available we are for interactions with other minds.

Neuroscience research conducted by Professor John-Dylan Haynes at the Bernstein Centre for Computational Neuroscience adds a new a fascinating piece to the puzzle as discussed in a YouTube entry entitled *"Neuroscience and Free Will."*[7] In the research, participants are placed inside an MRI scanner and their brain is scanned while they are asked simple yes or no questions. The subject pushes a button with a left or right hand to provide an answer. Certain regions of the brain become active in a yes response, and other regions are active in a no response. The study revealed that six seconds before the question is even asked, the area of the brain representing what the participant will eventually answer is activated. This allows the researchers to determine what the answer to each question will be prior to the person hearing the question.

For some reason, the researchers jumped over the logical next question of how the brain knew what the question was going to be. Instead, they focused on the brain making a decision without our conscious and free will. For me, what is important is that we are all receiving and processing information through an energy field that is received first by the body. Perhaps our awareness lags behind the information because we have stopped paying attention to our body cues. When we do listen, we have access to a whole new arena of information. Maybe the communication happens through our motor neurons, as described in Chapter 3, or maybe it happens through our energy sense, or both.

The net result is the realization that we are on a path—a trajectory through space that has been calculated. Like the lunar probes, we have been released onto this trajectory and, if all goes well, we will reach our intended destination. On the other hand, nothing is a given. The journey we are on requires our attention and our intent to fulfill its potential.

The Power of Intention

In her book *The Hidden Power of the Heart: Discovering an Unlimited Source of Intelligence,* Sara Paddison writes, "One of the basic tenets of quantum physics is that we are not merely discovering reality; we are participating in its creation."[8] She writes that, according to Dr. David Loye, "When we act upon a premonition and appear to alter the future, what we are really doing is leaping from one hologram to another."[9]

Several scientifically based groups are working on using intention for positive impacts in the world. This began in the early 1990s with the World Peace Organization and now includes groups around the world. An Internet intention forum called Future Earth is on my Website to facilitate healing and wellness of the Earth. Through this forum I am asking others to join in this very simple expression of love.

Gerald Hawkins said that we cannot see where a mindstep will take us before we arrive. The new vista is too foreign for us to grasp. Nonetheless, the following well-established projects show why the most important single action we can take today is to embrace the call and act.

The Intention Experiment

According to her Website, Lynn McTaggart, author of the Intention Experiment, is working with leading physicists and psychologists from the University of Arizona, Princeton University, the International Institute of Biophysics, Cambridge University, and the Institute of Noetic Sciences. Her projects include using intention to stimulate seed germination and plant growth, to promote peace and even to clean polluted water.[10]

German Intention Experiments

The Germination Intention Experiments were started in 2007 and conducted with psychologist Dr. Gary Schwartz and his laboratory team at the University of Arizona to test whether intention can affect the growth rate of plants. The background to the study includes:

+ Studies by Canadian psychologist Bernard Grad, who demonstrated that seeds irrigated with water held by a healer had a faster germination rate and growth than controls. [11]

+ A study by British researcher Serena Roney-Dougal and parapsychologist Jerry Solfvin, who tested the healing intention on lettuce seeds. Results of the first study did not demonstrate faster sprouting or growth, but did demonstrate better health and resistance fungi and predators. [12]

+ Results from six studies with the Intention Experiment using one seed bed for intention and three controls confirmed the positive results of sent intention on plant germination rates with a significance of $p<0.0000001$ and a 0.00001 percent possibility that the result was chance.

The Peace Intention

The Peace Intention took place from September 11 to 18, 2011. Dr. Salah Al-Rashed and his community of tens of thousands of Arabs throughout the Gulf States joined meditators in the West to transmit the intention to lower violence for the eight-day period of the experiment. The targeted areas to receive intention were two southern provinces of Helmand and Kandahar in Afghanistan. The results were as follows:[13]

+ Civilian causalities dropped an average of 37 percent.

+ Attacks with explosive devices dropped 16 percent compared to the average attack rate for the previous two years.

+ Overall enemy attacks dropped 12 percent from October to December 2011 compared to 2010.

+ Attacks in the Southwest dropped overall by 29 percent compared to the year before.

+ Attacks over the whole of Afghanistan were 9 percent lower.

The Global Coherence Initiative

Lynn McTaggart's Intention Experiment is one of many such endeavors. The Global Coherence Initiative sponsored by HeartMath is a "science-based, co-creative project whose mission is to unite people in heart-focused care and intention to facilitate the shift in global consciousness from instability and discord to balance, cooperation and enduring peace."[14] In this initiative people enter "care rooms" that send intentions three times per day. Intentions are based on environmental and peace concerns, and monitoring stations monitor conditions. You can join any or all sessions; participation is free. Members can "see" each other as signals from around the world are shown on a Google Earth map.

The organizers say: "This project has been initiated because millions of people sense that this is an extraordinary time; that a paradigm shift of human consciousness is now under way; that we are at the crossroads of change and must move toward the healing of ourselves and our planet. Many people are feeling a strong desire to help change our present and future conditions and are looking for ways to use their heart, spirit-aligned wisdom and care to make a meaningful difference."[15]

The fact that people are feeling the need to help change future conditions is a good sign; even better are the results showing that the process works.

The World Peace Project

The World Peace Project is one of the first intention initiatives. Since the early 1990s the originators have been engaged in using intention to decrease violent crime.[16] In June 2008, World Peace Project began a consciousness project that took place from June 7 to July 30, 1993, when a Transcendental Meditation (TM) peace group met in Washington, DC, to focus on reducing crime. Soon after the start of the study, violent crime began to decrease, with a total decrease of 23.6% by the end of the study. Violent crime was measured by FBI Uniform Crime Statistics and the probability of chance was less than two parts per billion ($p < .000000002$). The study concluded that the drop in crime could not be attributed to other possible causes including prior causative factors, temperature, precipitation, weekends, and police and community anti-crime activities.[17]

Currently the World Peace Project is encouraging members from faith-based organizations, meditation assemblies, community groups and individuals to implement peace initiatives within their own traditions. According to their Website, targeted areas have "produced a significant decrease in rapes, homicides and assaults, and a significant increase in other factors associated with improved quality of life. Over 41 studies, mostly in peer-reviewed journals, have shown repeated demonstration of these positive effects."[18]

One project set out to decrease the crime rate in the capital regions of the Philippines, United States, and India. In all three cases, when groups of meditators gathered for periods of weeks or months to meditate on reducing crime, the crime rates dropped significantly below pre-existing levels. "Time series analysis showed that this drop was not based on prior causative factors, and could not be accounted for by weather, seasonal cycles, or changes in police coverage."[19]

Healing Intention

Scientific studies to assess the effects of intercessory prayer were conducted between August 1982 and May 1983. In San Francisco General Hospital's Coronary Care Unit, 393 patients participated in a double blind study. Patients were randomly selected by computer to either receive or not receive intercessory prayer. All participants in the study, including patients, doctors, and the conductor of the study, remained blind to who was in what group throughout.

The patients who received prayer as a part of the study were healthier than those who had not. The prayed-for group had less need for CPR (cardiopulmonary resuscitation) for the use of mechanical ventilators. They had diminished need of diuretics and antibiotics, less occurrences of pulmonary edema, and fewer deaths.[20]

Final Words

We can influence the world with heartfelt intention. It requires two essential elements: first, that we begin by working on our own inner issues and polarities to become clear in our motives, needs, and intent; and second, that we approach this work with sincere honesty and love. With these accomplished, we are well placed to lead our leaders.

I have been lucky in my life to have met Pat Delgado and Synthia, two people who follow the internal compulsion to trust inner senses to guide their life. Both have demonstrated to me that subtle energy is real, as is our connection to other dimensions. They have been catalysts through whom I have seen miracles take place.

When Pat and I joined forces to become part of the first team to investigate crop circles, we could not have imagined where that path would take us. We did not travel it hoping to write books or be featured on hundreds of television programs; those things occurred incidentally. We traveled because, once engaged, there was no other path. Similarly with Synthia, I had no idea the adventure we embarked on when we joined our lives. Through our relationship I have learned what is possible when action is fueled with love and guided by intuition.

Now is the time for us all to step forward and be our true selves. At the core of who we are is the capacity to generate and promote love. The word is overused and its power diminished through sentimentality. Love is the force of life. Nothing less is required at this time.

All pretensions must be dropped. Fear of being judged and ostracized can no longer control our actions. Sincerity must prevail. We cannot access inner truth and connection to the greater whole without sincerity. Equally, if we don't act on what we receive, the conduit will close.

The adventure awaits, and our children are watching.

F*irst the Earth, then our souls. While we all argue, our Earth, our soul is dying.*
—Colin Andrews, in the movie
Circular Evidence

W*hen we truly understand that love is the only force, all life is family and Earth is our mother, we will find peace.*
—Synthia Andrews

Authors

Colin Andrews (*www.ColinAndrews.net*)

Synthia Andrews, ND (*www.thepathofenergy.com/* and *www. andrewshealingarts.com/*)

Consciousness

Andrews, Synthia, ND, with Colin Andrews, *The Complete Idiots Guide to the Akashic Record* (Alpha Books, Penguin, 2010)

Andrews, Synthia, ND, *The Path of Energy* (Career Press/New Page Books 2011)

Bodanis, David, $E=mc2$: *A Biography of the World's Most Famous Equation* (The Berkley Publishing Group, 2000)

Consciousness and Quantum Mechanics (*www.plato.stanford.edu/entries/ qm-copenhagen/*)

Consciousness Research Laboratory (*www.deanradin.com/default_ original.html*)

Gribbin, John, *In Search of Schrodinger's Cat, Quantum Physics and Reality* (Bantam Books, 1984)

Grof, Stanislav, and Hal Zina Bennett, *The Holotropic Mind: The Three Levels of Human Consciousness and How They Shape Our Lives* (HarperOne, 1993)

Hawking, Stephen, *The Illustrated A Brief History of Time/The Universe in a Nutshell—Two Books in One* (Bantam Books, 2007)

The Institute of Noetic Sciences (*www.noetic.org/?from=5*)

Kafatos, Menas, and Robert Nadeau, *The Conscious Universe: Parts and Wholes in Physical Reality* (Springer, 1999)

Kenyon, Tom, *Brain States* (World Tree Press, 2001)

Mapping the Brain (*www.xfinity.comcast.net/video/researchers-to-build- map-of-brains-activity/19308611572*)

McTaggart, Lynn, *The Field: A Quest for the Secret Force of the Universe* (Harper Perennial, 2002)

Mitchell, Edgar, and Arnan Dwight Williams, *The Way of the Explorer: An Apollo Astronaut's Journey Through the Material and Mystical Worlds* (New Page Books, 2008)

Pert, Candace, PhD, *Molecules Of Emotion: The Science Behind Mind- Body Medicine* (Simon & Schuster, 1999)

Princeton Consciousness Project (*www.noosphere.princeton.edu/*; *www.boundaryinstitute.org/randomness.htm*; *www. boundaryinstitute.org/articles/timereversed.pdf*)

Radin, Dean, *Entangled Minds: Extrasensory Experiences in a Quantum Reality* (Paraview Pocket Books, 2006)

Radin, Dean, *The Conscious Universe* (HarperEdge, 1997)

Radin, Dean, *Entangled Minds: Extrasensory Experiences in a Quantum Reality* (Paraview Pocket Books, 2006)

Sheldrake, Rupert, *A New Science of Life* (Park Street Press, 1995)

Sheldrake, Rupert. *The Presence of the Past: Morphic Resonance and the Habits of Nature* (Park Street Press, 1995)

Talbot, Michael, *The Holographic Universe* (HarperCollins, 1992)

Targ, Russell, *Mind-Reach: Scientists Look at Psychic Abilities* (Hampton Roads Publishing, 2005)

Targ, Russell, and Jane Katara, *Miracles of Mind, Exploring Non-Local Consciousness and Spiritual Healing* (New World Library, 1998)

Wilbur, Ken, *The Theory of Everything* (Shambhala, 2001)

Crop Circle Studies

Andrews, Colin, *The Andrews Catalog* (Archive House Media, 2011)

Andrews, Colin, with Stephen J. Spignesi, *Crop Circles: Signs of Contact* (New Page Books/Career Press, 2003)

Andrews, Colin, *Conscious Circles* (DVD; Samdog Films, 2011)

Circlemakers TV (*www.circlemakerstv.org/*)

Colin Andrews Research (*www.ColinAndrews.net*)

Crop Circle Connector (*www.cropcircleconnector.com/interface2005.htm*)

Dowsing

The American Society of Dowsers (*www.dowsers.org/*)

The British Society of Dowsers (*www.britishdowsers.org/*)

Electronic Voice Phenomenon (EVP) and Life After Death

Bayless, Raymond, *Phone Calls from the Dead* (New English Library Ltd., 1980)

EVP Recordings (*www.trueghosttales.com/how-to-record-evp.php*)

ITC images (*www.worlditc.org*)

Lonnerstrand, Sture, *I Have Lived Before: The True Reincarnation of Shanti Devi* (Ozark Mountain Publishing, 1998)

Macy, Mark, *Spirit Faces: Truth About the Afterlife* (Weiser Books, 2007)

Newton, Michael, *Destiny of Souls: New Case Studies of Life Between Lives* (Llewellyn Publications, 2000)

Newton, Michael, *Journey of Souls: Case Studies of Life Between Lives* (Llewellyn Publications, 2002)

Raudive, Konstantin, *Breakthrough: An Amazing Experiment in Electronic Communication with the Dead* (1968; Taplinger Publishing Company, translated into English in 1971)

Schwartz, Gary, and William Simon, *The Afterlife Experiments: Breakthrough Scientific Evidence of Life After Death* (Pocket Books, 2002)

The Scole Experiment (*www.thescoleexperiment.com/*)

Solomon, Grant, and Jane Solomon, *The Scole Experiment* (Campion Books, 2006)

Steiner, Rudolf, *Re-Incarnation and Immortality* (Harper and Row Publishers, 1970)

Stevenson, Ian, *20 Cases Suggestive of Reincarnation* (University of Virginia Press, 1980)

Stevenson, Ian, *Children Who Remember Previous Lives: A Question of Reincarnation* (McFarland & Company, 2000)

Wamback, Helen, *Life Before Life* (Bantam, 1984)

Zammit, Victor (*www.victorzammit.com/book/chapter05.html*)

Frequency Healing

Andrews, Synthia, ND, *The Path of Emotions* (New Page Books, 2013)

Andrews, Synthia, ND, *The Path of Energy* (New Page Books, 2011)

Frequency (Sound) Healing (*www.frequencyhealing.org/articles/*)

Gerber, Richard, *Vibrational Medicine: The #1 Handbook of Subtle-Energy Therapies* (Bear & Company, 2001)

International Alliance for Animal Therapy and Healing (IAATH; *www.iaath.com/treatments/radionics.shtml*)

Radionics Subtle Energy and Vibrational Medicine (*www.raydionics.com/*)

HAARP

HAARP Website (*www.haarp.alaska.edu/*)

View Zone (*www.viewzone.com/haarp00.html*)

Norway Spiral

Colin Andrews's Research (*www.colinandrews.net/UFO-MysteryLightNorway3.html*)

Universe Today (*www.universetoday.com/47219/what-was-the-norway-spiral/*)

Reg Presley Dedication

Colin Andrews's Research (*www.colinandrews.net/Reg-Presley_
AGetWelFromlColin-Andrews.html*)

Remote Viewing

Buchanan, Lyn, *The Seventh Sense: The Secrets of Remote Viewing as Told
by a "Psychic Spy" for the U.S. Military* (Pocket 2003)

Brown, Courtney, PhD, *Cosmic Voyage* (Dutton, published by Penguin
Books, 1996)

Hein, Simeon, Dr., (*www.NewCrystalMind.com*)

Hein, Simeon, Dr., *Open Minds: A Journey of Extraordinary Encounters,
Crop Circles, and Resonance* (Mount Baldy Press, 2002)

Institute for Resonance (*www.InstituteforResonance.org*)

McMoneagle, Joseph, *Remote Viewing Secrets: A Handbook* (Hampton
Roads Publishing Company, 2000)

Morehouse, David, *Remote Viewing: The Complete User's Manual for
Coordinate Remote Viewing*
(Sounds True, Incorporated, 2007)

Swann, Ingo (*www.biomindsuperpowers.com/*)

Targ, Russell, *Limitless Mind: A Guide to Remote Viewing and
Transformation of Consciousness*
(New World Library, 2004)

UFO

Center for the Study of Extraterrestrial Intelligence
(CSETI; *www.cseti.org/*)

Hopkins, Bud, *Missing Time* (Ballantine Books, 1988)

Mack, John E., *Abduction* (Scribner, 2007)

The National UFO Reporting Center (NUFORG; *www.nuforc.org/*)

The Paradigm Research Group (*www.paradigmresearchgroup.org*)

Woodpecker

The Sound (*www.youtube.com/watch?v=hH6C0kun5DU*)

Chapter 1

1. Hawkins, Gerald. *Mindsteps to the Cosmos* (HarperCollins, 1983), p. 295.

2. Mails, Thomas E., and Dan Evehems. *Hotevilla: Hopi Shrine of the Covenant-Microcosm of the World* (Marlow and Company, 1995), p. 494.

3. Hawkins, *Mindsteps,* p.301.

4. Tierney, Bil. *Dynamics of Aspect Analysis: New Perceptions in Astrology,* 2nd Edition (CRCS Publications, 1993).

5. "2012 Astrology Report," The Official Website of Colin Andrews, *www.colinandrews.net.*

6. Tierney, *Dynamics.*

7. The Official Website of Colin Andrews, *www.colinandrews.net/Israeli-VirusAttack-Iran.html.*

Chapter 2

1. NASA Website, *www.nasa.gov.*

2. Hough, Andrew, "Nasa Warns Solar Flares From 'Huge Space Storm' Will Cause Devastation," T*he Telegraph* Website, *www.telegraph.co.uk/science/space/7819201/Nasa-warns-solar-flares-from-huge-space-storm-will-cause-devastation.html.*

3. "March 13, 1989—The Quebec Blackout Storm," Space Weather Website, *www.solarstorms.org/SS1989.html.*

4. Behr, Peter, "This Week's Solar Flare Illuminates the Grid's Vulnerability," *The New York Times* Website, June 9, 2011, *www.nytimes.com/cwire/2011/06/09/09climatewire-this-weeks-solar-flare-illuminates-the-grids-63979.html?pagewanted=all.*

5. Thompson, Andrea, "Timing of Seasons Is Changing," LiveScience Website, *www.livescience.com/5296-timing-seasons-changing.html.*

6. Westerling, A.L., H.G. Hidalgo, D.R. Cayan, and T.W. Swetnam, "Warming and Earlier Spring Increase Western U.S. Forest Wildfire Activity," *Science*, volume 313, number 5789 (August 18, 2006), published online July 6, 2006, *www.sciencemag.org/content/313/5789/940.full.*

7. "USDA Designates an Additional 76 Counties in 6 States as Primary Natural Disaster Areas Due to Worsening Drought," News Release, July 25, 2012, United States Department of Agriculture Website, *www.usda.gov/wps/portal/usda/usdahome?contentid=2012/07/0250.xml&navid=NEWS_RELEASE&navtype=RT&parentnav=LATEST_RELEASES&edeployment_action=retrievecontent.*

8. Cook, Edward R., Connie A. Woodhouse, C. Mark Eakin, David M. Meko, and David W. Stahle, "Long-Term Aridity Changes in the Western United States," *Science*, volume 206, number 5698 (November 5, 2004), published online, October 7, 2004, *www.sciencemag.org/content/306/5698/1015.short.*

9. Wald, Matthew L., "Heat Shuts Down a Coastal Reactor," *The New York Times*, August 13, 2012, *green.blogs.nytimes.com/2012/08/13/heat-shuts-down-a-coastal-reactor/.*

10. Light, Malcolm, "Global Extinction Within One Human Lifetime as a Result of a Spreading Atmospheric Arctic Methane Heat Wave and Surface Firestorm," Arctic News blog, *arctic-news.blogspot.ca/p/global-extinction-within-one-human.html.*

11. Roach, John, "Earth's Magnetic Field Is Fading," *National Geographic*, September 9, 2004, *news.nationalgeographic.com/news/2004/09/0909_040909_earthmagfield.html.*

12. Lovett, Richard A., "North Magnetic Pole Moving due to Core Flux," *National Geographic*, December 12, 2009, *news.nationalgeographic.com/news/2009/12/091224-north-pole-magnetic-russia-earth-core/*

13. Simkin, Tom, and Lee Siebert, *Volcanoes of the World*, 2nd Edition (Tucson, Ariz.: Geoscience Press, Inc., 1994).

14. Kluger, Jeffrey, "How Chile's Earthquake Shortened Earth's Days," *Time* Website, March 2, 2010, *www.time.com/time/health/article/0,8599,1969081,00.html.*

15. Voigt, Kevin, "Quake Moved Japan 8 Feet, Shifted Earth's Axis," CNN.com, April 10, 2011, *www.cnn.com/2011/WORLD/asiapcf/03/12/japan.earthquake.tsunami.earth/index.html.*

16. Walsh, Dylan, "The Baffling Nexus of Climate Change and Health," *The New York Times* Website, September 6, 2012, *http://green.blogs. nytimes.com/2012/09/06/the-baffling-nexus-of-climate-change-and-health/.*

17. "Public Health Community Announces Major Initiative on Climate Change," News Release, American Public Health Association Website, *www.apha.org/about/news/pressreleases/2007/ climatechangeannouncement.htm.*

18. "Morgellons Disease: Managing a Mysterious Skin Condition," Mayo Clinic Website, *www.mayoclinic.com/health/morgellons-disease/ sn00043.*

19. "CDC Study of an Unexplained Dermopathy," Centers for Disease Control and Prevention Website, *www.cdc.gov/ unexplaineddermopathy.*

20. "World Population Prospects, the 2010 Revision" (question #4: "How do we know that the world population reaches 7 billion on 31 October 2011?"),United Nations, Department of Economic and Social Affairs Website *esa.un.org/unpd/wpp/Other-Information/faq. htm#q4.*

21. Hinrichsen, Don, and Bryant Robey, "Population and the Environment: The Global Challenge," actionioscience.org, October 2000, *www.actionbioscience.org/environment/hinrichsen_robey.html.*

22. Belpomme, Dominique, "Rise in Cancers From Environmental Chemicals," Pesticide Action Network UK Website, *www.pan-uk.org/ pestnews/Issue/pn63/pn63p6.htm.*

23. Glynn, Sarah, "Pesticides in Tap Water Responsible for Food Allergy Increase," Medical News Today Website, December 3, 2012, *www. medicalnewstoday.com/articles/253513.php.*

24. Fischlowitz-Roberts, Bernie, "Plan B Updates: Air Pollution Fatalities Now Exceed Traffic Fatalities by 3 to 1," Earth Policy Institute Website, September 17, 2002, *www.earth-policy.org/plan_b_ updates/2002/update17.*

25. "Fluorescent Bulbs," Rethink Recycling Website, *www. rethinkrecycling.com/residents/materials-name/fluorescent-bulbs.*

26. Fishman, Charles, "How Many Light Bulbs Does it Take to Change the World? One. And You're Looking at It," *Fast Company,* September 2006, *www.fastcompany.com/57676/how-many-lightbulbs-does-it-take-change-world-one-and-youre-looking-it.*

27. Harrell, Eben, and James Marson, "Apocalypse Today: Visiting Chernobyl, 25 Years Later," Time.com, April 26, 2011, *www.time.com/time/health/article/0,8599,2067562,00.html.*

28. "Statement on the *Annals of the New York Academy of Sciences* Volume Entitled 'Chernobyl: Consequences of the Catastrophe for People and the Environment,'" The New York Academy of Sciences Website, April 28, 2010, *www.nyas.org/AboutUs/MediaRelations/Detail.aspx?cid=16b2d4fe-f5b5-4795-8d38-d59a76d1ef33.*

29. Jamail, Dahr,"Fukushima: It's Much Worse Than You Think," Aljazeera.com, June 16, 2011, *www.aljazeera.com/indepth/features/2011/06/201161664828302638.html.*

30. Wood, Janice, "Worldwide Economic Collapse a Result of Shared Manic Behavior," Psych Central Website, *psychcentral.com/news/2012/06/10/worldwide-economic-collapse-a-result-of-shared-manic-behavior/39870.html.*

31. "Spending Under President George W. Bush," Working Paper, Mercatus Center at George Mason University: No. 09-04, March 2009.

32. Agence France-Presse, "Vatican Condemns American Nuns for Liberal Stances," The Raw Story Website, April 19, 2012, *www.rawstory.com/rs/2012/04/19/vatican-condemns-american-nuns-for-liberal-stances/.*

33. "Vatican Astronomer Cites Possibility of Extraterrestrial 'Brothers,'" *The New York Times* Website, *www.nytimes.com/2008/05/14/world/europe/14iht-vat.4.12885393.html?_r=1&.*

34. "2012 Debaite-Politics," The Official Website of Colin Andrews, *www.colinandrews.net/2012-Debate-Politics.html.*

35. "More Believe in Space Aliens Than in God According to U.K. Survey," The Huffington Post Website, October 18, 2012, *www.huffingtonpost.com/2012/10/15/alien-believers-outnumber-god_n_1968259.html.*

36. "Public Corruption," The Federal Bureau of Investigation Website, *www.fbi.gov/about-us/investigate/corruption.*

Chapter 3

1. "Public Opinion About Life and Death—Life After Death," Library Index Website, *www.libraryindex.com/pages/607/Public-Opinion-About-Life-Death-LIFE-AFTER-DEATH.html.*

2. Moore, David M., 'Three in Four Americans Believe in Paranormal,"
    Gallup Website, June 16, 2005, *www.gallup.com/poll/16915/three-four-
    americans-believe-paranormal.aspx.*
3. Moore, C.M., and H. Egeth (1997), "Perception Without Attention:
    Evidence of grouping Under Conditions of Inattention," *Journal of
    Experimental Psychology: Human Perception & Performance*, 23(2):
    339–352.
4. Chabris, Christopher, and Daniel Simons, *The Invisible Gorilla: And
    Other Ways Our Intuitions Deceive Us* (Crown, 2010), p. 32.
5. Pert, PhD, Candace, *Molecules of Emotion: Why You Feel the Way
    You Feel* (Scribner, 1997).
6. Ramachandran, V.S., "Mirror Neurons and Imitating Learning as
    the Driving Force Behind 'The Great Leap Forward' in Human
    Evolution," Edge.org Website, June 1, 2000, *www.edge.org/3rd_
    culture/ramachandran/ramachandran_index.html.*
7. Than, Ker, *National Geographic* Website, "'God Particle' Found?
    'Historic Milestone From Higgs Boson Hunters," July 4, 2012, *news.
    nationalgeographic.com/news/2012/07/120704-god-particle-higgs-
    boson-new-cern-science/.*
8. "What Exactly Is the Higgs Boson? Have Physicists Proved That it
    Really Exists?" *Scientific American* Website, *www.scientificamerican.
    com/article.cfm?id=what-exactly-is-the-higgs.*
9. The TED Forum at Amerstam, November 20, 2009, available at
    www.youtube.com/watch?v=eaV-GeAPSlE.
10. Radin, Dean, *Entangled Minds: Extrasensory Experiences in a
    Quantum Reality* (Pocket Books, 2006), pp. 164–69.
11. Andrews, Synthia, *The Path of Emotions* (New Page Books, 2013).
12. Schwartz, Gary E.R., and Linda G.S. Russek (1999), "Registration
    of Actual and Intended Eye Gaze: Correlation With Spiritual Beliefs
    and Experiences, *Journal of Scientific Exploration,* Vol. 13, No. 2:
    213–29.
13. McCraty, PhD, Rollin, *The Energetic Heart: Biomagnetic Interactions
    Within and Between People* (Institute of Heart Math, 2003), p. 7.
14. Persinger, MA, Makarec K. (1999), "The Feeling of a Presence and
    Verbal Meaningfulness in Context of Temporal Lobe Function:
    Factor Analytic Verification of the Muses?" *Brain Cognition* 20(2):
    217–26.

15. Bartlolmei, F., et al (2012), "Rhinal-Hippocampal Interactions During Deja-Vu," *Clinical Neurophysiology* 123(3): 489–95.

16. Benor, Dr. Daniel. *Healing Research: Holistic Energy Medicine and Spirituality, Vol. 1* (Helix Editions, Ltd., 1993)

Chapter 4

1. "Lifelong Health & Ageing: LHA National Survey of Health and Development: NSHD," Medical Research Council Website, *www. nshd.mrc.ac.uk.*

Chapter S

1. Andrews, Colin, and Pat Delgado, *Circular Evidence* (Bloomsbury Publishers, 1989), p. 45.

2. Adamiak, Shari, "The Story Behind the CSETI Triangle Logo," UFO Evidence Website, *www.ufoevidence.org/documents/doc237.htm.*

3. Ibid.

4. "New Swirled Order (CropCircle [sic] Documentary by NuoViso)" YouTube video, posted by NuoVisoProductions, March 28, 2009, *www.youtube.com/watch?v=8mAdrSvOgwI.*

Chapter 6

1. Andrews, Colin, *The Assessment* DVD, Andrews Archives, 2002.

2. Macnish, John, *Cropcircle Apocalypse: The Answer Is Here* (Shropshire, UK: Circlevision Publications, 1993), p. 180.

3. "Circlemakers Video," YouTube video, posted by Matthew Williams, *www.youtube.com/watch?v=AErU25oKqSY.*

4. "Strange Phenomena Inside Crop Circle," interview with Matthew Williams," YouTube video posted by On the Edge Media TV, *www. youtube.com/watch?v=_RrMnDtADYM.*

5. Ibid.

6. Ibid.

7. Ibid.

8. "Circlemakers Video."

9. Hein, Dr. Simeon, *Opening Minds: A Journey of Extraordinary Encounters, Crop Circles and Resonance* (Boulder, Colo.: Mount Baldy Press, 2002), p. 137.

10. Andrews, Colin, and Stephen Spignesi, *Crop Circles: Signs of Contact* (New Page Books, 2003), p. 145.

Chapter 7

1. Macnish, *Cropcircle Apocalypse.*
2. Andrews and Spignesi, *Crop Circles,* p. 40.
3. Ibid., p. 39.
4. Delgado, Pat, and Colin Andrews, *Circular Evidence: A Detailed Investigation of the Flattened Swirled Crops Phenomenon* (Bloomsbury, London, 1989), p. 81.
5. Radin, *Entangled Minds,* pp. 164–69.
6. Associated Press, "British Experts: Stonehenge Was Place of Healing," *USA Today,* September 22, 2008, *usatoday30.usatoday.com/tech/science/2008-09-22-stonehenge-healing_N.htm.*
7. Devereux, Paul, *Secret of Ancient and Sacred Places: The Worlds Mysterious Heritage* (Blandford Press, 1996), p. 22.
8. "Strange Phenomena Inside Crop Circle."
9. "Circlemakers Video."

Chapter 8

1. "Science: Foo Fighter," *Time,* January 15, 1945, *www.time.com/time/magazine/article/0,9171,775433,00.html.*
2. Stothers, Richard, "Unidentified Flying Objects in Classical Antiquity," *The Classical Journal* 103.1 (2207): 79–92.
3. Ancient Astronaut Society Website, *www.ancientastronautsociety.com/.*
4. "More Believe in Space Aliens...."
5. "FBI FILE OF DR. JAMES E. McDONALD," CUFON: The Computer UFO Network Website, *www.cufon.org/cufon/fbimcdon.htm* AND "Power Outages (Blackouts) and UFOs," UFO Evidence Website, *www.ufoevidence.org/documents/doc906.htm.*
6. The Fox News report can be viewed at *www.colinandrews.net/UFOs-NuclearOver-ride.html.*
7. "Mexican UFOs—Jaime Maussan Mexico in 1991," Disclose TV Website, uploaded December 6, 2010, *www.disclose.tv/action/viewvideo/61884/MEXICAN_UFOs___JAIME_MAUSSAN_Mexico_in_1991_.*
8. Phoenix Lights Network Website, *www.thephoenixlights.net/.*
9. "New Jersey Mystified by Strange Lights," ABC News Website, July 17, 2001. *abcnews.go.com/US/story?id=92865#.UBqde0QZFGE.*

10. Davenport, Misha, "History Channel Devotes Hour to Tinley Park Sightings," UFO Casebook Website, October 28, 2008, *www.ufocasebook.com/2008c/ufohunterstinleypark.html.*

11. "UFO Spotted by Police Helicopter," BBC News Website, June 20, 2008, *news.bbc.co.uk/2/hi/uk_news/wales/7465041.stm.*

12. The MUFON report can be downloaded from *www.ufocasebook.com/2008b/mufonstephenvillereport.html* and *transcripts.cnn.com/TRANSCRIPTS/0801/18/lkl.01.html.*

13. "Richard Dolan on CNN's Glenn Beck Show," Keyhole Publishing Company Website, January 3, 2007, *www.keyholepublishing.com/CNN-Beck.htm.*

14. "UFO Claim Over Wind Farm Damage," BBC News Website, January 8, 2009, *news.bbc.co.uk/2/hi/uk_news/england/lincolnshire/7817378.stm.*

15. Alexander, PhD, John B., *UFO's: Myths, Conspiracies, and Realities* (St. Martin's Press, 2011), p. 161.

16. Walton, Travis, *Fire in the Sky.*

17. "Ufo Sighting the Phoenix Lights News and Witnesses," YouTube video, posted by mainstream72, August 10, 2012, *www.youtube.com/watch?v=EWqFJ6fzDrA.*

18. Associated Press, "Arizona: O.K.,. [sic] It Was a UFO," *The New York Times,* March 24, 2007, *www.nytimes.com/2007/03/24/us/24brfs-OKITWASAUFO_BRF.html?_r=0.*

19. "Governor Admits to Government UFO Coverup!!! The Phoenix Lights," YouTube video, posted Americanrevolution02, by August 25, 2011, *www.youtube.com/watch?v=z3wr6_-XoRE.*

20. "Frances Barwood Presents How Did I Get Here?" OpenMinds Website, *store.openminds.tv/products/Frances-Barwood-Presents-How-Did-I-Get-Here%3F.html.*

21. Phoenix Lights Network Website.

Chapter 9

1. "Magnificent Orbs," Spiritlite.com, *www.spiritlite.com/orbs.php.*

2. "XCon 2005—Lynn Kitei—Seeing "WAS" Believing—'Phoenix Lights' Researcher," YouTube video, posted by LostArtsMedia, July 6, 2012, *www.youtube.com/watch?v=pJsiPiL99So.*

3. "UFO Sightings Bring Town to a Standstill," *Daily Mail* Online, July 26, 2007, *www.dailymail.co.uk/news/article-470579/UFO-sightings-bring-town-standstill.html.*

4. "Sighting Report" (11/10/2012), National UFO Reporting Center Website, *www.nuforc.org/webreports/094/S94321.html.*
5. "Milk Hill UFO 1990," YouTube video, posted by MrAstralwalker, August 5, 2011, *www.youtube.com/watch?v=grTTo2U6rUw.*

Chapter 10

1. "Inquiring Minds Meets CircleMakers' TV," July 8, 2011, Inquiring Minds Website, *inquiringminds.cc/inquiring-minds-meets-circlemakerstv.*
2. Private correspondence between Julian Richardson and the author, February 12, 2013.
3. "UFO Falls From the Sky in Amsterdam," Unexplained Mysteries Website, August 8, 2011, *www.unexplained-mysteries.com/viewnews.php?id=211681.*
4. "Sighting Report" (8/23/2011), National UFO Reporting Center Website, *www.nuforc.org/webreports/083/S83381.html.*
5. Kelleher, Colm. A., and George Knapp, *Hunt for the Skinwalker: Science Confronts the Unexplained at a Remote Ranch in Utah* (Paraview Pocket Books, 2005).
6. Private correspondence between Peter Sorenson and the author, February 8, 2013,
7. Two videos taken from cars that are recordings of the real event are "Norway Spiral" by Dylan Doug (*www.youtube.com/watch?v=ax2ITilnHlc* and "Norway Spiral * Best Video" by Linda Menzies (*www.youtube.com/watch?v=80__LLZK4zg*). The simulated version created based on eye witness accounts and mathematical projections that is often portrayed as the actual footage is "Norway Cloud Spiral" by Jadzia 2009 (*www.youtube.com/watch?v=wilTf3zPeoE*).
8. Private correspondence via e-mail between Dr. Jean-Noel Aubrun and the author, March 18, 2013.
9. Australian spiral: "New Spiral in Sky in Australia" by Top10UFO (*www.youtube.com/watch?v=iOXKhKKTRy0*); China spiral: "Norway Type Spiral Swirl Seen in Chinese Sky New Footage" by lucas911 (*www.youtube.com/watch?v=HarYTcr46RE*); Yemen, Armenia: "UFO Spiral in Armenia 2012—in Night Sky" by armmovie (*www.youtube.com/watch?v=cJ-xeI7s4tM* and *www.youtube.com/watch?v=MpcbHuYONyw*).

10. "Conquering an Infinite Cave," *National Geographic* Website, *ngm.nationalgeographic.com/2011/01/largest-cave/peter-photography#/19-stalagmites-714.jpg.*

Chapter 11

1. Alexander, Jame, "Have You Heard 'the Hum'?" BBN News Website, May 19, 2009, *news.bbc.co.uk/2/hi/uk_news/8056284.stm.*

2. Klein, B.E., R. Klein, W.E. Sponsel, T. Franke, L.B. Cantor, J. Martone, and M.J. Menage (1992). "Prevalence of Glaucoma: The Beaver Dam Eye Study," *Ophthalmology* 99(10):1499–504, *www.ncbi.nlm.nih.gov/pubmed/1454314.*

3. Saito, Y.A., P. Schoenfeld, and G.R. Locke III (2002), "The Epidemiology of Irritable Bowel Syndrome in North America: A Systematic Review," *The American Journal of Gastroenterology* 97(8):1910–5, *www.ncbi.nlm.nih.gov/pubmed/12190153.*

4. Wilson, S., L. Roberts, A. Roalfe, P. Bridge, and S. Singh (2004), "Prevalence of Irritable Bowel Syndrome: A Community Survey," *The British Journal of General Practice* 54(504):495-502 *www.ncbi.nlm.nih.gov/pubmed/15239910.*

5. "The Hum," *www.johndawes.pwp.blueyonder.co.uk/.*

6. "Report of the Taos Hum Investigation," November 22, 1993. Can be viewed at *www.colinadrews.net.*

7. Hutcheon, Stephen, "Mystery Humming Sound Captured," *The Sydney Morning Herald,* November 17, 2006, *www.smh.com.au/articles/2006/11/17/1163266756133. html?page=fullpage#contentSwap1.*

8. The World Hum Map and Database, *www.thehum.info.*

9. "Better Than a Hearing Aid? Better Hearing Without Bone Conducted Sound," Science Daily Website , July 9, 2009, *www.sciencedaily.com/releases/2009/06/090622194227.htm/*

10. Frey, Allan H. (1962), "Human Auditory Systems Response to Modulated Electromagnetic Energy," *Journal of Applied Physiology* 17(4):689–92.

11. Elder, J.A., and C.K. Chou (2003), "Auditory Response to Pulsed Radiofrequency Energy," *Bioelectromagnetics* Volume 24, Issue S6: S162–73.

12. "From The Secret War Against Medford, Oregon by Mark Metcalf," Bariumblues.com, *www.bariumblues.com/mind_control_medford_oregon.htm.*

13. "The Hum," *www.johndawes.pwp.blueyonder.co.uk/.*

14. "The Hum," The Official Website of Colin Andrews, *www. colinandrews.net/The-Hum-County-Durham-Colin_Andrews.html.*

15. "The Trumpets of Revelation—Strange Sounds Reported Around the Globe," YouTube video, posted by Rob Daven, January 11, 2012, *www.youtube.com/watch?v=Lpg_0Y_iB8w.*

16. Rapetti, Steve, February 3, 2012, The Official Website of Colin Andrews, *www.colinandrews.net/Sounds-More-reports-2012-Colin_Andrews.html.*

17. Ibid.

18. "UFO Emits Terrifying Sound? 2012," Disclose.tv, *www.disclose.tv/action/viewvideo/86969/UFO_Emits_Terrifying_Sound__2012/.*

19. "Malaysia Ministry Seeks Recordings of Strange Noises in Sky," asiaone.com, January 23, 2012, *www.asiaone.com/News/Latest+News/Science+and+Tech/Story/A1Story20120123-323459.html.*

20. Ibid.

21. Choi, Charles Q., "Mysterious 'Booming Sounds' Perplex Scientists," NBCnews.com, September 16, 2001, *www.nbcnews.com/id/44550343/ns/technology_and_science-science/t/mysterious-booming-sounds-perplex-scientists/#.UYledMo8GUM.*

22. Hill, David, "What Is That Mysterious Booming Sound?" (2011) *Seismological Research Letters* volume 82, pp. 619–22.

23. http://www.msnbc.msn.com/id/44550343/ns/technology_and_science-science/t/mysterious-booming-sounds-perplex-scientists/

24. Kalunian, Kim, "House-Rattling Boom Remains a Mystery," *Warwick Beacon* Website, December 6, 2012, *www.warwickonline.com/stories/House-rattling-boom-remains-a-mystery,77412?category_id=4&town_id=1&sub_type=stories.*

25. Ortega, Zavier, "Indianapolis Booms: Strange Lights & Explosions," Ghost Theory Website, January 10, 2013, *www.ghosttheory.com/2013/01/10/indianapolis-booms-strange-lights-explosions* AND "Late-Night Booms Waking Up Evansville Residents," wthr.com, January 10, 2013, *www.wthr.com/story/20553759/late-night-booms-waking-up-evansville-residents.*

26. "Mysterious Boom and Tremors Rattle South Carolina," The Extinction Protocol Website, September 30, 2011, *theextinctionprotocol.wordpress.com/2011/09/30/mysterious-boom-and-tremors-rattle-south-carolina/*.

27. Mystery Booms.Skyquakes Website, *mysterybooms.blogspot.com*.

28. If the site is still active, the video can be seen at *www.youtube.com/watch?v=4m5uB0xHmE8*.

Chapter 12

1. Instrumental Communication: EVP and ITC, *www.transcommunication.org/*.

2. Wagner, Stephen, "Edison and the Ghost Machine," About.com, *paranormal.about.com/od/ghostaudiovideo/a/edison-ghost-machine.htm*.

3. Ibid.

4. "Electronic Voice Phenomena," Mystic New Website *www.members.tripod.com/cryskernan/electronic_voice_phenomena.htm*.

5. "Chapter 5: Tesla and Electronic Voice Phenomena," Biblioteca Pleyades Website, *www.bibliotecapleyades.net/tesla/lostjournals/lostjournals05.htm*.

6. "Electronic Voice Phenomena."

7. "History of EVP," Michigan Paranormal Alliance Website, *www.m-p-a.org/EVPHistory.html* AND "Chapter 5: Tesla and Electronic Voice Phenomena."

8. "History of EVP."

9. Oliver, Rosalind, "The Scole Experiments," The Scole Experiment Website, *www.thescoleexperiment.com/artcl_05.htm*.

10. The Scole Experiment Website, *www.thescoleexperiment.com*.

11. Solomon, Grant, and Jane Solomon. *The Scole Experiment: Scientific Evidence for Life After Death* (London: Judy Piatkus Publishers Ltd., 1999), pp. 86–7.

12. Ibid., p. 22.

13. Ibid., pp. 23, 173.

14. Ibid.,,, p. 76.

15. Ibid., p. 22.

16. Ibid., p. 79.

Chapter 13

1. AviationExplorer.com, *www.aviationexplorer.com/aircraft_airliner_ contrails.htm.*
2. Environmental News Service Website, *e ns-newswire.com/.*
3. "Carnicom Institute Community Page," Carnicom Institute Website, *www.carnicominstitute.org/html/articles_by_date.html.*
4. World Affairs Brief Website, *www.worldaffairsbrief.com/keytopics/ Chemtrails.shtml.*
5. "Chemtrail Ground Sample: Microscopic Views," Carnicom Institute Website, *www.carnicominstitute.org/articles/micro.htm.*
6. Thomas, William, and Erminia Cassani, "Chemtrail Sky Samples Analyzed," Educa-te-yourself Website, April 22, 1999, *educate-yourself.org/ct/ctarticle12.shtml.*
7. Carnicom, Clifford E., "Atmospheric Magensium Discolsed," Carnicom Institute Website, June 10, 2001, *www.carnicominstitute. org/articles/mag1.htm* AND Carnicom, Clifford E., "Electrolysis & Barium" May 27, 2002, Carnicom Institute Website," *www. carnicominstitute.org/articles/precip1.htm.*
8. "Visitors to www.carnicom.com," Carnicom Institute Website, *www. carnicominstitute.org/articles/visitors.htm.*
9. "Ex Government Employee Talks About CHEMTRAILS," YouTube video, posted by COUNTCARDULAR, July 27, 2009, *www.youtube. com/watch?v=udEtOc2IFO8.*
10. "Kim Johnson's Chemtrail Analysis—UPDATED," New Mexicans for Science and Reason Website, *www.nmsr.org/mkjrept. htm#new2010.*
11. Petkewich, Rachel, "Cooling the Planet Atmosphere" (2008) *Chemical & Engineering News* 86 (17): 14.
12. Thomas and Cassani, "Chemtrail Sky Samples Analyzed."
13. Blair, Mike, "Military Said Behind up to Four Different Chemtrail Programs," Rense.com, *rense.com/general11/chmmill.htm* AND "Ex Government Employee talks about CHEMTRAILS part 2," YouTube video, posted by COUNTCARDULAR, July 27, 2009, *www.youtube.com/watch?v=M4c0FRYqlJQ.*
14. "Former FBI Chief Ted Gunderson Says Chemtrail Death Dumps Must Be Stopped," YouTube video, posted by aircraporg, January 13, 2011, *www.youtube.com/watch?v=gR6KVYJ73AU.*

15. Chemtrail Australia & International Website, *www.chemtrailaustrali-ainternational.com/*.

16. Carnicom, C.E., "A Mchanic's Statement," Carnicom Institute Website, May 19, 2000, *www.carnicominstitute.org/articles/mech1.htm*.

17. Murphy, Michael J., "What in the World Are They Spraying?" Countercurrents.org, March 3, 2010, *www.countercurrents.org/murphy030310.htm*.

18. All quotations from the exchange are from "What in the World Are They Spraying. Full Video," YouTube video, posted by poodle559, December 29. 2010, *www.youtube.com/watch?v=ybWku-lJe6I*.

19. Griffin, G. Edward, Michael Murphy, and Paul Wittenberger (producers), *What in the World Are They Spraying? The Chemtrail-Geo-Engineering Coverup*, *www.realityzone.com/whatspray.html*.

20. "Lifetime Risk of Developing or Dying From Cancer," American Cancer Society Website, *www.cancer.org/cancer/cancerbasics/lifetime-probability-of-developing-or-dying-from-cancer*.

21. "Visitors to www.carnicom.com."

22. "The Release of Censored 2012 in September Celebrates 35 Years of Project Censored," Project Censored Website, *www.projectcensored.org/top-stories/articles/the-release-of-censored-2012-in-september-celebrates-35-years-of-project-censored*.

Chapter 14

1. "Ionosphere," Encyclopedia.com, *www.encyclopedia.com/topic/ionosphere.aspx*.

2. "Was the Chernobyl 1986 Nuclear Plant Meltdown an Act of Sabotage?" Northerntruthseeker blog, April 14, 2012, *northerntruthseeker.blogspot.com/2012/04/was-chernobyl-1986-nuclear-plant.html*.

3. *Paranoia* magazine, issue 48, fall 2008.

4. Coppens, Philip, "The Russian Woodpecker: Experiments in Mind Control, Philip Coppens's Website, *www.philipcoppens.com/woodpecker.html*.

5. Ibid.

6. Coppens, Philip, "The Russian Woodpecker: Experiments in Mind Control," *Paranoia* magazine Website, *www.paranoiamagazine.com/2013/01/the-russian-woodpecker-experiments-in-global-mind-control-2/*.

7. "An Overview of the HAARP Program," The High Frequency Active Auroral Research Program Website, *www.haarp.alaska.edu/haarp/gen1.html.*

8. Ibid.

9. "ARCO ROADMAP," Agriculture Defense Coalition Website, *www.agriculturedefensecoalition.org/sites/default/files/pdfs/15C_Eastlund_Bernard_2008_ARCO_HAARP_ROADMAP.pdf.*

10. Zey, Michael G., *The Future Factor: Forces Transforming Human Destiny* (Transaction Publishers, 2004), p. 39.

11. "An Overview of the HAARP Program."

12. Haarp.net, *www.haarp.net/.*

13. "DoD News Briefing: Secretary of Defense William S. Cohen," official transcript, U.S. Department of Defense Website, April 28, 1997, *www.defense.gov/transcripts/transcript.aspx?transcriptid=674.*

14. "Atmosphere Above Japan Heated Rapidly Before M9 Earthquake," MIT Techonology Review Website, May 18, 2011, *www.technologyreview.com/view/424033/atmosphere-above-japan-heated-rapidly-before-m9-earthquake/.*

15. Butler, Declan, "Rat Study Sparks Furor Over Genetically Modified Foods," *Scientific American* Website, September 25, 2012, *www.scientificamerican.com/article.cfm?id=rat-study-sparks-furor-over-genetically-modified-foods.*

16. "New Weather Modification Research Papers by Dr. Bernard J. Eastlund," rense.com, March 31, 2000, *rense.com/general/neww.htm.*

Chapter 15

1. "Observatory," The Official Website of Colin Andrews, *www.colinandrews.net/WeatherObservatory-ColinAndrews.html.*

2. Private correspondence with the author, January 18, 2010. Name intentionally not disclosed.

3. Private correspondence between an employee of the Bureau of Meteorology, who has requested his name and details be kept private, and the author.

4. E-mail correspondence between BOM agent James Butler and the author, November 23, 2011.

5. Noone, Richard, "Bizarre Theories Circling Weather Bureau," *The Telegraph* Website, August 2, 2010, *www.dailytelegraph.com.au/news/weird/bizarre-theories-circling-weather-bureau/story-e6frev20-1225848752599.*

6. Ibid. AND Noone, Richard, "Bureau of Meteorology Images Show Mysterious Patterns on Radar System," *The Telegraph*, April 2, 2010, *www.news.com.au/weird-true-freaky/bueau-of-mereology-cant-explain-mysterious-patters-on-radar-system/story-e6frflri-1225848774377*.

7. Hambling, David, "Weatherwatch" Australia's 'Big Dought' Officially Over After a Decade," *The Guardian* Website, May 11, 2012, *www.guardian.co.uk/news/2012/may/11/weatherwatch-drought-australia-floods*.

8. "Australia in Summer 2012–13," Australian Government Bureau of Meteorology Website, March 1, 2013, *www.bom.gov.au/climate/current/season/aus/summary.shtml*.

9. Private correspondence with the author, January 25, 2010. Name intentionally not disclosed.

10. Private correspondence between Dr. Bruce Maccabee and the author, March 10, 2010.

11. Private correspondence between Malcolm Kitchen of the British Meteorological Office and the author, March 14, 2010.

12. Cristian, Arthur, "US Military H.A,A.R.P. Facility in Exmout,,Western Australia That Is Even More Advanced Than the One in Alaska," Love for Life Website, January 26, 2011, *loveforlife.com.au/content/11/01/26/us-military-haarp-facility-exmouthwestern-australia-even-more-advanced-one-alaska*.

13. "Worldwide Succcess," Weather Modification Incorporated Website, *www.weathermodification.com/projects.php*.

14. "ATLANT™ Technology," Australian Rain Technologies Website, *www.australianrain.com.au/technology.html*.

15. Reeves, Chris, "Cloud Seeding Gets Go Ahead," *Cooma-Monaro Express* Website, September 18, 2012, *www.coomaexpress.com.au/story/339965/cloud-seeding-gets-go-ahead/?src=rss*.

16. "What Caused Queensland Rain Floods?" SOS-NEWS Website, May 6, 2011, *sosnews.org/index.php?mact=News,cntnt01,print,0&cntnt01articleid=156&cntnt01showtemplate=-false&cntnt01returnid=56*.

17 "Comment," e-mail from Andrea Psoras to Commodity Futures Trading Commission (CFTC), May 5, 2008, *www.cftc.gov/ucm/groups/public/@lrfederalregister/documents/frcomment/08-004c002.pdf* AND Aindrais, Mac Ghille, "Leaked Weather Modification Document," USAHITMAN.com, *usahitman.com/leaked-weather-modification-document/*.

18. "Rain Dance," Indians.org (Website of the American Indian Heritag Foundation), *www.indians.org/articles/rain-dance.html.*
19. Skyhawk, Sonny, "Do You Still Do the Rain dance, and Does it Work?" Indian Country Today Media Network, May 19, 2012, *indiancountrytodaymedianetwork.com/article/do-you-still-do-the-rain-dance%2C-and-does-it-work%3F-113740.*

Chapter 16
1. "Tag Archives: DARPA," Disinformation Website, *www.disinfo.com/tag/darpa/.*
2. Steinberg, Jeffrey, "MindWar: How Military PsyOps Plan to Control Your Mind," *Mind Power News* Website, *www.mindpowernews.com/MindWar.htm.*
3. Sample, Ian, "Neuroscience Could Mean Soldiers Controlling Weapons With Minds," *The Guardian* Website, February 6, 2012, *www.guardian.co.uk/science/2012/feb/07/neuroscience-soldiers-control-weapons-mind.*
4. "Brain Waves 3: Neuroscience, Conflict and Security," The Royal Society Website, February 7, 2012, *royalsociety.org/policy/projects/brain-waves/conflict-security/?f=1.*
5. "Future Fighting All in the Head," *New York* Post Website, April 8, 2012, *www.nypost.com/p/news/national/future_fighting_all_in_the_head_BJXoN9Uska7ZpeMJcNOqiO#ixzz1slii3uUT.*
6. "Pentagon Plans for Telepathic Troops Who Can Read Each Others' Minds... and They Could Be in the Field Within Five Years," *The Daily Mail* Website, April 8, 2012, *http://www.dailymail.co.uk/news/article-2127115/Pentagon-plans-telepathic-troops-read-minds--field-years.html.*
7. Ibid.
8. "Brain Waves 3: Neuroscience, Conflict and Security."
9. Dillow, Clay, "Brain-Scanning Binoculars Harness Soldiers' Unconscious Minds to Locate Threats," popsci.com, July 5, 2012, *www.popsci.com/technology/article/2012-07/new-brain-scanning-binoculars-move-mind-melding-battle-tech-closer-deployment.*
10. "Dan Ariely Asks, Are We in Control of Our Decisions?" YouTube video, posted by TEDtalksDirector, May 19, 2009, *www.youtube.com/watch?feature=player_embedded&v=9X68dm92HVI.*

310 On the Edge of Reality

11. Collins, Dan, "4 Wives Slain in 6 Weeks at Fort Bragg," CBSNews. com, February 11, 2009, *www.cbsnews.com/2100-201_162-517033. html.*

12. "JetBlue Pilot Who Disrupted Flight to Be Freed," NBC 4 New York Website, November 9, 2012, *www.nbcnewyork.com/news/local/JetBlue-Pilot-Clayton-Osbon-Not-Guilty-Insanity-Federal-Mental-Health-Facility-161280035.html.*

13. Associated Press, "American Airlines Jet Delayed by Flight Attendant's Meltdown," News 10 ABC Website, March 9, 2012, *www. news10.net/news/article/183245/5/American-Airlines-jet-delayed-by-flight-attendants-meltdown.*

14. Andrews, Colin, "Saturday May 17th 2008 M6 Motorway England," The Official Website of Colin Andrews, September 5, 2010, *www. colinandrews.net/StrangenessOnM6-England2008.htm.*

15. Wilkes, David, "Woman Locked Up for Making Mad Dash Across M6 Stabbed Stranger to Death the Day After She Was Released From Jail," *Daily Mail* Website, September 3, 2009, *www.dailymail. co.uk/news/article-1210953/Woman-locked-making-mad-dash-M6-stabbed-stranger-death-day-released-jail.html#ixzz0z4GSZxTp.*

16. *Fate* magazine, February 2005, volume 58, number 2, issue 658, p. 100.

Chapter 17

1. "Global Extinction Within One Human Lifetime as a Result of a Spreading Atmospheric Arctic Methane Heat Wave and Surface Firestorm," Arctic News blog, *arctic-news.blogspot.ca/p/global-extinction-within-one-human.html.*

2. Interview with the authors, July 24, 2010.

3. Andrews, Colin, *Conscious Circles, www.createspace.com/303684.* Can be ordered at *www.colinandrews.net.*

4. All quotations attributed to Belbruno are from private correspondence between Dr. Edward Belbruno and the author, March 1, 2013.

Chapter 18

1. *Cell Biophysics* (1984) 6(1): 33–52.

2. Abbott, Alison, "Four-Strand DNA Structure Found in Cells," Nature.com, January 20, 2013, *www.nature.com/news/four-strand-dna-structure-found-in-cells-1.12253.*

3. "Biophotons: DNA Radiance of Health or Disease," Mind Science News Website, *http://news.pillaicenter.com/archives/92.*

4. Emoto, Masaru, *Messages From Water, Vol. 1* (Hado Publishing, 1999).

5. Strassman, Rick, Dr. *DMT: The Spirit Molecule* (Park Street Press, 2000).

6. Kristic, R. "Pineal Calcification: its Mechanism and Significance" (1986) *Journal of Neural Transmission Supp.* 21: 415–32.

7. Baconnier, S., S.B. Lang, M. Polomska, B. Hilczer, G. Berkovic, and G. Meshulam (2002), "Calcite Micro Crystals in the Pineal Gland of the Human Brain: First Physical and Chemical Studies," *Bioelectromagnetics* (7): 488–95.

8. McMoneagle, Joseph, *The Ultimate Time Machine* (Hampton Roads Publishing, 1998), p. 21.

9. "Statement by Ingo Swann on Remove Viewing," Biomindsuperpowers.com, December 1, 1995, *www.biomindsuperpowers.com/Pages/Statement.*

10. McMoneagle, *The Ultimate Time Machine,* p. 22.

11. McMoneagle, Joseph, *Remote Viewing Secrets* (Hampton Roads Publishing, 2000), pp. 48–49.

12. Private correspondence between Dr. Simeon Hein and the author, January 27, 2012.

13. "Remote Viewing/Changelings," Coast to Coast with George Noory, February 20, 2013, *www.coasttocoastam.com/show/2013/02/20.*

Conclusion

1. Wall, Mike, "Largest Structure in Universe Discovered," SPACE.com, January 11, 2013, *www.space.com/19220-universe-largest-structure-discovered.html.*

2. Sheldrake, Rupert, *A New Science of Life* (Park Street Press 1981, 1987, 1995).

3. "2012: TIPPING POINT The Prophets Conference Cancun January 22-24, 2010 Conference January 22-28 Conference + Pilgrimage to Mayan Temple Sites," Great Mystery Website, *www.greatmystery.org/nl/cancun2012hopi.html.*

4. Ibid.

5. Moran, Andrew, "Former Gov. Buddy Roemer: Washington Is Not Broken, It's Bought," *Digital Journal,* February 7, 2012, *digitaljournal.com/article/319192#ixzz2MUszSOR5.*

6. Radin, *Entangled Minds,* pp. 164–9.

7. "Neuroscience and Free Will," YouTube video, posted by LennyBound, October 24, 2009, *youtu.be/N6S9OidmNZM.*

8. Paddison, Sarah, *The Hidden Power of the Heart: Discovering an Unlimited Source of Intelligence, Revised Edition* (Heartmath LLC, 1998), p. 170

9. Ibid.

10. The Intention Experiment Website, *theintentionexperiment.com.*

11. *International Journal of Parapsychology* (1964): 6473–98.

12. *Journal of the Society for Psychical Research* (2002) 66: 129–43. A replication study showing enhanced growth as well as health was published in the *Journal of Parapsychology* (2003) 67: 279–98.

13. "The 9/11 Peace Intention Experiment," The Intention Experiment Website, *theintentionexperiment.com/pdf/09112011_The_9-11_Peace_Intention_Experiment.pdf.*

14. Global Coherence Initiative Website, *www.glcoherence.org.*

15. Ibid.

16. "World Peace Project News, Events, Articles," World Peace Project Website, *worldpeaceproject.org/news/index.php.*

17. *Social Indicators Research* (1999) 47: 153–201.

18. World Peace Project Website, *worldpeaceproject.org.*

19. Ibid.

20. Williams, D.D., Debra, "Scientific Research of Prayer: Can the Power of Prayer Be Proven?" Plim Report Website, *www.plim.org/PrayerDeb.htm.*

COLIN ANDREWS is an electrical engineer and 30-year veteran investigator into unusual phenomena. He is best known for his research into crop circles, a term he coined in the 1980s after founding Circles Phenomenon Research (CPR) International, the original crop circle research team. He coauthored the first book published on the subject, *Circular Evidence* (Bloomsbury, 1989), which imparted the hallmark features of the phenomena. Andrews's research has extended into many areas of unusual phenomena such as UFO, for which he has been presented with a number of prestigious awards. For the past 20 years, he has focused on investigating consciousness, spirituality, and non-ordinary reality with his wife and coauthor, Synthia Andrews. He is the author of three books and coauthor of six books, and continues to participate in innumerable television programs, documentaries, and video/DVDs. His work can be viewed at *www.colinandrews.net.*

SYNTHIA ANDREWS, ND, is a licensed naturopathic physician who focuses on the role of subtle energy and emotions in the dynamics of health and healing. For the past 20 years she has joined her husband in the exploration of consciousness, spirituality, and non-ordinary reality, offering insights into the physiology involved in changing states of consciousness. She focuses on the impact encounters with non-ordinary reality have on a personal level. She is the author of *The Path of Energy* (New Page Books, 2011) and *The Path of Emotions* (New Page Books, 2013), and coauthor of four additional books. Visit her at *www.thepathofenergy.com.*